Routes to Child Language

This remarkable book provides a detailed comparison of non-human primates and human infants with regard to key abilities that provide the foundation for language. It makes the case for phylogenetic continuity across species and ontogenetic continuity from infancy to childhood. Examined here are behaviors fundamental to language acquisition, such as vocalizations, mapping of meaning onto sound, use of gestures to communicate and to symbolize, tool use, object concept, and memory. The author provides evidence linking these abilities with language acquisition. This volume goes a step further to analyze the similarities and differences across species in these precursors and how these may have influenced the evolution of language. Fascinating hypotheses about the origins of language are described.

Joanna Blake is Associate Professor of Psychology at York University, Toronto, Ontario, Canada.

Routes to Child Language

Evolutionary and Developmental Precursors

JOANNA BLAKE
York University, Toronto, Canada

CABRINI COLLEGE LIBRARY
610 KING OF PRUSSIA ROAD
RADNOR, PA 19087

CAMBRIDGE
UNIVERSITY PRESS

P
118
.B584
2000

#42667950

PUBLISHED BY THE PRESS SYNDICATE OF THE UNIVERSITY OF CAMBRIDGE
The Pitt Building, Trumpington Street, Cambridge, United Kingdom

CAMBRIDGE UNIVERSITY PRESS
The Edinburgh Building, Cambridge CB2 2RU, UK   http://www.cup.cam.ac.uk
40 West 20th Street, New York, NY 10011-4211, USA   http://www.cup.org
10 Stamford Road, Oakleigh, Melbourne 3166, Australia
Ruiz de Alarcón 13, 28014 Madrid, Spain

© Cambridge University Press 2000

This book is in copyright. Subject to statutory exception
and to the provisions of relevant collective licensing agreements,
no reproduction of any part may take place without
the written permission of Cambridge University Press.

First published 2000

Printed in the United States of America

Typeface Sabon 10.25/13   *System* Quark XPress™   [HT]

A catalog record for this book is available from the British Library

Library of Congress Cataloging-in-Publication Data is available

ISBN 0 521 59299 2 hardback

This book is dedicated with love and gratitude to my family,
Eugene, Nicholas, and Rebecca Maiese.

Contents

Preface

The purpose of this book is to address the issue of continuity, both phylogenetic continuity across species and ontogenetic continuity across infancy to childhood. The focus is on behaviors that have been proposed as essential precursors of language: nonmeaningful sound production; early mapping of meaning onto sound; communicative hand and body movements (communicative gestures); movements that represent actions and objects (symbolic gestures); pretend play involving toy animation and imaginary use of objects; use of an object to achieve a goal (tool use); understanding of how objects behave in space, whether visible or not (object permanence); and memory for spatial layouts, objects in arrays, actions and events (delayed imitation), and lists of items (auditory memory). All of these precursors have been investigated in human infants with regard to their impact on early language, as well as others that will not be treated. Emotional factors that may be crucial for language, namely early processing of facial expressions and attachment, will not be included. These precursors have been addressed in recent books by Bloom (1993) and Locke (1993). I will also focus on language production with less emphasis on language comprehension, except for standardized tests of receptive language. This is because the vast majority of research on the precursors that I have selected is focused on their relation to language production. Speech perception will also not be covered; it has been reviewed recently by Jusczyk (1997).

This book extensively reviews research findings, both from our own studies and from those of other investigators, regarding the development across infancy of these abilities purported to underlie language. In the case of memory, the review includes results from children as well, because much of the research relating memory to language has been conducted with this group. The goal is to establish the degree to which the findings support a relation between the proposed precursor and language abilities. The review spans a relatively long time period, since this issue was first addressed by Bates (1979). More recent research has redefined the relation to language of such abilities as tool use, object concept, symbolic gestures, and symbolic play, however, and some of this research needs to be evaluated. The impact of some developments on language has only recently been addressed suffi- ciently, namely prelinguistic vocalizations and memory.

In addition, each chapter begins with a review of findings with regard to the presence of the precursor in nonhuman primates. The focus, where possible, is on great apes in the wild, with some treatment of apes in captivity or in rehabilitation centers when important findings pertaining to the topic exist, for example, for tool use and delayed imitation. When research with apes is scarce, findings on monkeys are more extensively reviewed, for example, for sound–meaning correspondences and memory for lists. Although a few captive apes have been experimental subjects in the domains addressed by the book, recent experimental research has been heavily focused on monkeys. For this reason, the nonhuman primate studies cited cover a wide range of years in order to include some interesting early experiments with apes, as well as important older studies of ape vocalization in the wild.

The purpose of the review of nonhuman primate abilities is to clearly juxtapose them against the abilities of human infants to determine just where the similarities and dissimilarities lie. In some cases, there are few dissimilarities, whereas in others there are few similarities. Some believe that such comparisons are not useful, either because the species being compared are of different ages (often adult ape and human infant) or because such a comparison is anthropomorphic. For those of us who are interested in the roots of language, however, I think such a comparison is one that we continually make and that such a juxtaposition of findings can contribute to a clarification of the continuity issue.

Each chapter, then, progresses from observations on nonhuman primates with respect to the precursor, to its development in human infants, and finally to its relation to language. Chapter 6 is a separate discussion of the issue of representation in infants, and Chapter 7 deals with memory in nonhuman primates and the relation of memory to language in children. Chapter 8 is an attempt to evaluate various hypotheses about the origin of language in the light of the findings reviewed.

Many people contributed to the research cited in this book. The graduate students who worked on the Italian-Canadian infant project were Grace Borzellino Vitale, who collected all the data; Esther Olshansky, who coded the gestures; Silvana Macdonald, who coded the communication task and acted as general statistician; Patricia Osborne, who phonetically transcribed the vocalizations; Elizabeth Stevens, who assisted in the coding; and Debbie Mason, who calculated mean length of utterance for the speech samples. Debbie also provided the memory data for the older language-impaired children, and Connie Kushnir conducted the study of younger language-impaired children. Lorraine Chiasson provided some symbolic play data, and Robin Holloway contributed some findings on Piagetian tasks of means–ends and object permanence. Sheilah McConnell, an ethologist at heart, devised the original coding scheme for the gestures and did much of the original filming. Evelyn Vingilis and Georgia Quartaro collected the memory and language data in the early stages and transcribed the speech samples. Paula O'Rourke conducted the study of gestural development over the first year.

Many undergraduate students also assisted in various capacities: Roy Abraham, Wendy Austin, Marsha Cannon, Nancy Dranitsaris, Joanne Cleyn, Susan Dolgoy, Helen Downie, Gayle Horton, Amanda Lisus, Diane Massum, Shirley Messer, Joanne Messere, Nurit Nadler, Susan Onorati, Mary-Lynn Stordy, Anabel Vaughan, and Linda Woods. This book has clearly been a group effort.

Our first study, of the older English-Canadian infants, as well as the original research on memory and language, were supported by the National Sciences and Engineering Research Council of Canada. The study of French infants was funded by a fellowship from the Foundation Fyssen in Paris, while the study of Italian-Canadian infants was supported by the Mario Elia Fund. All of the research received funding from the Faculty of Arts at York University.

I am indebted to Suzanne MacDonald, Lorraine McCune, and Anne Russon for their comments on selected chapters. I am also indebted to Anne Russon for allowing me to use her wonderful photographs of orangutans. I am especially grateful to all the families in the longitudinal studies for their gracious reception during our many visits. Finally, I thank my family for their encouragement and their participation, both behind and in front of the camera.

CHAPTER ONE

Prelinguistic Vocalizations

Among the most intriguing aspects of human language is its sound system and how the human infant comes to acquire it. Three major questions are addressed in this chapter. First, are there any similarities to be
found between features of animal vocalizations and those of early
infant vocalizations? In other words, can possible phylogenetic origins
of human infant vocalizations be found in the vocalizations of nonhuman primates? If so, where exactly is the overlap? Alternatively, are
even the earliest stages of human infant vocalizations quite distinct
from animal vocalizations? Second, what are the major developments
in the early ontogeny of the human vocalization system, and do they
vary across infants with different characteristics or backgrounds? The
focus here is on such features of vocal development as the onset of
canonical (reduplicated) babbling, phonetic preferences, consonantal
repertoire, consonantality (degree of consonant use), and complexity
(combination of different consonants). Third, do variations in features
of babbling across infants make a difference in language acquisition? Is
just babbling itself an important precursor to language, or is the quality of babbling also important?

In this chapter, infant prelinguistic vocalizations are considered to be
all phonated sounds (with vibration of the vocal cords) that are audi-
ble and are *not* crying, fussing, laughing recognizable words, imitated
animal sounds, or imitated conventionalized expressions *(uh-oh)*.
These criteria are consistent with those used in most research on early
infant vocalizations except that some researchers exclude also grunts
(for example, Oller & Lynch, 1992) and some include words (for
example, Vihman & Greenlee, 1987). Grunts, even those that are simple vegetative effort sounds, need to be included because they have
been emphasized in phylogenetic continuity (McCune, Vihman, Roug-

1

Hellichius, Delery, & Gogate, 1996, see below). For some infants, they have early situational meaning (see chapter 2). Treating prelinguistic vocalizations as a separate category from adult-modeled words or expressions allows the relationship between them to be more easily assessed. The distinction between the two categories is not always an easy one, however (compare also Vihman, Macken, Miller, Simmons, & Miller, 1985).

This chapter treats only the phonetic aspects of vocalizations. Mapping of vocalizations onto context, or the origin of meaning, is the subject of the next chapter. The relationship between vocalizations and gestures is discussed in chapter 3.

Phylogenetic Origins of Human Infant Vocalizations

Unlike the case of communicative gestures, as is apparent in chapter 3, the evolutionary roots of human vocalizations are difficult to trace. Nonhuman primates emit a number of sounds that have been categorized, often with the aid of sound spectrograms, into barks, grunts, roars, screams or screeches, howls, squeals, growls, chatters, hoots, and pants. These categories are sometimes subdivided into different types, such as waa barks versus shrill barks. (Laughter, whines, and whimpers are not included here because they are eliminated from our definition of human infant vocalizations.) The categories appear to be quite similar across several species, for example, baboons (Hall & DeVore, 1965), langurs (Jay, 1965), chimpanzees (Goodall, 1965, 1986; Reynolds & Reynolds, 1965), mountain gorillas (Fossey, 1972; Schaller, 1965), orangutans (MacKinnon, 1974), and pygmy chimpanzees (bonobos) (Mori, 1983; De Waal, 1988). But not all categories are used by each species. Marler (1976) compared acoustic aspects of chimpanzee vocalizations from his recordings on the Gombe Reserve in Tanzania with spectrograms of gorilla vocalizations provided by Fossey (1972). By merging acoustically similar calls while ignoring their contexts and the characteristics of the sender, Marler reduced Van Lawick-Goodall's (1968) original 24 categories for the chimpanzee to 13, all of which overlapped with Fossey's vocalization categories for the mountain gorilla (Table 1–1). Fossey reported 3 additional categories, roar, growl, and a sound idiosyncratic to a single individual. Reynolds and Reynolds (1965) reported roar and growl for the chimpanzees of the Budongo Forest, but apparently the chimpanzees at Gombe do not use these calls. Mori (1983) suggested that *roar* should

Table 1–1. Morphological Equivalents in Vocalization of the Chimpanzee and Gorilla

	Chimpanzee Call	Probable Gorilla Equivalent
A1	Pant–hoot	Hoot series
A2	Laughter	Chuckles
A3	Scream	Scream
A4	Rough grunt	Belch
A5	Pant	Copulatory pant
B6	Squeak	Cries (1)
B7	Whimper	Cries (2) (also whine ?)
B8	Waa–bark	Wraagh (1) (short form)
B9	Wraaa	Wraagh (2) (long form)
B10	Grunt	Pig grunt (1) (given in train)
B11	Cough	Pig grunt (2) (given singly)
C12	Pant–grunt?	Pant series?
C13	Bark?	Hoot–bark? (Also hiccup–bark and question–bark?)

Note: The correspondence is deemed most reliable in pairs labeled A and least in those labeled C.
Source: From P. Marler (1976), Social organization, communication, and graded signals: The chimpanzee and the gorilla. In P. P. G. Bateson & R. A. Hinde (Eds.), *Growing points in ethology* (p. 246). London: Cambridge University Press. Reprinted with permission from Cambridge University Press.

be merged with *wraah,* and then the same vocalization is common to gorillas, chimpanzees, and bonobos.

An interesting difference between vocalizations in gorillas and chimpanzees, which was highlighted by Marler (1976), is that most call categories were found across age and sex groups in the Gombe chimpanzees but restricted to the silverback male in Fossey's gorillas. High-ranking male chimpanzees do engage in one particular type of vocalization, the pant–hoot, more than do low-ranking chimpanzees, and the alpha male responds less to the pant–hoot of other males (Mitani & Nishida, 1993). In general, in the intergroup communication of most primate species, "the loud calls are a male attribute" (Deputte, 1982, p. 68). Female chimpanzees also have a different pant–hoot from males in that it lacks a "climax" section; in addition, they bark more than males (Marler, 1976). It is claimed in later research (Harcourt, Stewart, & Hauser, 1993) that Fossey's (1972) finding of vocalization dominance by the silverback gorilla was due to lack of habituation of the animals in her study. Although Fossey admitted this problem for the early period of her study, data were collected over 40 months, so it seems unlikely that all of her findings are distorted by reactivity. Nevertheless, Harcourt et al. (1993) did find more distribution of vocalizations across the sexes. At least close contact vocalizations, such as the grunts that are predominant in gorillas, were more widely used, although adult males still grunted the most. Such vocalizations were not heard in infants younger than 1.5 years, and they increased with age. The majority occurred as part of a vocal exchange within 1 second of each other. Lone gorillas (always male) were quite silent (See also Schaller, 1965; Stewart & Harcourt, 1994).

Harcourt et al. (1993), unlike Fossey (1972), did not record any roars or growls in their observations of gorillas. The frequency of "close" gorilla calls was about 8 per hour for adults, whereas Marler reported a rate of 10 to 100 per hour for chimpanzees. The chimpanzee rate is inflated because it includes all types of vocalizations and is based on recordings done at a feeding station where vocalizing is typically higher. Nevertheless, the comparison reflects a real difference in vocalizing tendencies between the species. Although chimpanzees remain silent for long periods, particularly during patrol and consortship, they can also be extremely vocal, even engaging in choruses of calling that resemble singing (Goodall, 1986). Bonobos also engage in "contest hooting," but this appears to be a more rapid vocal dialogue (De Waal, 1988).

Although researchers have been able to formulate discrete categories for nonhuman primate vocalizations, they stress that by comparison with birdsong, vocalizations of monkeys and apes are variable and grade into each other. In the graded vocal repertoire of the chimpanzee, the fundamental frequency and duration of calls also vary independently (Marler, 1975). Many years ago, Marler (1965) pointed to these characteristics as presaging the human vocalization system, which is also variable and continuous even though humans impose discrete sound categories on their perception of the acoustic signal. Nonhuman primates also impose categorical boundaries in that they do not respond to a call whose duration exceeds its norm in call production (Snowdon, 1982). Marler (1975, 1976) has suggested that only non-territorial, multimale primate groups that communicate over short distances on the forest floor can use graded sounds. Such characteristics are consistent with speculations about the social organization of early humans (Marler, 1975). Discrete, species-typic signals are also less essential in an environment where the sounds of other species rarely intrude to cause confusion. The danger of alien sound intrusion is minimal "when a species is living out of earshot of organisms similar in size and structure and when sounds are used at sufficiently close range that visual or other cues can confirm the identity of the signaling animal" (Marler, 1965, p. 565). Pure, discrete sounds, such as hoots, are still used by nonhuman primates to communicate over long distances. In contrast, birdsong is composed of stereotypic sounds that are discontinuous, very unlike human vocalizations, in part because each species competes with others for the sound space. More recently, however, describing birdsong as discrete and primate calls as graded has been termed an oversimplification (Marler & Mitani, 1988). Newman and Symmes (1982) argued that in fact, the graded nature of primate vocalizations is found only in the young and that these vocalizations become more discrete and less variable with maturity.

There appears to have been early general agreement that birds are uniquely similar to humans in exhibiting vocal learning (Nottebohm, 1975). Absence of vocal learning in apes was supported by the absence of local dialects in vocalizations (Marler & Tenaza, 1977). Snowdon (1982) did report subspecific differences in the long calls of saddleback tamarin monkeys living in different areas of the Amazon, but this finding is complicated by the possibility of interbreeding among subspecies. Snowdon (1982) also reported that pygmy marmosets that lost their parents never attained a fully adult vocal repertoire; this seems to be stronger evidence for vocal learning. In addition, Mitani and Gros-Louis (1998) recently documented vocal accommodation between adult male chimpanzees in chorusing – that is, calling bouts of overlapping pant–hoots. Two male pairs were found to produce calls when chorusing together that were acoustically more similar than calls they made with other males. One male's chorused calls were closer acoustically to those his partner produced alone than to his own calls produced alone. Thus, this single chimpanzee provides preliminary evidence that chimpanzees are able to alter their calls during choruses of pant–hoots to match another's calls.

The clearest link between human and nonhuman primate vocalizations appears to lie in the prosodic features displayed by nonhuman primate signals, namely pitch, timing, and intensity. These three features are physically described as follows: "the fundamental frequency contours, which give a language its characteristic melody; the duration

. . . measures, which give a language its characteristic rhythm; and the amplitude patterns, which give a language its characteristic patterns of loud versus soft syllables" (Levitt, 1993, p. 385). Pitch variation in nonhuman primate signals can be seen in the waa–barks of chimpanzees (wieew–barks of bonobos), the melodious "legato hooting" of bonobos (De Waal, 1988; Marler & Tenaza, 1977), the intergroup spacing calls of cotton-top tamarins with energy distribution across several formants (Snowdon, 1982), the long-distance J-calls of pygmy marmosets (Snowdon, 1982), and the harmonically structured clear calls of macaques (Brown, 1982). Such frequency modulation, along with repetition, makes calls more localizable (Snowdon, 1982). Prosody or the musical quality of speech is sometimes proposed as the earliest form of hominid vocal communication, and the roots of pitch contours associated with human emotions may be quite ancient, evolutionarily speaking (Hauser, 1996). In birds and mammals, high-pitched vocalizations tend to be associated with either fear or affiliation, and low-pitched, with aggression (Hauser, 1996). Darwin (1877) suggested that early hominids' first form of vocal communication was expressed in song, often for emotive purposes in courtship (see review in Donald, 1991). Studdert-Kennedy (1991) speculated that prosody "perhaps first followed an independent course of evolution, to be modified and integrated into the linguistic system only as longer utterances and more finely differentiated syntactic functions emerged" (p.9). Prosody is also, as we shall see shortly, among the earliest developments in human ontogeny; and Ferguson and Macken (1983) have suggested that the "ontogenetic primacy of prosodic phenomena may reflect a phylogenetic primacy" (p. 238).

Differences between the Nonhuman Primate and Human Vocal Tracts

According to Bastian (1965), monkeys and apes differ from humans in the simplicity and steadiness of upper vocal tract configurations produced by their auditory signals. Human linguistic signals are distinguished by the "incessant occlusions of the vocal tract" (p. 595) to produce transient resonant patterns. Thus, although all mammals possess respiratory muscles that blow air through the vocal tract, features of the human upper vocal tract allow articulatory capabilities beyond the reach of nonhuman primates. "The open-to-closed and closed-to-open articulatory actions may occur at various places in the upper vocal tract; they may be partial or complete; they may or may not be accompanied by concurrent glottal action; and, most important, they may be readily combined in many different sequences" (Bastian, 1965, p. 592).

Lieberman (1984, 1991) has discussed at length the changes in the human vocal tract that have contributed to our extraordinary vocal capabilities. The most important are the descent of the larynx into the neck to create a pharyngeal cavity, the change in the form and position of the tongue, and the right-angle bend between the pharyngeal (throat) and oral (mouth) cavities (Figure 1–1.) The larynx was originally a simple valve to protect the lungs of fish from the influx of water and foreign objects (Negus, 1949, cited in Lieberman, 1984). In ter-

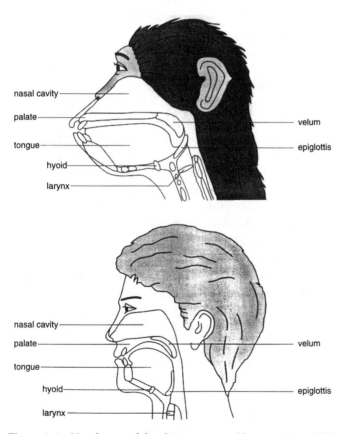

Figure 1–1: Vocal tract of the chimpanzee and human. From Whitney, P. (1998). *The Psychology of Language*. Figure 1.2, p.6. Copyright © 1998 by Houghton Mifflin Company. Used with permission.

restrial mammals, the larynx converts the flow of air from the lungs into phonation. The rate of opening and closing of the vocal cords sets the fundamental frequency of phonation (the lowest pitch) (Lieberman, 1975). The supralaryngeal vocal tract acts as a filter, maximizing acoustic energy at particular frequencies (formants) depending on its general configuration—that is, its length and shape (Lieberman, 1991). The basic structure of the larynx of the great apes is similar to humans' (Negus, 1949). However, apes also have laryngeal air sacs that may serve as resonators during loud vocalizing to compensate for the lack of a pharynx (Marler & Tenaza, 1977). Apes are capable of changing the filtering properties of the supralaryngeal vocal tract to produce variations in formant frequency, and the range of variation is similar to that found in the human neonate (Lieberman, 1975).

At birth, the human infant's vocal tract resembles that of lower mammals in that the larynx is high and can rise to seal off the nasopharynx (nasal cavity). This has the survival advantage of protecting the neonate from choking, because food can pass to either side of the raised larynx into the pharynx (Lieberman, 1984). Very young infants are further protected by being programmed to breathe only through their noses, and they can breathe while they eat, a feat that adult humans cannot (or should not) attempt. Human infants are also born with a thin tongue situated entirely in the mouth. By 3 months of age, the human infant's vocal tract has begun to resemble the human adult's in several ways: (1) the palate begins to move back, (2) the larynx has begun to descend in the neck and to become more mobile, (3) the tongue has become rounder and protrudes into the throat to form a movable anterior wall, and (4) the oral and pharyngeal cavities have become positioned more at right angles. The right-angle bend now helps the velum at the back of the throat to close off the nasal cavity, making possible the more easily perceptible non-nasal sounds (Lieberman, 1991). It may also be important in producing "stop" consonants (those with full occlusion) (Kimura, 1993) and the extreme high vowels /i/ as in *beet* and /u/ as in *toot* (Lieberman, 1975). In addition, the infant's ribs have moved from a perpendicular orientation to the spine to a downward slant, allowing the intercostal muscles and diaphragm to inflate the lungs. This last adaptation is not specifically human, because adult chimpanzees and gorillas also have downward-slanting ribs (Lieberman, 1984).

We know from computer simulations (Lieberman, Klatt, & Wilson, 1969) that the nonhuman primate vocal tract (and the human infant's vocal tract before 3 months) will not allow production of the full range of vowels, particularly the extremes of the high front vowel /i/, the high back vowel /u/, and the low midvowel /a/ as in *mama*. However, non-human primates do not fully utilize the vowel space that they do have, whereas 3-month-old human infants do (Lieberman, 1984). Thus, the evolution of human speech-producing capacity cannot be entirely explained by changes in the vocal tract. Another important evolutionary change is that nonhuman vocalizations are controlled by the cingulate (old motor) cortex, the basal ganglia, and midbrain structures and not by the neocortex, as they are in humans (Lieberman, 1991, 1995). Neocortical stimulation produces vowel-like sounds in humans but no vocalizations in squirrel or rhesus monkeys, although chimpanzees might be an exception (Kimura, 1993; Ploog, 1988; Ploog & Jurgens, 1980). Most of the vocal repertoire of captive squirrel monkeys can be elicited by stimulating areas within the midbrain and limbic system (Hauser, 1996). We also know from a century of research on brain-damaged patients that Broca's area (Figure 1–2), which may have a structural homologue but no functional counterpart in nonhu-

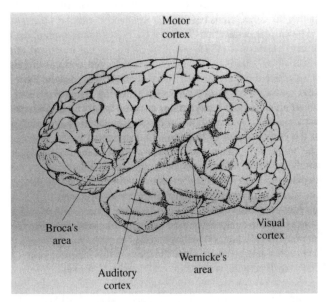

Figure 1–2: Left hemisphere of a human brain showing Broca's and Wernicke's areas. From Noble, W., and Davidson, I. (1996). *Human evolution, language and mind: A psychological and archaeological enquiry* (p. 17). Cambridge: Cambridge University Press. Reprinted with permission from Cambridge University Press.

man primates, is involved in the motor programs necessary for speech production (but see chapter 8). The prefrontal cortex also is clearly implicated in both language and thought (Bates, 1996; Hauser, 1996; Lieberman, 1991, 1995).

Voluntary neocortical control of complex vocal motor patterns thus seems to be restricted to humans. Cortical control means a "measure of independence of the signal from the limbic system and the direct, unconscious expression of individual emotion" (Lancaster, 1968, p. 453). Goodall (1986) has also stressed that chimpanzee calls are closely tied to underlying emotions and that these primates are unable to vocalize at will, even having difficulty in suppressing their vocalizations in situations of danger that require silence. This last statement, however, seems to be contradicted by her observation that chimpanzees on patrol of their territory are quite silent. Learning when to release or inhibit calls appears to be regulated by the anterior cingulate cortex, and rhesus monkeys with lesions to this area are no longer able to master operant conditioning tasks (Jurgens, 1995). Several species of non-human primates have been successfully operantly conditioned to produce a vocalization under certain conditions and not produce it when these conditions are absent in order to receive a reward (Pierce, 1985). Although it is claimed that these findings indicate that nonhuman primate vocalizations are modifiable, the acoustic structure of their vocalizations was not apparently modified, but only their frequency or duration. Lieberman (1995) has proposed that "the ability of humans to 'free up' the stereotyped motor acts that make up nonhuman primate calls derives from prefrontal cortex 'overriding' basal ganglia coded patterns" (p. 278). Researchers studying the semioticity of primate calls do not, of course, agree that primate vocalizations are strictly emotive and involuntary. Others argue that a strict dichotomy that posits limbic and involuntary against neocortical and voluntary is not useful (Steklis, 1985). The question of semioticity, and its potential voluntary aspect, is revisited in chapter 2.

It is nevertheless clear that the vocal tract of nonhuman primates does allow them to produce humanlike sounds that they do *not* produce. They *could* occlude their supralaryngeal vocal tracts to produce some of the stop consonants, namely /b/, /p/, /d/, and /t/, and they are capable of producing /s/ as well (Lieberman, 1991). In fact, Hauser and Marler (1992) found that rhesus macaques do use their lips to produce variants of clear tonal calls ("coos") and tongue movements to produce acoustic changes in alarm barks. These are the articulatory movements needed to produce labial sounds (/b/ and /p/) and dento-alveolar sounds (/d/ and /t/). Rhesus macaques also appear able to compensate for perturbations of the vocal tract, which may imply some voluntary control over call targets. Nonhuman primates should also be able to reproduce nasalized versions of human words (Lieberman, 1991). As we know from Vicki, the chimpanzee raised by Hayes and Nissen (1971), imitation of human words is extremely difficult for apes (although informal reports claim that it is easier for bonobos). At this stage of our knowledge, it appears that both brain mechanisms and vocal tract changes evolved to facilitate human speech. There is a "direct motor pathway from laryngeal representation in the primary motor cortex to laryngeal motoneurons in the medulla that does not exist in the monkey. This direct connection serves as the neuronal basis for the voluntary control of the vocal folds in man which is not possible in the monkey" (Ploog, 1988, p. 195; see also chapter 8). Bilateral destruction of the motor cortex in humans destroys the ability to produce learned vocal utterances, whereas it has no effect on monkeys' vocalization (Jurgens, 1995). It is probable that prosody in humans is still controlled by the anterior cingulate cortex (Ploog, 1988). It is unclear why vocalizations became increasingly cortically controlled in humans and how such remarkably rapid vocal articulation and encoding evolved, at the rate of 20 to 30 segments per second (Lieberman, 1975). Some proposals for this evolution, particularly from Deacon (1997), are discussed in chapter 8.

Continuity between apes and humans with regard to vocal sounds is thus clearly more apparent in involuntary sounds, such as squeals and screams (Figure 1–3), than in speech sounds. Humans have retained some nonhuman primate signals in nonlinguistic expletives; and crying in the human infant closely resembles that of ape infants, particularly when it builds up into screaming or temper tantrums (Fossey, 1972). These sounds are specifically those that we have eliminated from our definition of human infant vocalizations. Such signals are typically involuntary, emotive, and controlled by the limbic system in both human and nonhuman primates (Ploog, 1988). One type of infant vocalization, included in our definition, that is said to demonstrate clear overlap, however, is the "grunt" sound (McCune et al., 1996). A human "grunt" is defined by these researchers as a brief glottal closure, followed by an abrupt vowel-like release, with open or closed lips. These grunts are said to "index physiological functioning under condi-

Figure 1–3: A juvenile female orangutan (Sariyem) at Wanariset, Borneo, screaming because her food was stolen. Photograph by Anne Russon.

tions of respiratory challenge, effort, and locomotion" in many species (p. 30).

Marler and Tenaza (1977, p. 990) described the chimpanzee grunt as "an acoustically simple sound produced on a single exhalation through a mouth that is closed or only slightly open." Plooij (1978) reported observations in which the tonal grunt in chimpanzees appeared to serve as an attention-getting device directed at a hand gesture indicating a desired spot for grooming, a gaze toward a food source, or a movement indicating the onset of travel. Bonobos also use grunts as an attention-getting device (De Waal, 1988). Infant chimpanzees as early as 3 months of age have been found to emit effort grunts when reaching for things (Plooij, 1984). Grunts have also been uttered by infant chimpanzees when stimuli change suddenly, such as a change in illumination, a sudden move of an object, or a move of the infant. Grunts also occur in apparently strictly social contexts. Low-ranking chimpanzees give a distinctive call, known as the pant–grunt, to higher-ranking individuals (Mitani & Nishida, 1993). Similarly, a rhythmic series of greeting grunts is uttered by subordinate bonobos to the dominant male (De Waal, 1988). These are just a few examples of the functions proposed for ape sounds classified as grunts by human observers. More discussion of the function of grunts in nonhuman primates is found in chapter 2.

McCune et al. (1996) proposed that human infants show a developmental progression from effort grunts to attention grunts to communicative grunts, with the last type signaling the advent of referential word production or comprehension. Although it may be true that the infant's success in using such vocalizations communicatively launches it on the route to sound–meaning correspondences (see the next chapter), there are at least two problems with the claims of McCune et al. (1996). First, the situations are quite globally defined, and they overlap. For example, reaching is categorized as effort but reaching towards the mother as communication. In general, such a three-category contextual system seems too simplistic for infants in their second year. Second, what animal researchers call grunts in nonhuman primates and what McCune et al. (1996) have called grunts in human infants may be quite dissimilar acoustically. No direct comparison has apparently been made. Such a comparison might be difficult because, according to Marler (1976, p. 247), "by their nature, grunting sounds are difficult to characterize acoustically." Despite these cautions, our research (Blake & de Boysson-Bardies, 1992; Blake & Fink, 1987) on sound–meaning correspondences, reported in chapter 2, provides several illustrations which appear similar to the grunt vocalizations and their functional mappings described by McCune et al. (1996).

Ontogeny of Vocalizations in Human Infants over the First Year

Various stage models of the development of infant vocal production over the first year have been proposed, and they tend to be in general agreement (for example, Oller, 1980; Stark, 1980, 1981). During the first 2 months, vocalization is called reflexive (Stark, 1980) or phonatory (Oller, 1980). Stark divided infant sounds into crying/fussing versus vegetative sounds (coughing, burping, swallowing, glottal catches, grunts, and sighs). Sounds were first grossly categorized on the basis of a running commentary regarding the infant's facial expression, direction of gaze, limb movements, and mother's behavior. Selected sounds in each category were then subjected to further acoustic analysis, which revealed differences in the two general categories (Stark, Rose, & McLagen, 1975). Cry vocalizations contain prosodic features (intensity, pitch, rhythmic patterning) and vocalic elements. Vegetative sounds contain consonantal elements (transitions from a closed to an open vocal tract). There is as yet, however, no systematic contrast between open and closed vocal tract at this stage (Oller, 1980), even though Irwin (1947) did classify some sounds during this age period as consonants, namely [h], glottal stops, and, less commonly, velars [g/k]. Stark viewed crying as the source of prosody and vowels; like vowels, cries have an open vocal tract and vowel-like formant structure (Studdert-Kennedy, 1991). Vegetative sounds are seen as the source of consonants because there is often some constriction of the vocal tract (Stark et al., 1975). Netsell (1981) has questioned the relevance of crying to speech; he argues that only nondistress sounds approximate the respiratory laryngeal controls used in speech. He also believes that the relation of vegetative sounds to speech is questionable because they may be controlled subcortically. Vegetative sounds are closely tied to breathing and eating and thus potentially overlap with the sounds of nonhuman mammals. What may be most closely related to speech in this stage are the quasiresonant nuclei vowel sounds, called quasiresonant owing to the short length of the vocal tract (Oller, 1980). The length of the supralaryngeal vocal tract is closely correlated with overall growth during this period (Lieberman, 1980). Quasiresonant nuclei vowels have frequencies (pitch) concentrated in the low range, with a nasal air flow (Oller, 1986), and Oller did not consider them to be reflexive. They appear to be similar to what McCune et al. (1996) described as grunts in older infants. In fact, they are the grunts and sighs subsumed under vegetative sounds by Stark (1981) and viewed by her as responses to effort. Irwin (1948) did classify the vowel sounds consistently used at this age as [ɛ], [ɪ], and [ə], but more recent researchers would not consider these sounds to be phonetically classifiable.

At 2 to 4 months, with the incipient changes in the vocal tract, infants enter what is termed the cooing or gooing stage, during which occlusions at the back of the vocal tract may produce uvulars and faint velar sounds [g/k], from which the stage gets its name. Irwin (1947), however, found only a small increase in velars at this age, at least as a proportion of "consonants," but a larger increase in [h] sounds. Kent and Murray (1982) cautioned against interpreting transient noises at this stage as phonetic sounds. The tongue movements are still large and relatively undifferentiated (Kent, 1981), and the dorsum of the tongue and the epiglottis are still high and in close con-

tact with the soft palate most of the time (Oller, 1981), hence producing back sounds. Stark (1978, 1980) called these back sounds
"comfort" sounds and believed that they show increased control over
voicing. During this stage, the infant begins to produce a basic opposition between opening and closing of the vocal tract (Oller, 1980).
The "consonantal" elements in comfort sounds are typically nasals,
stops (with full occlusion), or friction and trill-like noises. Irwin's
(1947) data, however, showed nasals as definitively present only at 5
to 6 months. The most common vowels are [æ] and [ɛ] (Lieberman,
1980). Although the inner cell layers of the cerebral cortex are fairly
well developed during this period, especially the primary motor and
sensory areas, subcortical neural mechanisms are still considered to
be dominant (Netsell, 1981).

The next stage, termed expansion or vocal play, continues the
development of stage 2, with fully resonant adultlike vowels now
heard, as well as "marginal" consonants with closures at various
places in the vocal tract and not just at the back (Oller, 1980). The
formant transitions are still too slow for these consonants to be considered as "true" consonants (Oller & Lynch, 1992). Overlap with
nonhuman primate vocalizations can be seen in the squeals, yells,
growls, nasal murmurs, laughter, and to a degree in the prosodic variations that the human infant engages in during this stage. However,
the vowels are clearly more fully resonant and varied in the human
infant. The infant's vowels are not simple imitations of adult formant
frequencies but have a spectral patterning consistent with the short
length of the vocal tract; formant frequencies fall with growth
(Lieberman, 1980). By 24 weeks, the acoustic pattern begins to
resemble a rudimentary vowel triangle, demarcated by /ɪ/, /æ/, and /u/
(Buhr, 1980), but improvement in vowel production continues at
least through age 3 (Lieberman, 1980).

By this stage, dialogues have begun between infants and their parents, at least in middle-class homes. Such dialogues on the part of the
infant involve clear turn-taking, resonant vowels, long vowel strings
with sing-song intonation, and laughter (Figure 1–4). Some would also
argue that with the development of dialogues, human infants begin to
voluntarily control their vocalizations, because they can now at least
inhibit them while the parent is taking a turn (Ginsburg & Kilbourne,
1988). This argument would then also apply to the duetting songs of
male and female gibbons (Deputte, 1982). Vocal dialogues with signal

adjustment have been reported as well in the contest hooting of captive bonobos (De Waal, 1988). However, as discussed above, inhibition of vocalizations may not imply cortical control.

Human infants are now increasingly able to match both the absolute vocal pitch of their mothers' speech and the intonation contour, particularly contours that are falling and bell-shaped (containing both a rise and a fall) (Papousek & Papousek, 1989). Over the first 5 months, Japanese infants increasingly matched the contours in their mothers' speech (Masataka, 1992a) and did so with a greater than expected frequency when mothers were instructed to exaggerate the contours of their verbalizations (Masataka, 1992b). This matching is a clear indicator of voluntary control and vocal accommodation. Similar matching of musical tones has also been found in infants of this age (Kessen, Levine, & Wendrich, 1979). Thus, the musical aspects of pitch alone are sufficient to elicit matching, even without the affective, attention-getting component of exaggerated motherese or even without the mother.

It is debatable whether these first three "stages" should be termed such, because development is quite continuous across them (Stark, 1981). Each stage does, however, represent the incorporation of some new features into the infant's repertoire (Oller, 1980). At about 7 or 8 months, a clear discontinuity occurs, which is the sudden onset (Roug, Landberg, & Lundberg, 1989) of canonical or reduplicated babbling (Figure 1–5). Stark (1981) viewed this stage also as essentially continuous but with increased voluntary control over the opening and closing of the vocal tract. Canonical babbling (CB) refers to the production of "true" consonant–vowel (CV) syllables with adultlike timing (i.e., less than 140 milliseconds between consonant and vowel) (Oller & Lynch, 1992) and with smooth changes in formant frequency. It is very salient in its onset, easily recognized accurately by parents from a wide range of backgrounds as confirmed by laboratory evaluation (Oller, Basinger, & Eilers, 1996). It usually begins with a clear CV syllable, such as [ba], followed quickly by a reduplicated string [baba]. In normally developing infants, CB has quite a restricted age range of onset (typically 7 to 11 months) (Oller & Eilers, 1988), which is invariant across socio-economic status (SES) (Eilers, Oller, Levine, Basinger, Lynch, & Urbano, 1993), across monolingual versus bilingual environments (Oller, Eilers, Urbano, & Cobo-Lewis, 1997), and across the several languages that have been

Figure 1–4: A precanonical vocalizing 5.5-month-old male infant. Photograph by Eugene Maiese.

Figure 1–5: A canonical vocalizing 8-month-old female infant. Photograph by Eugene Maiese.

Figure 1–6: A (noncanonical) adult female wild orangutan hooing. Photograph by Anne Russon.

investigated (Locke, 1993). In deaf infants, onset is delayed until at least 14 months (Oller & Eilers, 1988). Canonical babbling represents a clear discontinuity both ontogenetically and phylogenetically; there is no counterpart in nonhuman vocalizations (Figure 1–6), even though nonhuman primates should be able to produce something resembling the stop consonants which are most commonly found during this stage (Lieberman, 1991). It is probably not a coincidence that the onset of canonical babbling occurs after the supralaryngeal vocal tract of human infants has become almost fully adultlike (Ploog, 1988), but it seems likely that peripheral changes are insufficient to explain its appearance in humans. Despite the stagelike onset of CB, there are some isolated observations (Oller, 1980; Roug et al., 1989) of such babbling occurring earlier and then disappearing.

It has recently been claimed that something resembling babbling occurs in the early vocalizations of pygmy marmosets (Elowson, Snowdon, & Lazro-Perea, 1998). Infant and juvenile pygmy marmosets produce long sequences of calls; and in the 8 infants observed by these researchers over their first 20 weeks, such calling bouts contained many reduplicated call types. It should be emphasized, however, that reduplicated or canonical babbling in the human infant literature means specifically the repetition of the same CV syllable. Elowson et al. (1998) also pointed out that infant pygmy marmoset sequences are not used in the appropriate adult context; that is, single J-notes were not given or received as warning calls, a finding they viewed as suggestive of vocal practice. This is perhaps a more interesting area of potential overlap, but there is no information given concerning the contexts in which the infants' calls did occur. Thus, we do not know if these infant monkeys engage in any idiosyncratic mapping of calls onto contexts as human infants do (see next chapter).

For human infants, it is posited that following reduplicative babbling, there is a stage of variegated babbling beginning at about 10 months, in which the consonants and/or vowels in an utterance vary rather than reduplicate. According to Elbers (1982), the babbling of her son followed an operating principle in which single sounds were exercised separately before being combined into complex (variegated) babbling. Other researchers (Mitchell & Kent, 1990; Smith, Brown-Sweeney, & Stoel-Gammon, 1989) have claimed, however, that both reduplicated and variegated babbling are present at the onset of CB. Over the first 4 to 6 months after this onset, the two kinds of babbling are also said to be used equally often (Davis & MacNeilage, 1995). Smith et al. (1989) focused on consonant variation in place of articulation only and on "substantial" vowel variation and still found variegated babbling in about 40% of polysyllabic utterances between 6 and 9 months, most involving consonant change. Variegated babbling did increase after the first year to constitute a majority of polysyllabic utterances (66%). Roug et al. (1989) also found an increase in variegated babbling but somewhat earlier. In contrast, Vihman, Ferguson, and Elbert (1986) reported that in their 10 infants followed from age 9 to 16 months, combining consonants with different places or manners of articulation in a single vocalization was relatively infrequent.

Development of Vocalization in Human Infants during the Transition to Language

My colleagues and I have conducted longitudinal investigations of infants belonging to three different cultural groups: English-Canadian, Parisian-French, and Italian-Canadian. Studies of the first two groups involved small samples followed intensively (usually recorded biweekly) from 9 to 14 or 15 months. In addition, an older group of English-Canadian infants was followed for a 3- to 5-month period during the second year until they had acquired a 30-word vocabulary. The Italian-Canadian group was observed at 9 and 10 months, at 15 months, and again at 3 years. It was a much larger sample than the other groups (30 infants) in order that babbling measures could be statistically correlated with other measures of interest. Infants in all groups were videorecorded at home in interaction with a parent to obtain approximately a half-hour corpus of babbling during each of the visits. In addition, the older group of English-Canadian infants was also videorecorded in a day-care center over the first 2-month period.

Crying, fussing, laughing, animal sounds, and recognizable words were omitted from the corpora before phonetic transcription. For the younger infants, recorded over 9 to 15 months, reliability was determined on at least 20% of the corpora, chosen to represent different age periods, after coders had discussed their disagreements. Percent agreement on consonants, disregarding voiced–voiceless distinctions, on combinations of consonant types, and on vowels used alone was at least 80%. For the older sample, two coders transcribed all corpora, and a third judge decided between the two transcriptions in cases of disagreement. Details of the procedure for the three small samples are provided in Blake and Fink (1987) and in Blake and de Boysson-Bardies (1992). These published reports focus on the mapping of phonetic categories onto contexts, the subject of the next chapter. In this chapter, unpublished data on developmental change in phonetic preferences in all groups are presented, as well as data from the larger Italian-Canadian sample on developmental change in consonantality, consonantal repertoire, and variegated babbling.

Phonetic Preferences

Tables 1–2, 1–3, and 1–4 show the phonetic preferences of one boy and one girl from the younger English-Canadian group and one boy and one girl from the Parisian-French group, for the age periods 9 to

Table 1-2. Change with Age in the Relative Frequency (%) of Consonantal Categories for Younger English-Canadian and French Infants

Age in months	English-Canadian				Parisian-French			
	Female		Male		Female		Male	
	9–11	12–14	9–11	12–14	9–11	12–14	9–11	12–14
Phonetic categories								
b/p	.02	.02	.03	.03	.10	.05	.01	.004
m	.19	.38	.30	.15	.05	.12	.21	.12
f/v	.005	.003	.01	0	.01	.004	.005	0
d/t	.07	.03	.11	.17	.04	.04	.03	.09
g/k	.02	.03	.04	.05	.04	.02	.03	.02
n	.01	.003	.01	.03	.002	.01	.02	.004
l	.003	.001	.01	.02	.01	.008	.003	.006
s/z	0	.004	.02	.01	.01	.004	.002	.01
w	.01	.03	0	0	.03	.06	.005	.004
j	.04	.02	.04	.04	.07	.06	.02	.09
r	.003	.001	0	0	0	.009	.003	0
TOTAL single consonants (supraglottal)	.37	.52	.57	.50	.36	.38	.34	.35

Table 1-3. Change with Age in the Relative Frequency (%) of Combined Consonantal Categories for Younger English-Canadian and French Infants

| | English-Canadian | | | | Parisian-French | | | |
| | Female | | Male | | Female | | Male | |
Age in months	9–11	12–14	9–11	12–14	9–11	12–14	9–11	12–14
Phonetic categories								
Labial combinations	0	.02	.05	.02	.06	.06	.02	.01
Labial plus velar (sonorant/j)	.01	.03	.01	.01	.04	.07	.01	.005
Labial plus sonorant/strident(j)	.025	.03	.03	.02	.08	.12	.01	.003
Dento-alveolar plus labial (sonorant/j)	.02	.01	.02	.03	.09	.06	.02	.004
Dento-alveolar plus velar (sonorant/j)	.01	.01	.03	.01	.01	.006	.002	.009
Dento-alveolar plus sonorant/j	.02	.02	.04	.05	.01	.03	.002	.008
Dento-alveolar plus labial plus velar (sonorant/strident)	.002	.005	0	0	.01	.01	.002	.001
Velar plus sonorant/strident/j	.02	.025	.01	0	.02	.02	.01	.004
Sonorant/j/strident	.01	.001	0	.01	.01	.01	.003	.01
Other combinations	.004	.002	0	0	.01	.02	0	.005
TOTAL combined consonants	.12	.15	.19	.15	.34	.41	.08	.06

Table 1-4. Change with Age in the Relative Frequency (%) of Vowel Categories for Younger English-Canadian and French Infants

| | English-Canadian | | | | Parisian-French | | | |
| | Female | | Male | | Female | | Male | |
Age in months	9–11	12–14	9–11	12–14	9–11	12–14	9–11	12–14
Phonetic categories								
I/i	.005	.004	.02	.02	0	.002	.002	.009
e	.002	.005	.01	0	0	0	.03	.008
ε	.06	.02	.04	.05	0	.004	.12	.06
æ	.05	.02	.01	.01	0	.002	.04	.04
ə/ʌ/œ/ɤ/ø	.08	.10	0	.01	.01	.004	.04	.07
a/ɑ	.04	.01	0	.01	.01	.02	.11	.25
o/ɔ	0	0	0	.03	.01	.01	0	.002
u/ʊ	.01	.01	0	.02	0	.002	0	.002
Vowel plus j/w	.002	.01	0	0	.01	0	0	0
Vowel combinations	.09	.04	.06	.14	.01	.02	.22	.13
TOTAL vowels	.34	.22	.14	.29	.05	.06	.56	.57

11 months and 12 to 14 months. The corpora from which these preferences were derived contained 390 to 977 utterances for each age
period based on 4 to 6 sessions. The relative frequencies for single consonants, disregarding voiced–voiceless distinctions, are based on
counts of first consonants only in reduplicated babbling; repeated consonants were not counted (compare also Vihman et al., 1986). Those
for vowels are based on utterances in which there were no consonants.
This may actually result in a more accurate representation of vowel
preferences if it is true that vowels are not articulated independently of
initial consonants in the syllable at this stage (Davis & MacNeilage,
1995; but see de Boysson-Bardies, 1993, for counterevidence). Again,
repetition of the same vowel in an utterance was not counted.

First, it is clear from Table 1–2 that very little change in preferences
for single supraglottal consonants is found across the two age periods.
(Note that relative frequencies of glottal stops and [h] phones are omitted from Table 1–2, so that the frequencies on Tables 1–2, 1–3, and
1–4 combined do not total 100%.) Davis and MacNeilage (1995) also
found little change in relative frequency of consonant place categories
over the babbling period. The major changes for our infants are found
for [m], which decreases for two infants and increases for two infants;
for dento-alveolars (mostly [d/t]), which increase for two infants and
decrease for one; and for [w], which increases for two infants. Overall
rank order remains quite similar across the age periods: most frequent
is either [m] or [b/p], next is [d/t] or [j], and third is [g/k]. Thus, these
infants, in both English- and French-learning environments, preferred
the three stop articulation positions: closure with the lips, with the
tongue against the alveolar ridge, and with the raised back of the
tongue. These preferences have been found in the babbling of infants
from many cultures (Locke, 1983; Roug et al., 1989). "Stops present
the sharpest possible contrast with vowels and provide the most obtru-
sive break in the acoustic stream of speech sounds. . . . [Their] production is relatively undemanding" (Vihman, 1996, p. 117). We did
not analyze phonetic preferences according to position in the syllable,
but others have found that the preference for stop consonants is limited to initial position (Kent & Bauer, 1985). The relative frequencies
of Table 1–2 accord well with the data of Irwin, Fisichelli, and Pierce
and Hanna reported by Locke (1983) for infants of 11 to 12 months
of age. The major discrepancy between Locke's Table 1–1 and my
Table 1–2 is in the higher relative frequency of [m] for our infants. A
strong preference for [m], as well as for [d], however, is congruent with

the findings of Davis and MacNeilage (1995) for four of their six subjects and with Irwin's (1947) finding of an abrupt increase in the relative frequency of [d] at 9 to 10 months. Two of our infants also
preferred [w], especially during the second age period. All four infants
showed very infrequent use of [r]. Use of the other infrequent consonants did not show a cultural pattern.

Similar to the single-consonant preferences, the preferred consonant
combinations for all infants were of different bilabials or labiodentals
([b/p], [m], [w], [f/v] and of these with other consonant types (see Table
1–3). Next were combinations of dento-alveolars [d/t] with consonant
types other than bilabials, and finally, combinations of velars [g/k] with
consonants other than bilabials. The two female infants increased their
bilabial–velar combinations across the two age periods, and the French
female infant increased her combinations of bilabials with [j], [n or l],
and [s]. The male infants did not show much developmental change in
consonant combinations and did not increase their total proportion of
utterances combining different consonant types during the second age
period.

Vowel preferences in utterances containing only a single vowel type
(and no consonants) (see Table 1–4) were for mid-/low-front or central
vowels, [ɛ], [æ], [ə/ʌ], [a/ɑ], as has been found in other studies (for
example, Buhr, 1980; Davis & MacNeilage, 1995; Holmgren,
Lindblom, Aurelius, & Zetterstrom, 1986; Irwin, 1948; Kent & Bauer,
1985; and Vihman, 1992). These infants rarely produced high front
vowels [ɪ/i] or high-mid back vowels [u], [o/ɔ], except for the English-
Canadian boy. As Buhr (1980) suggested, vowel preferences may be
anatomically based, arising from the faster development of the musculature of the lips, jaw, and front of the tongue as compared with the
slower descent of the larynx and back of the tongue into the neck.
However, our infants presumably had undergone most of these
anatomical changes.

The consonant preferences for the older sample of English-Canadian
infants are given in Table 1–5 across the age periods that they were
observed. In this group, there were two boys (Nic and Nik) and three
girls (Kar, San, and Lis). San withdrew before attaining the 30-word
criterion. The total number of babbled utterances in the corpora of
these infants ranged from 409 to 1881. For this group, glottal stops
and [h] were not coded. The most preferred consonants for these
infants were dento-alveolars [d/t] or velars [g/k]. Next in relative frequency were bilabials, either [b/p] or [m] (for Lis), and glides [w] or [j].

Table 1-5. Change with Age in the Relative Frequency (%) of Consonantal Categories for Older English-Canadian Infants

Age in months	Nic			Kar		San		Nik		Lis	
Phonetic categories	13–15	15.5–17	17.5–19	13–15	16–18	14–15.5	16–17	17–19	20–22	17–19	20–21
b/p	.03	.05	.05	.05	.11	.04	.04	.11	.16	.07	.07
m	.02	.01	.03	.01	.04	.02	.04	.05	0	.12	.05
d/t	.27	.33	.19	.17	.09	.20	.26	.19	.13	.12	.05
g/k	.02	.05	.03	.04	.13	.02	.07	.05	.03	.15	.11
n/l	0	.03	.01	.03	.01	.02	.01	.03	.03	.01	.07
s/z	.02	0	0	.01	.04	.01	0	0	.02	0	.01
w	.03	.04	.08	.07	.07	.13	.05	.06	.02	.01	.05
j	.03	.02	.03	.07	.01	.14	.13	.04	.01	.04	.05
r	0	0	0	0	0	0	0	0	.03	0	.04
TOTAL single consonants	.42	.53	.42	.45	.50	.58	.60	.53	.43	.52	.50

The most common changes with age were a decrease in the relative frequency of [d/t] (4 infants) and an increase in [b/p] (3 infants). Thus, this older group is similar to the younger groups in its preference for stops and glides but had a much greater preference for [d/t] and [w] and a lesser preference for [m]. Preference for [d/t] decreased in favor of other phones as these infants reached a 30-word vocabulary (when observations stopped).

All of the older infants show a clear developmental increase in the proportion of utterances in which different consonant types were combined (Table 1–6). The most common combination was labial plus dento-alveolar. Three infants also frequently used dento-alveolars or labials combined with [s/z] or [n/l], and two infants (Kar and Nik) used many other types of combinations.

Strictly vocalic utterances show a decline with age in this group (Table 1–7). The preferences are very similar to those of the younger groups: front-mid [ɛ] and [æ], midcentral [ə/ʌ], and low [a/ɑ]. The preference for [ə/ʌ] tended to decrease with age, except for Nic, while back vowels did not increase, contrary to what might be expected for infants of this age.

In the large Italian-Canadian sample, all consonants, even those repeated in the same utterance, were counted in order to measure consonantality, defined as the ratio of total number of consonants to number of utterances. Clear [h]'s and initial glottal stops were coded for this sample, but voiced–voiceless distinctions were again disregarded.

Table 1–8 gives the preferences for each *supra*glottal consonant type in terms of the number of male and female infants using it as one of their three most frequent consonant types at 9 to 10 months and at 15 months. These preferences are based on a mean of 118 utterances (range, 64 to 232) from two half-hour sessions at 9 to 10 months and a mean of 97 utterances (range, 47 to 157) from a single half-hour session at 15 to 16 months. The most preferred consonant for both male and female infants in this group is dento-alveolar [d/t] at 9 to 10 and 15 to 16 months, followed closely by velars [g/k] at 9 months and by [m] at 15 months. At both ages, [b/p] is also relatively frequent. The major changes across age are a preference for [j] at 9 months but not at 15 months, and a more frequent use of [s/z] by female infants at 15 months. These infants, then, resemble the older English-Canadian group in their more pronounced preference for [d/t], but they show a greater preference for [m], more similar to the younger English-Canadian and French infants.

Table 1-6. Change with Age in the Relative Frequency (%) of Combined Consonantal Categories for Older English-Canadian Infants

	Nic			Kar			San	Nik		Lis	
Age in months	13–15	15.5–17	17.5–19	13–15	16–18	14–15.5	16–17	17–19	20–22	17–19	20–21
Phonetic categories											
Labial combinations	0	.01	.04	.01	.08	.02	.01	.03	.01	.01	.01
Labial plus velar	.01	.02	.01	.01	.06	.02	.01	.01	.02	.03	.01
Labial plus sonorant/strident	.01	0	.02	.05	.05	0	0	.01	.08	.01	.01
Dento-alveolar plus labial (sonorant)	.04	.06	.08	.13	.07	.02	.05	.13	.16	.02	.05
Dento-alveolar plus velar	.01	.01	.01	.01	.03	0	.01	.02	.02	0	0
Dento-alveolar plus sonorant/strident	.03	.04	.02	.05	.02	0	0	.01	.04	0	.01
Dento-alveolar plus labial plus velar	0	0	.01	.01	.03	0	.01	.02	0	0	.01
Dento-alveolar plus labial plus strident	0	0	.02	.02	.05	0	0	0	.01	0	0
Other combinations	0	.01	.02	.05	0	0	0	.03	.14	.01	0
TOTAL combined consonants	.10	.15	.23	.34	.39	.06	.09	.26	.48	.08	.13

Table 1-7. Change with Age in the Relative Frequency (%) of Vowel Categories for Older English-Canadian Infants

Age in months	Nic			Kar		San		Nik		Lis	
	13–15	15.5–17	17.5–19	13–15	16–18	14–15.5	16–17	17–19	20–22	17–19	20–21
Phonetic categories											
ɪ/i	.03	.02	.02	0	0	.05	.02	0	.01	.02	0
e	.03	.01	.01	0	.02	.02	.01	0	0	0	.02
ɛ	.09	.06	.12	.01	.01	.04	.04	.01	0	.02	.10
æ	.05	.05	.02	.04	.01	.02	.03	.04	.01	.06	.02
ə/ʌ	.07	.07	.09	.07	0	.11	.07	.02	0	.12	.04
a/ɑ	.02	.01	.01	.01	.03	0	.03	.03	0	.05	.10
o/ɔ	0	0	.01	.01	.01	.01	.01	.01	.02	.01	.01
u/ʊ	.01	.03	.02	0	0	.02	0	.01	0	.01	.01
Vowel plus j/w	0	.01	0	0	0	0	.03	.01	.02	.02	.01
Vowel combinations	.16	.05	.04	.05	.04	.08	.06	.06	.02	.08	.05
TOTAL vowels	.46	.31	.34	.19	.12	.35	.30	.19	.08	.38	.36

Table 1–8. Number of Italian-Canadian Infants Whose Use of Each
Consonant Type is among Three Most Frequent at 9 and 15 Months

	9 Mo.		15 Mo.	
Single Consonants	Male	Female	Male	Female
d/t	9	11	12	13
m	5	5	11	11
b/p	5	8	5	9
φ/β	2	2	4	2
g/k	6	9	5	4
j	7	7	2	1
s/z	3	1	1	5
w	4	2	3	0

Features of Babbling

Table 1–9 gives the means and standard deviations for consonantality, consonantal repertoire, and complexity, at 9 to 10 months and
at 15 to 16 months, for male and female infants in the larger sample of
30 infants. Consonantality increased for these infants from a mean
ratio of 1.6 consonants per utterance (range, .4 to 3.0) at 9 to 10
months to a mean ratio of 2.3 (1.2 to 4.4) at 15 to 16 months, an
increase that was statistically significant; $F (1, 24) = 18.14$; $p < .0001$.

Table 1–9. Mean Measures of Features of Babbling by Sex and Age

	Male		Female	
Age	Mean	SD	Mean	SD
Consonantality				
9–10 mo.	1.60	0.72	1.69	0.79
15–16 mo.	2.27	0.83	2.38	0.77
Repertoire				
9–10 mo.	11.80	3.19	10.87	2.99
15–16 mo.	15.07	4.15	14.20	3.47
Complexity				
9–10 mo.	0.17	0.11	0.18	0.12
15–16 mo.	0.28	0.11	0.33	0.15

All but 4 infants (3 male and 1 female) showed this increase. This measure may be similar to the CB ratio of Oller, Eilers, Steffens, Lynch, and Urbano(1994), which is the proportion of syllables containing a consonant. Our measure, of course, is based on the utterance, not the syllable (but Oller's measure was previously based on the utterance). At 8 months, the infants studied by Oller et al. (1994) had a CB ratio of .2, which increased to .3 at 10 months and not much more at 14 months. Our findings, then, do not agree with the lack of increase at 14 months. They are more in agreement with the results of Menyuk, Liebergott, and Schultz (1995), who found an increase from .09 to .25 in the proportion of *syllables* containing a consonant from 8 to 12 months and a steep increase from 12 to 14 months (from .27 to .42 for "early fast developers" and from .17 to .24 for "late fast developers" and "slow developers" combined).

Consonantal repertoire also increased from a mean of 11.3 consonants at 9 to 10 months (range, 6 to 17) to a mean of 14.6 at 15 to 16 months (range, 7 to 22), an increase that was also statistically significant; $F(1, 24) = 13.27$; $p < .001$. For this measure, each consonant had to be used twice, in two different utterances, to be counted. The number of infants showing this increase was 23 of 30 (77%), with male and female infants equally represented. In contrast, Vihman et al. (1986) found an increase in consonantal inventory in 3 of 7 of their infants, fewer than half.

Complexity, or the proportion of utterances in which different types of consonants were combined, significantly increased from a mean proportion of .18 (range, .01 to .46) at 9 to 10 months to a mean proportion of .30 (range, .09 to .55) at 15 to 16 months; $F(1, 24) = 15.39$, $p < .001$. This measure indicates that variegated babbling was indeed increasing over this age period and contradicts the previous studies cited indicating no change. Discrepancies between our findings and those of Mitchell and Kent (1990) and Davis and MacNeilage (1995) may be because they did not study infants beyond the end of the first year.

Although the measures of consonantality, repertoire, and complexity could, in principle, vary independently, they did not. They were highly correlated with each other at each age level (r's ranging from .52 to .87; $p < .01$). The only measure that was stable across the two age levels, however, was consonantality ($r = .49$; $p < .01$).

It is clear from Table 1–9 that none of these measures interacted with sex; male and female infants showed equivalent increases in consonantality, repertoire, and complexity of babbling. However, the range of variation in these measures was large. The obvious question, then, is do these babbling characteristics make a difference for language acquisition? That is, is there an advantage for infants who show more complex babbling or a greater consonantal repertoire or simply a greater use of consonants in general? The next section addresses these issues, beginning with a brief review of studies that have shown relationships between babbling and early words.

Prelinguistic Vocalizations and First Words

For many years, the prevailing view was that of Jackobson (1941/1968), who saw babbling as irrelevant for language. This view was based primarily on other sources, such as Grégoire's diary study of his child. Grégoire stressed that the child at the peak of babbling is capable of producing all possible sounds. According to Jakobson, the child "then loses nearly all of his ability to produce sounds in passing over from the pre-language stage to the first acquisition of words" (p. 21); "phonetic abundance" is replaced by "phonemic poverty." This discontinuity view incorporated also a notion of temporal discontinuity in that a period of silence was thought to intervene between babbling and language, proper. Evidence for such a silent period is lacking (Locke, 1983), and evidence for continuity between babbling and language has been rapidly accumulating. Although it is largely true that first words are simpler than babbling, at least in English (Vihman, 1996), in that they are shorter and less complex, many similarities between babbling and early words have been established. Oller, Wieman, Doyle, and Ross (1976) first found that in the 10 infants whom they studied, 5 at 6 to 8 months and 5 at 12 to 13 months, features of early speech were also characteristic of babbling. Like language, over 90% of babbling contained single consonants rather than clusters; initial consonants outnumbered final consonants by 3 to 1; stops outnumbered fricatives by a wide margin in initial position, whereas the reverse was true in final position; glides, [w] or [j], outnumbered liquids, [r] or [l]; and alveolars and dentals were more frequent than palatals and velar-uvulars in the older group. Similarities between babbled utterances and early words have also been found in general preferences, but those phones which are the most frequent in babbling are not necessarily the most frequent in speech (Stoel-Gammon & Cooper, 1984). It is rather that if a phone is frequent in the babbling of an infant, "it is *available to be programmed* into a lexical unit" (Locke, 1983, p. 55). Babbling and early words have been shown to be generally similar in consonant place and manner of production and in number of syllables (Vihman, et al., 1985; Vihman & Greenlee, 1987). However, dentals and glottals are more associated with babbling and labials are more associated with words (Stoel-Gammon & Cooper, 1984; Vihman, et al., 1985).

The four older English-Canadian infants whom we followed into early word acquisition confirmed some of these findings. The most common initial consonant in their early words heard on the video-recordings or reported by parents was a labial (/b/p/). Between 24% and 44% of their words began with a /b/ or /p/, and they had several of these words in common: *bye-bye, ball, book, baby, button, bottle, bath, bus,* and *bed.* The next most frequent initial consonant was /d/ or /t/ for two infants and /g/ or /k/ for two infants. However, for none of these infants did the relative rankings of bilabials, dento-alveolars, or velars as initial phonemes in words match the relative frequencies of the corresponding phones in babbling. In addition, some very rare or absent phones in babbling were used as initial consonants in at least three early words – for example, /r/ for one infant and /s/ for two infants. Thus, only general parallels in preferences can be drawn between babbling and first words. More specific predictions for individual infants cannot be made. Early word choice is clearly both semantically and phonetically driven (Ferguson & Farwell, 1975).

During the period of transition to intelligible speech, the consonantal repertoire is richer in babbling than in early words (Vihman et al., 1986), a finding that appears to offer some support for Jakobson's views. The progression in consonantal repertoire in words, however, does seem to stem from babbling. Across sessions, some consonants (most commonly, [p], [j], and [w]) were seen first in babbling and then, subsequently, in words (Vihman et al., 1986). The relation between consonants practiced the most in babbling and those produced in words was strongest for those children who acquired words the fastest (Vihman, 1992), but some of these comparisons are concurrent and involve simply the mutual influence between babbling and words (Elbers & Ton, 1985).

The issue of whether more sophisticated babbling matters for early word acquisition has been addressed by very few studies. Menyuk et al. (1995) found that the proportion of syllabic vocalizations (those containing a consonant) at 14 and 16 months, but not earlier, was significantly related to the age of acquisition of a 50-word vocabulary. Similarly, McCune and Vihman (1996) found that earlier talkers (those with a larger cumulative referential lexicon at 16 months) were distinguished from later talkers by both their greater consonantality between 9 and 13 months and their larger consonantal repertoire. Both babbling and words were included in these measures, however.

Atypical babbling patterns have also been associated with delayed onset of meaningful speech in two otherwise normal infants (Stoel-Gammon, 1989). A study of an infant who was prevented from babbling by a tracheostomy revealed a delay in word acquisition after decannulation but only for a short period of time (Locke & Pearson, 1990).

In our 30 Italian-Canadian infants, there was not an advantage in early word acquisition at 15 months for babies with more advanced babbling at 9 months, in terms of either consonantality, consonantal repertoire, or complexity. At 15 months, however, complexity of babbling was moderately related to concurrent vocabulary size ($r = .37$; $p < .05$) (Blake, Osborne, Borzellino, & Macdonald, 1995). This vocabulary measure included both English and Italian words reported by mothers and/or produced during the observational session.

Prelinguistic Vocalizations and Later Language

Even less information is available about the long-term relation between babbling and language acquisition after the second year. Stoel-Gammon (1992) reviewed a few studies demonstrating relationships between precanonical *rate* of vocalization before 6 months and later language. However, none of these assesses relationships between qualitative aspects of postcanonical babbling and language. In a small sample of seven subjects, Vihman and Greenlee (1987) found a relationship between phonological accuracy at 3 years of age and the earlier proportion of utterances containing a nonfinal consonant, a measure of consonantality (but with glottals and glides disregarded), in both babbling and words. Early preferences for relatively unusual consonants (for example, fricatives or liquids) were unrelated to their mastery at 3 years.

In our longitudinal study of 30 Italian-Canadian children, a half-hour speech sample was audio- and videorecorded at 3 years 1 month while the child played with a collection of small toys brought to the home by the observer. The speech samples were transcribed, and mean length of utterance (MLU) and a measure of syntactic complexity were calculated using rules that we had previously developed (Blake & Quartaro, 1990) and applied to almost 90 speech samples of preschool children (Blake, Quartaro, & Onorati, 1993). Our measure of MLU at age 3 was correlated with complexity of babbling at 15 months ($r =$ .46; $p < .01$). This long-term relationship was not mediated by the concurrent relationship between complexity of babbling and vocabulary size at 15 months, because early vocabulary size was not related to MLU at 3 years ($r = .15$; $p > .05$) (Blake, Borzellino, Osborne, Mason, & Macdonald, 1997). Mirak and Rescorla (1998) also found that MLU at age 3 was not predicted by earlier vocabulary size (at 24 to 31 months) in a sample of late talkers.

Environmental Influences on Babbling

Although the onset of canonical babbling is generally considered to be biologically driven, in part by changes in the infant's vocal tract described above, sporadic investigations have been conducted regarding potential environmental impact on age of onset. As previously mentioned, socioeconomic status seems not to affect the onset of canonical babbling (Eilers et al., 1993), even among infants born into extreme poverty (Oller, Eilers, Basinger, Steffens, & Urbano, 1995). After onset, the rate of babbling is lower in infants from low SES families and from extremely poor families, but not the degree of well-formedness of consonants and vowels (Oller et al., 1994; Oller et al., 1995).

The mediating factor in the effect of SES on rate of vocalization is generally believed to be the greater maternal responsivity to infant vocalizations found in higher SES groups (Tulkin, 1977) of higher education levels (Bradley & Caldwell, 1984). However, maternal responsivity has received most attention with respect to its impact on *pre*canonical vocalizations. Experimental studies of 3-month-olds have shown that infants vocalize more frequently when spoken to than when faced with a silent adult, whether or not the adult's utterance is contingent on the infant's vocalization and whether it is verbal (*Hi* plus baby's name) or nonverbal *(tsk, tsk)*. Being contingent *and* verbal, however, is associated with infant vocalizations that are perceived by adults to be more syllabic (i.e., speechlike) and less vocalic (Bloom, 1988; Bloom, Russell, & Wassenberg, 1987). Under contingent responding, either verbal or nonverbal, infants paused longer as if waiting for the adult's turn, whereas under random responding they showed more quick bursts of vocalizations. Thus, simply being talked to apparently arouses infants and elicits more vocalizations, whereas contingent responding increases turn-taking behavior. Contingent verbal responding enhances the maturity of the speech sounds.

The effect of contingent verbal responding on the quality of precanonical vocalizations was replicated by Masataka (1993) in an experimental study of mother–infant dialogues in the home. Infants in this study also showed more bursts of vocalization under random responding. The effect of an active versus passive mother was extended by Legerstee (1991) to a comparison with a nonsocial stimulus (a doll). Precanonical infants produced more "melodic" sounds (syllable-like with varied pitch contours and longer durations) to an actively conversant mother than to both the passive adult and the doll, but they produced more vocalic sounds to a passive adult.

In our study of 30 Italian-Canadian infants, we found no relation between maternal education level and the qualitative aspects of babbling that we measured (consonantality, repertoire, and complexity) (Blake et al., 1995). Our lowest educational level was high school graduate (7 mothers); the mean years of education of our mothers was 14.3 (SD = 2.12), and the range was 12 to 18 years. Our findings, then, do not rule out a negative impact of lower education levels on babbling. None of the families in our study was impoverished. In addition, responding to infant vocalization may be a widespread practice of this subculture, although we did find variability. High school–educated mothers did respond more insensitively to their infants' vocalizations at 15 months than did more educated mothers; $F (2, 24) = 4.44$; $p < .02$. By insensitive responding we mean verbal responses that are not directly focused on the infant's vocalization. Consonantal repertoire at 15 months was negatively related to the proportion of maternal insensitive responding ($r = -.39$; $p < .05$), but there were no differences in repertoire among the infants of different maternal education levels. Verbal responses that were sensitive to infant communications at 15 months, and specifically those that were imitations of the infants' communications, were significantly related to infants' concurrent vocabulary size ($r = .36$, $p < .05$ for verbal sensitive responding, overall; $r = .62$, $p < .01$ for imitations, specifically) (Vitale, 1998). As in Menyuk et al. (1995), maternal responsivity was unrelated to consonantality.

Research on deaf infants appears to support the importance of environmental input for the onset of canonical babbling, because deaf infants begin this stage after the end of the range for hearing infants, with no overlap in distribution (Oller & Eilers, 1988). It is not just a question of delay, since 5 to 6 months after the onset of canonical babbling, only half of the deaf infants showed babbling patterns similar to those of hearing infants. Moreover, deaf infants have a *decreasing* consonantal repertoire, resulting in a much reduced repertoire at 15 to 18 months compared to that of normally hearing infants (Stoel-Gammon, 1988). Among the hearing impaired, glottal phones, [h] and [?], and labials were found to constitute a much higher proportion of the consonantal inventory and alveolars (mostly [d/t]) a much lower proportion than among those with normal hearing (Stoel-Gammon, 1988). Glottal phones are the easiest to articulate (being a kind of default phone), and labials have a visual component (moving the lips), which would make them easier to mimic. At the *onset* of canonical babbling, however, normally hearing infants were found to produce more labials, [b/p] or [w], than matched hearing-impaired infants, who continued to produce the back sounds (velar fricatives and trills) preferred by both groups in the early months (Clement & Koopmans-van Beinum, 1995). Profoundly hearing-impaired infants continued to show a higher number of velar fricatives and trills than their nonimpaired counterparts between 8.5 and 11.5 months (Clement, Koopmans-van Beinum, & Pols, 1996). These differences between deaf and hearing infants seem to support an important role for speech input during the transition to language. However, the study cited earlier of an infant who was tracheostomized during the normal babbling period (Locke & Pearson, 1990) casts some doubt upon this conclusion. This infant could hear sounds but not make them. Her babbling, upon decannulation, was more similar to that of hearing-impaired infants than to that of normal infants. These researchers concluded that what is most important to the normal development of babbling, then, is vocal *self*-stimulation, or the auditory feedback loop, which was first emphasized many years ago by Fry (1966).

The environmental variable that has received the most research attention is the ambient language of the infant's culture. Underlying this research is the notion of babbling drift: That is, as infants begin to make the transition into adult-modeled language, their babbling changes to reflect more of the phonetic features of the language of their culture and less of the features absent from their linguistic environment. Babbling drift is then a *post*canonical development, usually evident by 10 months of age but possibly beginning earlier. Evidence to support it is not clear-cut. The clearest effects seem to be for vowels.

The F2:F1 ratio, a measure of the relationship between the two lowest frequency bands in the acoustic signal, which distinguishes vowels on the compact–diffuse dimension, showed that 10-month-old English, French, Algerian, and Cantonese infants matched the ratios in the corresponding adult languages (de Boysson-Bardies, Halle, Sagart, & Durand, 1989).

Recent studies of prosody also show some clear environmental effects. By comparison to the reduplicative babbling of American infants, the reduplicative babbling of French infants during the latter half of the first year demonstrated a higher incidence of rising fundamental frequency contours, a greater proportion of long final syllables, and an increasingly regular timing of nonfinal syllables, all characteristics that differentiate French from English (Levitt, 1993). In contrast, American infants showed a greater proportion of falling intonation in their reduplicative babbling (Whalen, Levitt, & Wang, 1991).

The case for babbling drift in consonants is more difficult to make because infants in different cultures, as I have stressed earlier, prefer the same small set of consonants (Locke, 1983). Individual differences tend to be restricted to consonants of very low frequency (Vihman, 1991; Vihman et al., 1986). Despite this finding, when the patterns of distribution of place and manner in both babbling and early words were compared across four language groups, some differences were found in higher frequency consonants (de Boysson-Bardies, et al. 1992). Swedish and American infants used a higher percentage of stop consonants, whereas French and Japanese infants used a higher percentage of nasals, all tendencies reflecting differences in the target languages. In contrast, our two French infants previously described did not differ from the two English-Canadian infants in their preference for nasals versus stops. De Boysson-Bardies et al. (1992) also found that French infants produced more liquids (e.g., [r] and [l]) than did Japanese infants, differences again reflecting the target languages. With respect to place, French infants produced the highest percentage of labials and the lowest percentage of velars, whereas Swedish and Japanese infants showed the reverse tendencies, differences found in the respective target languages. In a study of syllable structure, de Boysson-Bardies (1993) found that Yoruba infants from Nigeria used more VCV (vowel–consonant–vowel) patterns, whereas French, English, and Swedish infants used more CVCV (consonant–vowel–consonant–vowel) patterns, corresponding to characteristics of nouns in their respective language environments.

In our study of Italian-Canadian infants, we evaluated babbling drift by examining the babbling of two groups of infants, one who heard much more Italian than English and one who heard either no Italian at all or very little. The proportion of infant-addressed maternal utterances that were Italian, English, or mixed was counted during one of the 9-month sessions and the 15-month session and was found to be quite stable over this age period ($r = .92$; $p < .01$). Five male and six female infants heard at least two-thirds Italian from their mothers, and typically much more, whereas five male and six female infants heard less than one-third Italian, and typically almost exclusively English. The Italian group did not have older siblings who spoke English to them. This comparison was done after phonetic transcription, so that transcribers were unaware of the language groups. Predominantly English-hearing infants were found to produce significantly more [d/t] phones in their babbling at both ages, F $(1, 20) = 5.13$, $p < .04$; whereas at 15 months, predominantly Italian-hearing infants produced significantly more Italian r sounds (trills and flaps), $t(20) = 2.26$, $p < .04$ (Blake et al., 1995). The mean frequencies for these phones for each group at 9 and 15 months are presented in Table 1–10. The latter finding recalls Locke's (1983) report of a relatively high frequency of [r] phones (4.2%) in an infant living in an Afrikaans language environment and recorded between 11 and 18 months. Afrikaans, like Italian, seems to have rolled [r]'s with flaps. Our results show, then, that even in an essentially bilingual environment, salient aspects of the dominant ambient language can affect babbling.

Table 1–10. Mean Relative Frequencies of Target Phones in the Babbling of Infants Hearing Mostly Italian Versus Mostly English

	Language Heard							
	Italian				English			
	9 Mo.		15 Mo.		9 Mo.		15 Mo.	
Target Phones	Mean	SD	Mean	SD	Mean	SD	Mean	SD
[d/t]	.129	.124	.116	.082	.246	.182	.174	.065
English [r]	.002	.004	.016	.017	.002	.003	.022	.021
Italian r	0	0	.011	.013	0	0	.002	.004

Conclusions

Phylogenetic continuity in sound production clearly ends with the
onset of canonical babbling (except for the involuntary, emotional
sounds that we continue to utter). Before 6 months, we can see similarities between human infant and nonhuman primate phonation, particularly in the prosodic features of pitch, timing, and intensity, and
also in dialogue and turn-taking. Perhaps the most important precursor found in nonhuman primate vocalizations is the frequency modulation apparent in long and repeated calls. Such modulation is
particularly striking when the elements vary following a pattern, as in
the calls of marmoset and cotton-top tamarin monkeys. Labeling such
patterns as syntax (Snowdon, 1982) is an exaggeration, but the speed
and complexity of the calls represent an evolutionary base for prosody
and sequencing of components.

It is unclear why nonhuman primates do not formulate the labial,
dental, nasal, and fricative sounds (with the exception of [h]) that they
could articulate. It is clear that production of these sounds would be
quite primitive, given limitations of the vocal tract. Before the human
vocal tract is fully developed and the neural circuits are myelinated (at
least to a degree), human infants' vocal production is also quite primitive. It is significant that babbling begins in all language communities
with those consonants that are easiest to articulate, the "default" stop
consonants, and gradually incorporates the more difficult fricatives
and sonorants. The infants whom we followed belonging to different
cultural groups showed stable stop preferences, with an increase in
preference for "unusual" consonants, such as [s], during the second
year. Combinations of consonants also were, first and foremost, of stop
consonants, with more varied types of combinations increasing during
the second year. Vowels also were preferred on the basis of ease of
articulation, with very few high and back vowels. Locke (1983) argued
that these preferences support a biological view of babbling because
the majority of sounds produced by infants are those easiest to articulate. Combinations of different consonant types in the same utterance,
even when they are all stop consonants, seem, however, to reflect vocal
play rather than automaticity or a fixed action pattern, as proposed by
Locke (1993). Furthermore, the tendency to combine different consonant types was related to early word production, even though early
words usually contain only a single consonant. Complexity of babbling
was also related to complexity of sentences at age 3 years (MLU).

Thus, the articulatory demands involved in producing complex babbled utterances clearly have some influence on language production
although the relationships are moderate. These findings and the evidence on babbling drift lead to a conclusion that, whereas the onset of
canonical babbling has characteristics that implicate a biological trig-
ger (universality and suddenness), the progression of babbling reflects
environmental influence and individual variability in sound exploration that affect language acquisition. In the following chapter, evidence regarding the mapping of sounds onto contexts further
demonstrates that the development of babbling in human infants is not
simply biologically controlled.

CHAPTER TWO

Sound–Meaning Correspondences

The issue of what meaning is and how to define it has occupied philosophers, linguists, and psycholinguists for a very long time. Linguists limit meaning to word meaning, or what Halliday (1975) has termed lexicosemantic. Halliday's pioneering observations of his son's prelinguistic vocalizations, however, revealed that Nigel had a functional system of meaning prior to adopting recognizable adult-modeled words. That is to say, he used many nonword expressions repeatedly with the same functional content relevant to particular situations. These early expression–content relations were grouped into categories that anticipated the later semantic system of the linguistic period. Halliday termed the early system bistratal, with meaning being directly mapped onto sound, in contrast to the later tristratal system in which sound and meaning are related via syntax. He stressed the continuity between the two systems, thus extending the ideas expressed in the previous chapter about phonetic continuity between babbling and language to continuity on the semantic plane as well. Although other observers have presented illustrations of "phonetically consistent forms" (Dore, Franklin, Miller, & Ramer, 1976) or "clusters of sounds exhibiting a functional content" (Gillis & De Schutter, 1986), it is only with Halliday's extensive and detailed observations of Nigel that a clear case has been made for a prelinguistic semantic system.

Similar efforts are currently ongoing among observers of nonhuman primates. These researchers have been concerned with the degree to which animal signals in the field can be viewed as referential, in that a certain signal transmits a particular meaning to conspecifics whereas other signals transmit a different meaning. A claim about reference, however, goes beyond Halliday's view of the prelinguistic system and borders on the lexicosemantic system of the linguistic period.

In this chapter I examine first the extensive observations concerning the functions of nonhuman primate calls in the wild, particularly the calls of great apes. These observations are similar to the sound–meaning correspondences described by Halliday in that they attempt to map calls onto general contexts. Playback experiments in the field attempt, instead, to demonstrate more precise reference to objects in primate calls; these are reviewed next. Sound–meaning correspondences in infant prelinguistic vocalizations will then be examined through illustrations from several observational studies conducted by other researchers, Halliday in particular, and from our own detailed longitudinal study of 11 infants. The major questions will be the following: (1) To what degree is there phylogenetic continuity in semioticity? (2) Do human infants display different kinds of sound–meaning correspondences from nonhuman primates? (3) What case can be made for ontogenetic continuity in the semantic system?

The Functional Meaning of Nonhuman Primate Calls

Spontaneous Calls of the Great Apes

Goodall (1986) mapped chimpanzee calls onto emotional meanings on the basis of her extensive observations of chimpanzees at the Gombe Reserve. Emotive states were associated with a single call or with several different calls. Conversely, some calls were associated with a single emotive state; whereas others, such as scream, bark, waa–bark, tantrum scream, crying, and pant–hoot, occurred with more than one state. The major difficulty with Goodall's mapping is that she provided associations with 32 different calls, whereas Marler (1976), as discussed in chapter 1, could find acoustic differences in only 13 of them. Some of Goodall's additional distinctions arise from combinations of call types – for example, pant–bark; whereas others are variations on the same call, apparently defined by the situation – for example, arrival pant–hoot, inquiring pant–hoot, and spontaneous pant–hoot. In agreement with Marler's earlier analysis, more recent work has not found consistent acoustic differences between these different types of pant–hoots (Mitani & Nishida, 1993). So, there is perhaps some circularity between the description of the call and the emotive state onto which it is mapped. In addition, clearer definitions of the emotional meanings and determination of observer reliability would strengthen the associations proposed. Nevertheless, some aspects of the mapping should be noted. First, Goodall (1986) stressed the emotive nature of the meaning and not the referential. She stated that although the calls "may alter, often in a highly predictable way, the behavior of individuals who hear them. . . , [they] are not necessarily made with the intention of influencing the action of others" (p. 125). Second, Goodall's observations that soft grunts are used by chimpanzees to regulate movement and cohesion among friendly individuals, specifically when pausing during travel, have been extended by other observers to mountain gorillas (see below). Third, some of the correspondences are quite similar to those that have been noted in human infants, particularly *huu* for puzzlement, soft bark for annoyance, and grunt for sociability. As for the communicative nature of these vocalizations, a revealing comment is that when chimpanzees are frightened, "they normally run off silently with no alarm call" (Goodall, 1965, p. 467), thus leaving the rest of the group unaware of the danger. This behavior is to be contrasted to the vervet alarm calls described below.

Mitani and Nishida (1993) argued that the pant–hoots of male chimpanzees are not just a manifestation of high arousal levels caused by social or feeding excitement, as in Goodall's (1986) mapping. Using a method similar to ours (see below), these investigators compared observed frequencies of calls occurring with particular behavioral activities with the frequencies that would be expected by chance. There were only three activities – feeding, traveling, and resting – but they could potentially occur at different times with respect to the calls – that is, before or after. Only traveling was associated with pant–hoots, and it both preceded and followed these calls with a greater than expected frequency in the two highest ranking males. Although feeding and resting activities would seem by their nature to preclude pant–hooting, it is possible for these behaviors to occur *before* or *after* calling, but they did not. Animals also called more frequently when conspecific allies were nearby. The authors concluded that the functions of pant–hooting are to maintain contact and to recruit allies.

The chimpanzees of the Budongo Forest also were observed to use pant–hoots when preparing to move on or while traveling, as well as at the meeting or splitting of large gatherings and sometimes when seeing bunches of fruit (Reynolds & Reynolds, 1965). The last mapping is similar to Goodall's (1986) association between pant–hoots and food enjoyment. Grunts were also used while traveling, in addition to accompanying feeding and nest building. The last functions are similar to Goodall's food grunts and nest grunts. Waa–barks were associated only with seeing the observer and thus might have expressed anger similar to what Goodall (1986) reported for the chimpanzees at Gombe. These observers argued against any spacing function of calls: "although different groups no doubt 'locate' each other by calling and answering over the forest, there was no evidence that this led to the spacing of groups" (Reynolds & Reynolds, 1965, p. 414).

Fossey (1972), like Goodall (1986), also categorized the calls of mountain gorillas according to associated situations but, in addition, recorded the responses given by conspecifics to the vocalizations. These are reproduced on Table 2–1. According to Fossey, panting occurred in females when observing a dispute among other group members and evoked positional changes in the latter. The hoot–bark was heard in all members of the group, it appeared to initiate or coordinate group movement, and it was the most effective vocalization in clustering group members. Hoots accompanied intergroup contacts and elicited other hoots or scattering of the group. The rest of the calls were made mostly by the silverback (see chapter 1). Roars were heard in threatening situations and evoked aggressive responses and positional changes in conspecifics. Growls accompanied annoyance at close approaches and evoked retreat in the approaching animal. Question–barks and hiccup–barks occurred in situations of mild alarm or curiosity and evoked positional changes in other group members. Alarm barks were given upon the initiation of a sudden or close contact, for example, with a buffalo, and also following loud noises or rock slides; they were followed by a retreat of the group. Pig grunts were heard more frequently when the group was on the move or when the silverback was pursuing a female, and they evoked movement in group members. Belching occurred when the group was stationary or feeding or toward the end of sunning, when group contentment was high. It evoked other belch vocalizations. Belching in gorillas appears both to be more frequent than its equivalent, rough grunting, in chimpanzees and to occur in a broader array of contexts (Marler & Tenaza, 1977).

Schaller's (1965) observations of the mountain gorilla confirm an association between grunts and movement and between belching (what he calls soft grunts) and both feeding and resting peacefully. Hoots made by silverbacks also were found to occur in the presence of another group (as part of a chest-beating display), and roars expressed anger or fear, usually as a reaction to the presence of an observer. Annoyance (at quarreling animals) was expressed by barks or harsh grunts, rather than by the growls observed by Fossey.

Table 2–1. Type and Number of Responses Given to Each Type of Gorilla Vocalization

Type of Call	Aggressive	Mild Alarm	Alarm	Positional Changes	Distress	Vocalizations Coordinating Group	Chest Beats	Hoot Series Plus or Minus Chest Beats	Total Responses for Each Vocalization
Roar (threat bark)	6 (5)	2		5 (2)			1		14 (7)
Growl	2	2		5 (1)		2			11 (1)
Pant series		1	3 (1)	6 (4)		2 (1)			12 (6)
Question–bark	2	1	1	13 (3)		2 (1)	4		21 (3)
Hiccup–bark				6		1	5	1	13
Screams	12	7	24 (9)	56 (28)	4	13	4		120 (37)
Wraagh (alarm bark)	7	46	104 (7)	222 (74)	1	15 (2)	41	1	437 (83)
Cries				11 (2)		3 (1)			14 (3)
Whines		1		4	1				6
Pig grunts	5	11 (1)	11	66 (13)	2	49 (12)	13	2	159 (26)
Hoot–bark		36	20	138 (35)	3	35 (3)	51	2	285 (38)
Belch vocalization		3		2		43 (8)	5		53 (8)
Hoot series plus chest beats	2 (1)	24 (1)	10 (1)	86 (9)	4	15 (5)	28	29	198 (17)
Hoot series minus chest beats		6	3	11 (2)		3 (2)	5	3	31 (4)
TOTAL of each type of response	36	140	176	631	15	181	157	38	

Note: All numbers in parentheses indicate that portion of responses given by group as opposed to an individual.
Source: From Fossy, D. (1972). Vocalizations of the mountain gorilla, *Animal Behaviour, 20*, p. 43. Reprinted by permission of Academic Press.

Belching in the gorilla was further investigated by Harcourt et al. (1993), who categorized these "close" calls into staccato syllable-like grunts and nonsyllable-like calls of longer duration. Close calls occurred most often during feeding but also sometimes during resting, and they typically were part of an exchange between animals quite close together, hence their name. These calls were given when gorillas were approaching another animal, when they were being approached, or in response to a movement. The end of a rest period was often preceded by an increase in syllable-like calls, and concerted group movement was the context most commonly associated with vocal choruses. Harcourt et al. (1993) concluded from their observations that close calls have two major functions: to coordinate activity of the group and to negotiate peaceful proximity in potentially competitive situations. With regard to the second function, syllable-like calls appear to signal threat, and nonsyllable-like calls, appeasement.

The first function, group coordination, was further explored by Stewart and Harcourt (1994), who focused on the syllable-like grunts that gorillas give while resting. The number of these grunts was higher during the last interval of the rest period than during other intervals, the increase occurring in both the number of animals vocalizing and in the number of calls per individual. The investigators interpret this increase as indicating a readiness to depart or at least to change activity.

Mori (1983) compared the functions of target vocalizations across gorillas, chimpanzees, and pygmy chimpanzees (bonobos), namely, *hoot* (*pant–hoot* in chimpanzees, *huii* in bonobos) and *wraah* (*roar* in gorillas). For all three groups, hoots were uttered at intergroup encounters. For the chimpanzees and bonobos only, they were also used between males inside a temporary group, for long-distance calling between temporary groups, and to prepare the group for movement. Wraahs were used by all three groups as a threat or alarm vocalization. For gorillas, they were also a long-distance call. For chimpanzees and bonobos, they were an initial response to hoots. The hoot thus appears to be a territorial call for all groups, except that bonobos show less antagonism and do not give choruses of hoots. Hoots also function as long-distance calls for chimpanzees and bonobos, whereas this function is associated with wraahs for gorillas.

Like the hoots of the gorillas, chimpanzees, and bonobos, the long calls of orangutan adult males also appear to have a territorial function, specifically to space out adult males and avoid encounters

(MacKinnon, 1974). Similarly, the songs of gibbons are hypothesized to have a spacing function (Deputte, 1982).

In captive bonobos, low hooting is a "contagious group response to environmental changes and disturbances, and an expression of general social excitement" (De Waal, 1988, p. 202). High hooting, which is apparently more gibbonlike than chimpanzee-like, is used between individuals who are out of sight of each other. Like low hooting, it is also used to express excitement or disturbance. Wieew–barks also occur in response to disturbance but, in addition, can be an attentional signal anticipating the expected appearance of food. In contrast, whistle–barks are an agonistic vocalization, often uttered in support of other group members or to recruit their help. High-pitched grunts (mentioned in the previous chapter) and soft peeps are used to draw attention to or to comment on objects, food, or events. Alarm peeps are typically given when an insect or snail is encountered and may correspond, at least in function, to the chimpanzee's huu of puzzlement (De Waal, 1988).

In summary, the kinds of mapping that have been observed in these apes are very general. Although in most species several different calls have been distinguished, both acoustically and observationally, their functions are quite limited. Repeatedly, they are said to be associated with agonistic behavior or with less intense annoyance; with traveling or, conversely, with feeding and resting; and with alarm or intergroup encounters. Responses typically involve aggression, positional changes, general retreat, or repetition of the call in exchanges. From these observational studies, then, the functions of calls that can be identified are not very specific. As we will see below, that is also true of some of the early mapping of sounds onto situations in human infants, although the functions of their vocalizations are much more varied.

This review has focussed on the great apes, but in the area of sound–meaning correspondences, much of the most interesting work has been done with monkeys, particularly cotton-top tamarins, pygmy marmosets, vervets, and rhesus macaques. In these species, playback experiments have been conducted in which responses of animals to the calls of their conspecifics or of other species have been systematically studied. These will now be briefly reviewed.

Playback Experiments

The long calls of cotton-top tamarins occur in at least three variant forms associated with three different contexts: while situated within the group, upon hearing vocalizations of strange animals, and when isolated or disturbed (Snowdon, 1982). In playback experiments, animals differentially responded to the first two call types and also discriminated between calls from their own group and other groups.

Pygmy marmosets use four variants of trill vocalizations. Of these, the closed-mouth trill, with a short duration, occurs during calm, relaxed movement, and the open-mouth trill, with a longer duration, precedes an agonistic encounter. Animals respond categorically to these trills in that they give differential responses to calls with different duration boundaries (Snowdon, 1993).

Sound–meaning correspondences in vervet monkeys are the most thoroughly investigated and the best known. Struhsaker (1967) first reported that vervets give different alarm calls to different predators. Further observation by Cheney and Seyfarth and their collaborators determined that they give a loud barking alarm call to leopards and other cat species, a short double-syllable cough to the martial eagle and the crowned eagle, and a chutter to pythons and poisonous snakes. In playback experiments (Cheney & Seyfarth, 1990; Seyfarth & Cheney, 1993), alarm calls were recorded and later played from a concealed speaker when no predator was in view. The monkeys were found to respond appropriately to the acoustic information in the call alone. That is, upon hearing the leopard alarm call, they ran up trees; when hearing the eagle call, they looked up or ran into bushes; and on hearing the chutter alarm, they stood bipedally peering into the grass and then mobbed the (absent) snake.

These observations were at first dismissed as being a simple expression of the intensity of fear, since the three calls fall on a continuum of loudness. However, variation in the length and amplitude of the calls did not change response distinctiveness between the three types of calls (Seyfarth, 1984). Furthermore, very similar sounding chutters were observed in situations involving not snakes but rather threats to a member of the group, a member of another group, or a human observer (Cheney, 1984). There are small but consistent acoustic differences in these four types of chutters. Thus, it is argued that these calls cannot be viewed simply as "iconic representations of the objects to which they refer . . . [but] that association between a given referent and a particular acoustic unit is relatively arbitrary" (Cheney, 1984, p. 62). Conversely, calls signaling the same predator can be acoustically quite different. For example, males give long, low barks to leopards, whereas females give short, high chirps. Yet vervets respond similarly to both types of calls, apparently demonstrating that they are classifying calls according to referent (Cheney & Seyfarth, 1990). They also transfer habituation within a class – that is, between two acoustically different alarm calls (chutter and wrr) that have the same referent (presence of another group) but not to an alarm call with a different referent (Seyfarth & Cheney, 1993). However, if chutters and wrrs are given by different individuals, then there is no transfer of habituation. This last finding appears to contradict the notion that vervets are classifying calls according to referent.

In a laboratory study using a two-choice operant conditioning procedure, vervets were immediately able to classify new snake and eagle alarm calls after extensive training on a single pair, even calls produced by monkeys of different ages and sexes (Owren, 1990a). Vervet responses to synthetic versions of snake and eagle alarm calls indicated that spectral patterning provided the most important cue (Owren, 1990b).

Playback experiments with vervet monkeys have also shown that recorded grunts to a dominant animal caused conspecifics to look toward the loudspeaker, whereas grunts recorded to members of another group caused conspecifics to look toward the horizon (Seyfarth, 1984). Although acoustic differences between these grunts are not easily identifiable, a classification based on 16 acoustic features did distinguish between grunts used in these two social contexts (Cheney & Seyfarth, 1990). Five of the features significantly discriminated between types for most of the monkey grunts recorded (Seyfarth, 1984). Despite the evidence that mapping exists between acoustic features of vervets' calls and specific referents, these researchers acknowledge the limitations of playback experiments. The precise meaning of a signal cannot be determined, but merely whether conspecifics discriminate between signals (Seyfarth, 1984). Also, we cannot tell if monkeys actually recognize a referential relationship between their calls and objects in the world around them (Cheney & Seyfarth, 1990). This, Cheney and Seyfarth noted, can be contrasted to chimpanzees trained in sign language, who clearly can identify the relation between a sign and its referent (see chapter 4).

Cheney and Seyfarth (1990) also denied that there is any pedagogy in vervet monkey culture, although Hauser (1996) disagreed. Infant vervets at an early age make appropriate alarm calls, but at first their predator categories are too broad. For example, they make eagle alarm calls to several avian species that do not prey on vervets. Adults give second alarm calls (following infant calls) more frequently when there is a real predator, and these may serve as reinforcers for the correct alarm calls (Cheney, 1984). Hauser (1996) argued that this is pedagogy, but according to Cheny and Seyfarth, there is no evidence that adults explicitly or intentionally teach their infants alarm calls. The issue of pedagogy has been addressed at length by King (1994) and is discussed in this book in chapter 8.

Playback experiments with rhesus macaques (Gouzoules, Gouzoules, & Marler, 1985) have indicated that mothers respond more frequently to their offsprings' screams when they are "noisy" rather than "arched." "Noisy" screams tend to occur in encounters with high-ranking opponents in which there is a high probability of physical contact, whereas "arched" screams are associated with a low probability of physical aggression. These researchers argue that the mothers are not simply responding to the degree of fear of injury expressed in juvenile screams. The fact that they responded at all to arched screams may mean that the mothers were more interested in preserving their matrilineal dominance rank than in protecting their offspring from injury (Gouzoules, Gouzoules, & Ashley, 1995). Gouzoules et al. (1985) considered the vervet alarms and grunts and the rhesus screams to be truly representational signal systems in that contextual or motivational information is not necessary for interpretation of the meaning of the signal. Whether the mapping is representational is further addressed in my discussion of such mapping in prelinguistic human infants.

Phonetically Consistent Forms in Prelinguistic Infants

Many of the early diary studies give examples of idiosyncratic expressions used with consistent meaning before the acquisition of recognizable words. Reviews of these studies can be found in Werner and Kaplan (1963), Dore et al. (1976), and Ferguson (1976). This review focuses on the illustrations found in more recent systematic observational studies.

Various labels have been applied to early sound–meaning correspondences: vocables (Werner & Kaplan, 1963), semiverbal signs (Piaget, 1962), self-language words (Winitz & Irwin, 1958), sensorimotor morphemes (Carter, 1974), patterns (Blake & de Boysson-Bardies, 1992), protowords (Stark, 1981), quasi words (Stoel-Gammon & Cooper, 1984), and phonetically consistent forms

(Dore et al., 1976). Although probably not the best choice because some variability is often present, phonetically consistent form seems to have become the label of choice.

Interestingly, the identification of these expressions in the stream of babbling has not been viewed generally as problematic. Halliday (1975, p. 245) stated that in practice, "the distinction between random vocalizations and systematic forms proved to be obvious." His specific criterion for a systematic form was that an expression had to be observed in at least three unambiguous instances with the same functional meaning. Dore et al. (1976, p. 15) characterize phonetically consistent forms as "readily isolable units, which are bounded by pauses," unlike babbling. According to these researchers, the phonetic elements of these expressions are more stable than in babbling, but not as stable as in words. Similarly, for Ferguson (1976, p. 9), "early vocables are more limited and more structured than babbling." Like Halliday (1975), Dore et al. (1976, p. 16) defined phonetically consistent forms as occurring repeatedly in "specifiable, recurring conditions." Phonetically consistent forms thus seem to be discriminated from "random" babbling, sound play, and practicing on the basis of their short length, distinctive phonetic structure, and recurrence under similar conditions, all features that are claimed to make them easily recognizable and easy to correlate with a particular context, even under the constraints of direct observation.

Review of Observational Studies

Dore et al. (1976) grouped phonetically consistent forms into four general categories: affect expressions (both protest and pleasure), instrumental expressions, indicating expressions, and grouping expressions. The defining criteria for the first three categories were nonverbal cues: facial expression, posture, and body movement for affect; reaching, grasping, and bodily straining in a certain direction for instrumental; pointing and directed gaze for indicating. Grouping expressions were vaguely defined as utterances addressed to objects that evoked the same feeling in the child – for example, frustration, contentment, or reassurance. Four children in their second year were videotaped in a nursery school interacting with their mother or teacher about once a month for 6 to 8 months. Despite all the data and the categorical criteria, only 16 examples of phonetically consistent forms are given: 4 in the affect category (from two children), 2 in the instrumental category (from two children), 7 in the indicating category (from two children), and 3 in the grouping category, 1 of which appears to be a word (*babi* for *baby*). The instrumental expressions involved either [m] or [ʌ], whereas most of the indicating expressions were one- or two-syllable [d] utterances with variable vowels. As we will see below, these forms are commonly found with these functions.

Carter (1974, 1978) drew her data for phonetically consistent forms from four one-hour videotapes made of a single infant between 12.5 months and 16.5 months. Functional categories were defined again largely on the basis of the gestures accompanying the vocalizations. Attention to self was expressed by variants of the infant's name (*David*) or of *Mommy*. Attention to object was expressed by initial [d] or [l]. Request object was expressed by initial [m], request disappearance by initial [b], rejection by [ə], and both request transfer of object and pleasure/surprise/recognition by [h] sounds. The expression for rejection was identified as a "general want expressor" used to gain attention and/or to express any request or state of dissatisfaction. This form appears to be quite similar to the grunt described by McCune et al. (1996).

Other examples come from observational studies not specifically focused on phonetically consistent forms. Bates's (1976) oldest Italian infant uttered [mm] as an imperative, [ayi] to point out novel objects and events, and [da] or [tieni] during give and take of objects. Her middle subject uttered [ha] for both imperative and declarative functions and [na na] also for imperative and to call to an adult. Scollon's (1976) infant, Brenda, said variants of [ne: ne:] to mean *sleep* (possibly a modeled Japanese word), and also to mean *milk, juice, bottle,* and *Mother*. Although this form appears to be a "general want expressor," it was also used *while* drinking juice. Expressions combining [a] or [æ] with [b], [w], or [l] were used to express desire or rejection. *Dædi* meant *Daddy,* but it also was used to label a picture in a magazine. *Ada* is interpreted as *another,* but this may represent an imposition of adult form on the infant's form. Greenfield and Smith's (1976) Nicky, like Brenda, used [dada] for his father but also with another meaning, as it accompanied all his actions. He also used [ada] while pointing to things around the house, and this time it was interpreted as meaning *there it is*. His general want expressor appeared to be [awa] or [awada]. McShane (1980) reported [eheheh] with high pitch as a request by one child up to the age of 17 months, when it was replaced by [dah].

More recently, Stoel-Gammon and Cooper (1984), in their longitudinal study of the lexical and phonological development of three children, found that two of these children used only one quasi word between 10 months and 16 months. One of them said [di:] for attention to object, and the other used [na ma ə] for general request. The third child, Will, used about a dozen quasi words, many of them with an initial [d] consonant, thus resulting in several homonyms. For example, his request form was [dæ dæ], and he used a similar form to refer to any object for which he did not know the name. Similar forms were also used to refer to airplanes or birds (things in the sky?) and to barking dogs, whereas a single syllable [də:] meant *nice* and [di:] meant *yes*. The expression [aha] was used for nudity or swimming and appears comparable to David's use of [h] for pleasure, surprise, and recognition. The expression [ga:ja] was used for calling people. Interestingly, for all three children in this study, quasi words first appeared either just before the first recognizable words or at the same time.

Kent and Bauer (1985) presented examples from four 13-month-olds of "recurrent phonetic forms" but with a distinct phonetic fluidity. The forms are said to have broad referential functions, but descriptions are not given. Some examples, however, appear to be various approximations of words – for example, *water* and *baby* or *bye-bye*. One set from Susan, consisting predominantly of [ɪs/z] preceded by a variable form [s,t,d,ʤ, or z], probably is an idiosyncratic form, since the easy interpretation of *this* may again be an imposition of an adult form.

Vihman and Miller (1988) reported consistent forms for three of their infants in a longitudinal study across the 9- to 16-month period. Many of these occur in the categories defined by Carter (1974). To express interest/surprise, one infant whispered [pwi], whereas another uttered an expression beginning with [h], like David. Excitement was associated with [dada] in one child. Pointing was accompanied by [tV] or [dV] in one infant and by [pah], [bʌʔʊ], or [ɛh] in another, who also used a word-based form, [ʔʌgæ], while pointing to or showing objects for which he could not produce a label. Reaching as a request was accompanied by "grunts" or stylized effort sounds (as defined in chapter 1) in several infants. In one infant, request to perform an action was briefly indicated by [hə].

The most detailed study of phonetically consistent forms, with the largest number of examples, still is Halliday's (1973, 1975) study of his son, Nigel, between the ages of 9 and 16 months. Every 6 weeks, Halliday categorized Nigel's expressions into functional categories.

At the first such summary, when Nigel was 10.5 months, he already had several expressions used with consistent functional meaning, although one, [bø], meaning "give me my bird," appears to have been a word. In terms of Carter's categories, request object was expressed by [na]; pleasure/recognition/interest (greeting) by [ø], [nŋ], or [a]; and attention to self by [ɛ] or [ə]. In addition, request action was indicated by [ə] or [mnŋ] and being sleepy by [ʔgxi]. These meanings are grouped by Halliday into the now well-known functional categories of instrumental (request object), regulatory (request action), interactional, and personal. The latter two categories both seem to overlap with Carter's (1974) category of pleasure/surprise/recognition. By 16 months, Nigel had many new expressions, even when those that seem word based are ignored. Requests for specific objects were accompanied by [aʔa] or [aha] and [yi]; request action by [a], [ə], [dɔ], [da], or [ɛ:da]; greeting by [a:] or [bæ] to a cat; response by [mɪʔ], [m], [da], or [ɛə]; pleasure/surprise/recognition by [ɛdɛ], [yi], [da], [ɛʔɛ], or [m]; dislike by [βɛʊ]; *what's that?* by [a::da]; and play by [ɛ] or [dida]. The last two functions are termed heuristic and imaginative, respectively. Interestingly, Halliday believes that his seventh function, the informative, is too sophisticated for an infant and thus did not appear in Nigel until 21 months. This may be because he defines this function similarly to Piaget's verbal recounting (McShane, 1980), in contrast to a simpler declarative function (Bates, 1976). That is, the informative function is said to involve dialogue, which for Halliday means communicating an experience to someone who has not shared that experience.

What is notable about the expressions is that many are homonymous, like the expressions of Stoel-Gammon and Cooper's Will. Thus, the infant repeats similar sounds across different types of situations. In addition, within a situation, there is often variability in the expression, as noted also by Vihman and Miller (1988). In giving only the general categories associated with the expressions, I have omitted the colorful glosses provided by Halliday for the meaning of each expression. For example, "Nice to see you and shall we look at this together" is said to be the content of [ʔdø]. These glosses have been criticized by others (for example., Bates, Benigni, Bretherton, Camaioni, & Volterra, 1977; Greenfield & Smith, 1976), and the description of the contexts is clearly not as empirical as psycholinguists would like. However, the general functions into which such glosses are grouped have had much heuristic value.

Prosodic Aspects of Sound–Meaning Correspondences

The review of Nigel's expressions ignores prosodic aspects, which Halliday stressed and which often distinguished one of Nigel's expressions from another, thereby decreasing some of the homonymy. For example, [ə] said with a midtone was mapped onto the regulatory category ("do that again"), whereas [ə] with a low tone was mapped onto the interactional category ("yes, it's me"). Similarly, [m] with a short, high falling intonation was instrumental ("give me that"), whereas [m] with a low falling intonation was regulatory ("yes, let's do that"), and [m] with a high rise–fall intonation was interactional ("yes, I see") or personal ("that's my best. . ."). At about 19 months, Nigel adopted a system according to which falling tones were mathetic (cognitive) in function and rising tones were pragmatic in function. Similarly, Marcos (1987) found that at close to the same age (15 to 16 months), pitch contours for elicited labeling versus request began to be differentiated. From this age, but not earlier at 14 months, initial pitch for requests was higher than for labels, whereas initial pitch for showing and giving tended to fall in between.

Whether intonation varies across different functional situations at younger ages has received contradictory answers. Menn (1976) found that her single subject over the second year did use particular intonation contours consistently with particular routines. Greetings were moderate in pitch, with first a falling contour and later a rising contour, the latter also being associated with "curiosity" routines. Thus, these two routines might be considered a single function comparable to the pleasure/surprise/recognition function of Carter (1974). Request object routines were associated with a high pitch and a rising contour, with a peak that was higher than that associated with request game routines. "Narrative" utterances were moderate in pitch with a falling contour. Contrary to Menn's results, Scollon (1976) stated that his single infant did not use intonation contrastively with different functional acts. Stoel-Gammon and Cooper's (1984) Will did distinguish between his many quasi words that involved the consonant [d] by variations in pitch and stress. At a much younger age (between 4 and 9 months), D'Odorico (1984) found that a primitive distinction could be made between request vocalizations, calls, and discomfort sounds in a laboratory situation. The request and call vocalizations of four infants exhibited more rising patterns, whereas discomfort cries showed more falling patterns. In addition, call vocalizations had a higher fundamental frequency than discomfort cries, with request vocalizations showing the lowest fundamental frequency.

Delack and Fowlow (1978) examined the association of contours with general contexts in a larger sample than the other studies – 19 infants. Corpora for 9 of these infants were recorded over the first half year, and for 10, during the whole first year. These infants tended to use fall–rise or rise contours when vocalizing alone and *not* to use rise–fall, whereas the reverse was true when they were vocalizing with their mothers. Vocalizing while *looking* at objects was associated with fall and *not* with rise–fall; in contrast, vocalizing while *touching* objects occurred more with rise–fall contours and *not* with fall or with fall–rise or rise contours. Thus, a simple contrast in contours was evident across these simple contrasting contexts. D'Odorico and Franco (1991) also found that for each of their five subjects, different contours were associated with different general situations. These were infant manipulation of a toy, infant manipulation of a toy while looking at an adult, adult manipulation of a toy while the infant looked at the adult or the toy, and infant looking at the adult with no focus on the toy. Between 4 and 9 months, rising contours, in particular, were associated with the second and third contexts for two infants and falling contours with the third context for another. Thus, there were individual differences in associations between acoustic parameters and contexts. These associations disappeared for all infants after 9 months.

It can be concluded from this summary that the evidence demonstrating the prelinguistic use of pitch or prosody to express differential meanings is not overwhelming. Those associations that have been found between contours and contexts are also not very informative, particularly in those studies of infants in their first year that focus on overly general contexts.

Our Research on Sound–Meaning Correspondences

In our research on sound–meaning correspondences (Blake & Fink, 1987; Blake & de Boysson-Bardies, 1992), we sought to examine a large babbling corpus from several infants. Six of the infants were followed from the last trimester of the first year to 14 months. Three of these were English-learning infants and three were French-learning, two in each language group being boys and one a girl. In addition, five older English-learning infants, three girls and two boys, were followed over a period of 3 to 6 months during the second year. The number of half-hour videorecorded sessions ranged from 5 to 13 across infants, and the size of the corpora varied accordingly. To determine sound–meaning correspondences, we conducted an exhaustive analysis on the corpus for each infant individually. All babbled utterances that were clear and *not* judged to be laughing, crying, words, animal sounds, or conventionalized expressions (*oh-oh*) were transcribed and categorized into single consonant types, single vowel types, combination of consonant types, or combination of vowel types. Consonant-type categories were formulated on the basis of both place and manner of articulation. As described in chapter 1, utterances categorized as vowel types contained no consonants.

The contexts for all utterances were also exhaustively categorized into 12 general categories, with most of these subdivided into several subcategories. Contexts were similar to many discussed above but more extensive; they reflected a focus, where possible, on the infant's actions. They are described in Table 2–2. Similar to the approach followed by Mitani and Nishida (1993), specific mapping of phonetic categories onto contextual categories was defined as deviations from expected cooccurrences, given the overall frequencies of each phonetic and contextual category. Results for the older English-learning infants showed that between 14% and 40% of each infant's babbling consisted of positive deviations from expected frequencies – that is, particular phonetic categories recurring more in a given context than relative frequencies would predict (Blake & Fink, 1987) results for the younger infants, both English- and French-learning, were quite similar: across infants, from 15% to 30% of babbled utterances showed mapping of phonetic categories onto particular contexts with a greater than expected frequency (Blake & de Boysson-Bardies, 1992). Because the analyses in these studies were quantitative, they did not provide a record of the infants' phonetically consistent forms. Rather, they revealed rudimentary but systematic contrasts between phonetic categories that an infant tended to use or *not* to use in a particular situation.

In the following section, these data are further examined in terms of the exact forms of the expressions that yielded nonrandom patterns in particular contexts. I proceeded, then, from the significant positive deviations reported previously to the actual utterances comprising the patterns. In this way, we can see the range of variations, and their limits, in the expressions that recurred in the same context.

Tables 2–3 through 2–8 present for each of the six younger infants the utterances that yielded certain selected patterns according to the ages when they were recorded (in months and days) and the general age range of the pattern found. The patterns selected are usually those

Table 2–2. Contextual Categories for Vocalizations

1. Fine object manipulation
   (a) Lifting up, holding up something (not to someone)
   (b) Poking, fingering, touching something; turning it over, examining object while holding it
   (c) Putting something into something, taking it out, putting it down; opening, closing something
   (d) Picking up something, grasping it, dropping it, letting it go
2. Gross object manipulation
   (a) Pushing, pulling, rolling something; turning it if being pushed
   (b) Banging, smashing, kicking, pounding, bouncing, swinging, shaking something; knocking it down, waving it, batting at it
   (c) Throwing something
3. Upright movement
   (a) Walking around, running with no apparent purpose
   (b) Walking, running with a purpose: to something, to someone, to pick up something
   (c) Going into/out of a room. Turning around or away (a change in direction)
4. Confined movement
   (a) Creeping, sometimes to get something
   (b) Sitting down (back), standing up, getting up on knees, crouching down, rolling over, climbing, getting up/down from lap or chair, standing on head
   (c) Leaning forward (not a request to be moved), bouncing, waving arms (not *bye-bye*), rocking in chair, clapping, clasping hands
   (d) Moving body parts (e.g., lifting leg) (not a gesture)
   (e) Bending over, usually to pick up something
5. Request
   (a) Trying to do something and looking at someone for help. Bringing (holding out) and/or giving something to someone, clearly wanting something done with it
   (b) Reaching for something (not in proximity)
   (c) Request to be lifted up, down, or moved (arms out, leaning, squirming, grabbing clothes)
   (d) Request for someone to play game (point in book, throw ball)
   (e) Taking adult's hand to go somewhere, get something, do something
   (f) Request for someone to do/give something without gesture (not a game)
   (g) Pointing as a request

(continued)

Table 2–2 *(continued)*

6. Comment
   (a) Watching something after doing something to it, watching as someone else does something to an object or to an infant, noticing something
   (b) Pointing at object or out of window and usually looking at someone (not a request or response)
   (c) Looking around room, at something without doing anything to it, out of window without pointing; looking up, down, back, or off (object of look undetermined)
   (d) Shaking head no/yes, waving bye-bye
   (e) Looking at someone (not a response) – conversation
   (f) Talking to equipment, into telephone

7. Book reading
   (a) Looking at book, sometimes in response to adult's request to show, find, point to something
   (b) Pointing in book
   (c) Book manipulation: touching book, turning page, turning book over, opening/closing book, pulling on it, picking it up, holding it up in front of face

8. Demonstrative
   (a) Holding up something to someone (not offering it)
   (b) Indicating object on request: picking it up, pointing to it, touching it when requested to bring it, say it, label it

9. Response (to adult's utterance): turning to someone, looking at someone, all in response to question or command

10. Give and take
    (a) Bringing (offering) and/or giving something to someone (without clearly wanting them to do something with it)
    (b) Taking something from someone and often dropping it/throwing it/putting it down; accepting something given to infant

11. Rejection/protest: pushing something away, hitting someone's hand, lying down on floor and kicking legs with negative affect, hand flapping in distress

12. Physical interaction: hugging someone, patting someone on head, pushing head into someone, poking someone's face

Source: From Blake, J., & de Boysson-Bardies, B. (1992). Patterns in babbling: A cross-linguistic study. *Journal of Child Language, 19*, pp. 56–57. Reprinted with permission of Cambridge University Press.

Table 2–3. Patterns for CA

9–11.5 Mo.			

Fine object manipulation with [d/t]

9:01	10:00	10:24	11:20
ɛdidɛd	dɛd	ødidæ	dɛd
didɛdɛ ɛ::ɛ::	didɪdɛ::	idɛ	
ɛ::d̪d̪deaʲ	dæ	dʌdʌtʌdʌ	
dæde:e:i::e::eʲ::	tada		

12–14 Mo.				

Fine object manipulation with [ɛ, ɜ, a or ɛa]

12:14	12:25	13:08	13:21	14:01
ɛ:ɛ:	ɛ::a::	ɛ::	ɜ:	ɛ:(2)
			ɜ̃	ɜ::
				ɛ::
				a::
				ɜ:ɛ::

Overall				

Sitting down/standing up with [m]

9:01	9:14	10:00	10:24	11:12
mmm	m̩mmm	m̩(5)	ɛ:: ɛm	m(2)
mmmmm	mi::	mmm		m::
m̩	mmm	mmmm		
m:m:m:		mm		
m::		mm::m̩m		
m̩m̩				

12:14	12:25		13:08	14:01
m̩m̩mm	mmmmmmmm		m̩	m̩
			mm	

Noticing/watching with [h]

9:01	9:14	11:22	13:08	13:21	14:01
he::i::i	ihhi	ɛhɛ	hɔ:hɔ:	hi	hɔ::(2)
hᵘiʔi	he::				hɔ::
aʲ:hi::i					

Note: Age is indicated in the form of months: days, so 9:01, for example, is 9 months 1 day.

Table 2–4. Patterns for JE

9–11.5 Mo.

Looking around with [d]

8:27	9:14	10:12	11:04
da aː a	dæh	haida	dæ ɐ ɒ
adæ dæ da	dæ ɔ̃ dæ dæ	aida(3)	dæ dæ dæ dæ
		da	

12–14 Mo.

Looking around with [ə]

12:06	12:21	13:08	14:08
ə(3)	ə(2)	ə (2)	əːːː
əː	əː	əːː(5)	

Reach/request with [m]

12:21	13:08	13:24	14:08
m̩(2)	əmː mː mː	mːaː mː ma	mːː
mː(2)	ɵʔmɵmʔə	m̩m̩m̩m̩ mː m	
	m	m̩m̩m̩mːː mːːːː mːː mːː	
	mːː mːː(3)		

Noticing with [ʔ/h]

12:06	13:08	13:24	14:08
ʊʔə	ɛʔɛʔæʔæː æʔæ	æhː	æːh
æh	əh	æhː æhː	æh æh
ə̰h	æh	æh(2)	hai
ə ə ʌʔʌ	əʔ əʔ æ	ɛh(2)	
hə		aʔəːː ih ʔaʔ	
ə əʔə		hæːː ɛːː æːː	
əː əʔə		hæ	

Overall

Rejection/protest with [m]

8:27	9:14	9:28	10:12	11:20	12:06	13:24
mːː	mːː	mː mː	mɛ	m̩m̩m̩m̩m̩mː	m	mː m̩
		m m m m m	mː mː m̩m̩			
			m m mːː mːː			

(continued)

Fine object manipulation with [w]

10:12	12:06	13:08	13:24
hai waia	wah	wːawa	ʉː ʉː wih
		wə wə awə	wæwæwæwæwæwæː
		awə waːː	ʉwa
		əwa	

Note: Age is indicated in the form of months: days, so 8:27, for example, is 8 months 27 days.

Table 2–5. Patterns for AD

11–12.5 Mo.

Fine object manipulation with [ɛ]

11:02	11:18	12:09
ɛ (2)	ɛː ɛ	ɛ (2)
ɛː	ɛ (3)	
	ɛ ɛː	
	ɛːː (2)	

Noticing/watching with [m]

12:09

mʉɛ
hm (4)
m m m
əmɛ
m (4)
m m

13–14.5 Mo.

Creeping with [b/p/m]

13:00	13:14	13:29	14:16
əm	əb	m m m m	bəp(2)
ɛm mɛ æ		m	bəp bəp
m		ba ba ba bæ	mə mə
m̩mɛ			

Note: Age is indicated in the form of months: days, so 11:02, for example, is 11 months 2 days.

Table 2–6. Patterns for PI

Overall

Fine object manipulation with [j]

10:22	11:05	12:02	12:23	13:16
hɪhəjəː	aːːœjœ	ɪːjeːʰ	jaʰ	ejeːːɐ
ajə ɛʰ		æ ɛjah	ʔæjiːːːija	jæjæʲʔjæ
		ahiji	ɨjɔjaː	ʔjæjɛ
		eːːja		
		jaːːː		
		ɨːːjahɨʔæ		
		æja		
		əjiːːɨ		
		æjaːː		
		əjijeʔ		
		ɵːːjɑɑ		
		əjiːjɑɑ		
		əjie		
		ejiɑː		
		ijɑjə		
		jaːːj jɛ ɑjɑjə		

Sitting down/standing up with [ɛ]

10:06	11:19	12:05	12:23	13:13	13:27
ʔɛ	ɛʰ	ɛ	ʔɛʰ	ʔɛʰ	ʔɛʰ (2)
ʔɛːːɛːɛ	ʔɛːfiɛ			ʔɛ	
	hɛːː			ɛ	

Give request with [a]

10:22	11:05	12:02	12:23	13:13	13:27
ʔaːːʰ	aʰ	aʰaːː	ʔaːːɐʰ	ʔ2ʰ	
aːː		ʔaːː			
aːʰ		ʔaːːʰ			
aʰːː		ʔaʰːːː			
aːːʰ					

Show with [æ] or [a]

10:06	10:22	11:05	12:02	12:23	13:13
ʔæːʰ	a (2)	æʰːː	aːːːʰ (2)	ʔaʰ	ʔaːːæʰ
	ʔaːː		æʰ (2)	æː æʰ	
			ʔaʰʔaʰːː		
			aʰ ʔaʰ		
			ʔaʰ		
			ʔa		
			æ		

Note: Age is indicated in the form of months: days, so 10:22, for example, is 10 months 22 days.

Table 2–7. Patterns for FL

9.5–11.5 Mo.

Looking around with [b/p/m]

9:20	10:01	10:15
hum	bu bæ	mm mm
pa	bab	pɛ obu^h
pæ	pa	mʔ
mmː mm mmː mmː	^{m}ba	mm a^h
m mmː	ba	mm
	mmː ^{h}əm m ^{h}um mu	
	b	
	pa	
	apø ø	
	pæː pa	
	ba ba	
	ʔmm^h	

12–14 Mo.

Looking around with [m]

11:27	12:17	13:07	13:21
m a^h	m mm	m	mm
m	ɔm	mø	m
mm (2)	muh		m^h

Picking up with labials (and [d/t] and sonorants/[j])

11:27		12:17	13:07	13:21
hm eh		hu pipæ	ɔβwuw	ɔvlaː ʔuʔ
wiːdijɛ		^{m}ba	bɔ	mu wɛa
iðiubiəiubiuː uwa		bej	ɔwejebwæːʰaː	maː
jaʔ ʔeɛh ʔeeɛh ʔja ʔe ʔeja ʔa hmm			jaboː^m	wawa
apida			idjaːpa	ʔapaːlu
			wo	
			wop	
			odjowowo	
			iɲɔmpabwo	
			ɲobwopabo	
			ʔɛwuwpœ	

(continued)

Table 2–7 *(continued)*

Overall

Sitting down/standing up with [j]

10:01	11:13	11:27	12:17	13:21
hæjæ	jæ	ja:	hajah haja	ija:
ʔjaʔ		ja (2)		
ja				
ja:h				

Note: Age is indicated in the form of months: days, so 9.20, for example, is 9 months 20 days.

Table 2–8. Patterns for LA

11–12 Mo.

Fingering with [g/k]

10:26

gə ɣgø əgø
ɛgi:g
gegø age ge
gagege
ɑ:gɛg
agø (2)
kah
xɑ ɑø
gø
ka:ɔø
øgo

12.5–14 Mo.

Fingering with [d/t]

12:21	13:04	13:25
ydɑ:da	dɑɛda	tata: dat
dø	adad	
ata	ædid	
dɑ:dɑ:	ɑ:dæt	

(continued)

12:21	13:04	13:25
εiεdada	tœːda	
daːda	dœd dødød dœ da	
	da dœ	
	tæːta	
	dø	
	tata (2)	
	ah ta ðæðæt	
	dɛd dœ ʔah	
	dø dadø dødɔ	

Overall

Lower movement with [b/p]

11:23	12:21	13:04
aːob	papap	ba
aːbɔ		bœː œː
ɔːbu		ba bœ
ba		
abua		
bø ø ø		
aːabœ		
pa		
aʔabuː		
aβa (2)		
baːaaaa		

Noticing/watching with [ʔ/h]

10:26	11:09	11:23	12:21	13:25
ahːa	εh	ʔaːh	ʔah ʔah	ʔε?
ahː	ʔæ			eh:
ah e	ʔhæ			ʔa? ʔε?
ah	ʔhaːe			haːh
ʔaːœ (2)	øh			a^h
ʔaːeː (2)				
ʔaː ʔeʔea				
ʔεaø				
eh				
ʔœ				
ʔa				

Note: Age is indicated in the form of months: days, so 10:26, for example, is 10 months 26 days.

for a *single* consonant type or vowel type, because these are the simplest. Where possible, patterns occurring in more specific contexts are also selected. The first three infants to be discussed were English-learning. For the child designated CA (see Table 2–3), a pattern of using [d/t] utterances with the general category of fine object manipulation was found prior to 12 months, whereas after 12 months this pattern changed to the vowels [ɛ], [ɜ], or [a] or their combinations. Examining the [d/t] utterances shows that they were primarily polysyllabic, that the consonant was almost exclusively [d] and rarely [t], and that it occurred most often in first position in the syllable and only three times in final position. The vowels were quite variable, although [ɛ] and [i] predominate. It is important to note that examples of this pattern were found across four of the six sessions, including the earliest and the latest, over the time period. The vowel pattern found after 12 months was much more consistent, with eight illustrations consisting of a single vowel type. Again, the pattern is distributed across the sessions. The next pattern, found across all the sessions from 9 to 14 months, is also quite consistent in containing [m] almost exclusively; only one example contains a vowel. This pattern was used with sitting down and standing up. Thus, it might be considered illustrative of the effort grunts described by McCune et al. (1996). The final pattern given for CA is the use of [h] with noticing/watching. Again, this pattern was found across several sessions, and the (h) was primarily initial, although three times it was preceded by a vowel. Again, the vowel was variable but predominantly [i] or [o/ɔ]. Most of these utterances were polysyllabic.

JE's patterns (see Table 2–4) also include one with fine object manipulation, but hers was with [w]. (Note that when [h] or [ʔ] was combined with another consonant, it was not counted.) This was an overall pattern but was found only during 4 of her 11 sessions. It was almost always polysyllabic, and [w] occurred in initial position of the syllable, sometimes preceded by a vowel. Another of JE's patterns, like one of CA's, involved [m] but this time with reaching for something not in proximity (reach–request). This pattern was found between 12 and 14 months in 4 of the 5 sessions. It began as a monosyllabic utterance and then shifted to a predominantly polysyllabic utterance. Only three times did it occur with a vowel. This pattern is like the request grunt described by McCune et al. (1996). During the earlier period prior to 12 months (although an overall pattern), [m] also occurred with rejection/protest with no vowel and primarily in repeated form. Some researchers (for example, Bates, 1979) have considered rejection to be instrumental like request, so it is interesting that JE used a similar utterance for both functions. She was, however, the only infant to do so, and the pattern was found predominantly over different age periods for each function. Like CA also, JE had a pattern with noticing/watching involving [h], but in her case the illustrations also contained [ʔ]. (The glottal stop had to occur in initial position in the syllable to be counted.) JE's pattern in this context occurred only after 12 months and was found in four of her five sessions. The phone [h] occurred both in initial and final position in the syllable, and the vowels were exceedingly variable. Finally, with looking around (at something undetermined), JE first used [d] utterances in four of her six sessions before 12 months and then shifted to [ə] after 12 months. In the earlier pattern, [d] was always in the initial position of the syllable but was sometimes preceded by a vocalic syllable. This expression was almost always polysyllabic. The [ə] utterance after 12 months was quite consistently monosyllabic but often extended. It might have been an attention grunt (McCune et al., 1996), but this category is less clearly attentional than other functions of comment (see Table 2–2).

Like CA, AD (see Table 2–5) had a vowel pattern with fine object manipulation, but his was a much more consistent [ɛ] utterance, almost always monosyllabic, and appearing at a younger age. He also had a noticing/watching pattern, but his was with [m]. This again might be illustrative of the attention grunts described by McCune et al. It was restricted to only one session, occurred only twice with vowels, and was predominantly monosyllabic. During his later sessions, AD had a pattern with [b/p] or [m] that occurred when creeping. This pattern was found in all sessions during the second age period, typically with the bilabial in initial position but sometimes in final position, and equally often in monosyllabic and polysyllabic form.

The next three infants to be discussed were French-learning. PI (see Table 2–6) also had a pattern with fine object manipulation, but his was with [j]. Many of the illustrations were polysyllabic utterances with the [j] in initial position in the last syllable(s), preceded by a vocalic syllable(s). The vowels were very variable. The remainder of PI's patterns are vocalic (his babbling was not very consonantal). In the case of PI, unlike the other infants, vocalic patterns were analyzed disregarding [ʔ/h] because he used glottals with most of his utterances. PI used [ɛ] with sitting down/standing up across most sessions, and almost all of these utterances were monosyllabic. He used [a] with give-request, and either [a] or [æ] with show, also across most sessions. Most of these, again, were monosyllabic utterances.

Before 12 months, FL (see Table 2–7) used [b/p] or [m] with looking around; but after 12 months, this pattern was narrowed to [m]. Combinations of other consonant types with bilabials were used during the later age period with picking up objects. These utterances were primarily polysyllabic. FL, like some of the other infants, also had a pattern with sitting down/standing up, but in her case it was with [j]. The [j] was typically in initial position in a monosyllabic utterance.

LA (see Table 2–8) had an early pattern (from session 1 only) of velar utterances with fingering/examining objects. This pattern changed to [d/t] utterances after 12 months. Most of these utterances were polysyllabic with the consonant in initial position in the syllable, sometimes preceded by a vocalic syllable. Like CA and JE, he also used [ʔ/h] with noticing/watching. With lower movement, he used [b/p] utterances in three of his sessions.

The three infants in the older English-learning group who were followed from early in the second year (Tables 2–9, 2–10, and 2–11) present several patterns that are similar to the ones already described. For these infants, as for PI, [ʔ/h] was not counted. NI, followed from 13 months, had a very large corpus that yielded many patterns. Again, only the simplest or most specific ones are presented on Table 2–9. NI had a pattern of using [æ] with gross object manipulation at every session between 15.5 months and 17 months. This pattern occurred primarily with throwing something and was always monosyllabic. It often had an initial glottal stop. This utterance probably expressed satisfaction in the action rather than effort, since it generally occurred with positive affect. In almost all sessions, NI used the classic [ə/ʌ] with reach-request. This utterance was typically a repeated syllable. NI used polysyllabic [d/t] utterances when walking or running around with no apparent purpose. The vowel varied across and within utterances, with

Table 2–9. Patterns for NI Overall

Gross object manipulation with [æ]			
15:22	16:04	16:19	17:05
ʔæ	æʔ	ʔæ (2)	æ (4)
ʔæː			ʔæ
æ			

Walking/running with repeated [d/t]

13:14	14:00	14:15	15:00
dæ diʲ	dʲɛdʲi ʔɛdʲɪdʲɪdʲɛdɛʰ dʲə dʲed ɛdʲədʲədʲədʲəʌdʲəːdʲə ɛʷdʲɪdʲɪdʲɛdʲɛ ɛtɛʷtɪ dede dædædæ	tɛətɛətitəhuː	dæʔi dædi dædi

15:22	17:05	18:16	19:00
dæt hədɛt	dədʲi dedə	ʔaʔ dɛtətætə	dʲɪdididɛde dɛdɛ dej dʲidʊ

Reach/request with [ə/ʌ]

13:15	14:00	14:15	15:22	16:04	16:20
hə hə həʔ	hə hə həʔə	hə	ʌː	ʔəʔʌʔʌ ʔəʔə	ʔəʔə

17:05	17:15	18:00	18:15	19:00
ə hə hə hə	əʔəʔə	ʔhə əː ʔəʔə	ʔəʰʔəʔəʰʔʌʔʌʔʌ	ʔəʔəʔə ʔəʔə

Watching/noticing with [ɛ]

13:00	14:15	18:00
ɛ (2)	ʔɛ ʔɛʔ (2) ɛːə	hɛ hɛ hɛ ʔhɛh hɛ (2) ʔɛ ʔhɛʔ ɛə ɛə ɛə ʔɛʔɛː hɛʔ

Indicating object on request with monosyllabic [d/t]

16:19	17:05	17:17	18:00	19:00
dɛə	dæ (3) dɛ (3) dɛə de	da dæːj	dɛ (2) dæ dɛhə tejː	dɪ də

Note: Age is indicated in the form of months: days, so 15:22, for example, is 15 months 22 days.

Table 2–10. Patterns for KA Overall

Object manipulation with labials

12:19	12:28	13:01	13:23	14:02
hʌvi pʲʌbʌʷ	ʔʌwə ʔʌp	ʔə wjəjʌjə wi əwʌja aː pe	bɔ bɔ bɔ bɔ	wəjej wəjej jəwej

14:18	15:03	16:12	17:12
ʔʌwi we we	bɔ bʊ wei aə	ʊbe əbɔ bʌbu u ʔɔ ʔaːwjɪ æ we bɔu bo o ajwoheæ	wæ

Conversation with [d/t] or [d/t] combinations

12:28	13:01	13:03		13:10
wədʌ ʔʌjdʲə wɛwetʲ	ʔəjəwdəwdʌdʌ udadaj hjɔwbædʲɪʔ wɔdɛi u netʃdəwadə mgadʲɛ	ediʃ ʔɪsʲːdɛp ɪgabɪdəbɪgadəwɪdblʌwʌ		dʲədəʲ

13:20	13:23	13:27	13:28
ʔʌdʌdʔəda:	ajdɛs dɛʃ awadʲdɪʃ	ʔʌdʲə dʲəb ʔʌʷ ʔʌdʲʌt dɔʷ	ʔuawt ʌ dʲɛ dʌjʌjʊ ʔʌjʊ ʊwʌːjej ʌjəwɛ

14:18	14:23	15:05	16:12	17:12
ʔʌdwen	dʲæ	dɛdʌ ɔ ɔ ʔɔgʌduɪi	de tʰugʌjbe dada	dɛdʲi gɛdʲi

Note: Age is indicated in the form of months: days, so 12:19, for example, is 12 months 19 days.

some reduplication in the same utterance. The first syllable typically began with the consonant. Final consonants occurred but were quite rare. The prevalence of [d] over [t] is clear in the examples. Illustrations of this pattern were found across most of NI's sessions. These polysyllabic [d/t] utterances can be contrasted with the monosyllabic [d/t] utterances used with indicating an object on request after 16 months.

Table 2–11. Patterns for SAN Overall

Pointing in book with [d/t]		
14:22	**15:02**	**15:06**
dædʲæ dʲæ dʲæ	dədiʲːɪ	dʌʔ
dʲa dʲædʲædʲæ ʔædʲædʲædʲæ	djɪdjɪʔ dʲɪʔ	
	diːjæ	
	djɪ	
	œ œ ti	
15:27	**16:00**	**16:13**
dɛʔ ʔʌ ʔʌij	hʌʌː adʲɛdʌhʌː	dəːw
		dɪʔ (2)
		dʊ
		daə (2)
		dɔ
		dʊʔ
		dɛ
		dæ dæ
		dij

Object manipulation with [ɛ]					
14:18	**15:02**	**15:27**	**16:00**	**16:13**	**16:27**
hɛ hɛ	hɛ	ʔɛhɛʔ	hɛ hɛʔ	ɛʲ	ɛ
hej	hɛ hɛ		ʔɛ	ɛ	ʔɛʰ
ʔɛʰ			ɛ		

Lower movement with [j]			
15:01	**15:02**	**15:27**	**16:00**
ɛjɛjə	hiʲə	ɛjəjɑj jəjə	ɑjeʲi
jəjʌː ʔæʔ			ʌːjʌjʌː ʌːjʌːjʌ
16:01	**16:12**	**16:13**	
jəijɑj ɑːj	jʌjʌjʌjʌjʌjʌjʌ	ɛjʊ	
	ʔʌjəjɛjɛjɛʔ	jɛjʊ	
	ji ɛjɪ	ʌjʌɛ	
	jæ jæ jæ jæ		

Note: Age is indicated in the form of months : days, so 14:22, for example, is 14 months 22 days.

The preferred dento-alveolar was clearly [d] again, combined most often with the vowels [ɛ], [ɛə], [æ], or [e]. These expressions were found at every session between 16:19 and 19 months. NI also used [ɛ] with watching/noticing in the earlier sessions and a later session. This vowel was often preceded by [ʔ/h] and is thus similar to the pattern found for CA, JE, and LA.

KA (see Table 2–10), like JE, used [w/v] or [b/p] with object manipulation. This pattern was typically polysyllabic, occurred across the sessions, and sometimes also included [j]. When KA "conversed," she used utterances with [d/t], sometimes combined with other consonant types. These utterances tended to be polysyllabic and were sometimes very long. They were exceedingly variable, as the illustrations indicate, but always contained the requisite [d/t].

SAN (see Table 2–11) used [d/t] utterances when pointing in a book, increasingly monosyllabic by the last session. Her preference was for [d] in initial position. Some of the utterances also included [j]. The vowels again are quite variable, but there is some reduplication. Like CA and AD, SAN also used [ɛ] with object manipulation; and, like FL, she used [j] with lower movement. The first pattern was primarily monosyllabic and the second polysyllabic.

The focus in this detailed presentation of patterns, for the most part, has been on the simplest ones, rather than on those that involve combinations of consonant types. Even so, it is clear from the illustrations that the utterances forming a pattern are not consistent in terms of number of syllables, position of consonant, and type of vowel used in a consonant pattern. The patterns were initially revealed in an analysis that focused on consistent consonant types only, with a focus on consistent vowel use only if the utterance contained no consonant. Thus, it is not surprising that the vowels vary in the illustrations of consonant patterns. These patterns, however, do not clearly fit a label of phonetically consistent form (see also Kent & Bauer, 1985). They are more fluid than constant, although they are consistent in repeating a critical consonant type in a context over time. In contrast, the single vowel patterns, by definition, were quite consistent in their form.

Patterns tended to be repeated in most sessions during a given age period, but sometimes they did change over time. The patterns found are not typically due to a transient mapping in a single session, however.

The patterns were quite idiosyncratic to the individual infants, but across infants there were some interesting recurring themes: [ʔ/h] with noticing/watching; bilabials or polysyllabic [d/t] utterances with movement; [d/t] with fine object manipulation; [ɛ] with fine or general object manipulation; and, for the older infants, [d/t] with pointing in a book or indicating an object. Because the statistical analysis used to determine patterns required a minimum frequency, how often the infants vocalized in a context was related to the number of patterns found. For example, infants vocalized less in object exchange contexts, and no patterns were found. However, infants could vocalize a great deal in a context without revealing a pattern. Because the analysis took account of both context frequency and phonetic preferences in determining expected frequencies of cooccurrence, the patterns are not the result of a simple conjunction of highly frequent contextual and phonetic categories. Rather, to yield a pattern, the conjunction had to significantly exceed the expected frequency of cooccurrence.

The three older English-learning infants overlapped in age with the younger infants in that they were followed from 13 or 14 months whereas the younger infants were studied until 14 or 14.5 months. The patterns of the older infants were generally found across their sessions, until 17 to 19 months. Thus, it is interesting that some of their patterns were similar to those of the younger infants: bilabials or [j] with movement and [ɛ] with object manipulation. However, there were also new patterns in the older group: monosyllabic [d/t] utterances with pointing in a book and [ə/ʌ] with request. Although in both younger and older groups, slightly more patterns with combinations of different consonant-types were found later in the study period, this tendency was not clearcut (see Blake & Fink, 1987, and Blake & deBoyssons-Bardies, 1992).

There was some variation across infants in the number of patterns found and in the percentage of their babbling that was patterned. These differences were due, in part, to the size of the corpus, as explained above, but not entirely. Both NI and JE had extremely large corpora (1,880 utterances for NI and 1,600 for JE), yet 40% of Nicholas's babbling was patterned, with more than 100 different patterns found, whereas only 28% of JE's babbling was patterned, with 33 different patterns found. Several infants had 700 to 800 utterances in their corpora (SAN, CA, LA, and AD), yet the percentage of babbling that was patterned ranged from 15% (AD) to 34% (SAN), although the number of different patterns for these two extreme infants was similar (18 and 19, respectively).

The question of whether variability in patterning is directly related to language acquisition is a difficult one to answer on the basis of these nine infants. We kept records of their progress in word acquisition; it was clear that the most advanced were AD, FL, and KA, whereas the slowest was NI, who reached the 30-word criterion for ending observations only at 19 months. For the younger infants, observations ended at 14 months, when CA, LA, and PI had almost no words. The results are suggestive of a negative relationship between the percentage of patterned babble and word acquisition, since the three most advanced infants in word acquisition had the lowest percentage of patterned babble (15%, 17%, and 21%, respectively). However, CA and LA had only slightly more (22% and 23%), and the *number* of patterns found for the three linguistically advanced infants was low only for KA (11).

Conclusions

The sound–meaning mapping found in nonhuman primates appears more comparable to the sound–meaning correspondences described above in human infants than to vocabulary acquisition. Proponents of a referential or representational view of meaning in monkeys' vocalizations would argue, instead, that their vocalizations are mapped onto specific objects – for example, predators. We have not argued that view for prelinguistic infants, nor does their mapping appear to be directed at particular objects. It is much more action or function based and thus more similar to the mapping reported for apes in the wild. Burling (1993) and Noble and Davidson (1996), among others, have argued that vervet alarm calls are not referential but are mapped onto a context, much as we have described for human infants. In both human infants and nonhuman primates, these mapping systems are closed and nonproductive. The same expression does not become more complex over time, as is clear in Tables 2–3 through 2–11, although it may become increasingly monosyllabic.

Most of the communicative functions of nonhuman primate signals revolve around very basic functions: movement, food, threat, and aggression. The functions of human infant prelinguistic vocalizations are already quite a bit more varied. Recurring patterns are associated not only with movement but also with manipulating objects, with requests, and with indicating objects. These functions are, of course, not part of primate life in the wild. The potentially overlapping contexts are movement, looking around, and noticing something. These are generally mapped onto stop consonants in human infants, except for the last which, as I pointed out earlier, seems similar to Goodall's

(1986) *huu* of puzzlement found in chimpanzees. Thus, I can conclude only that although the origin of the sound–meaning mapping process can be found in nonhuman primates, the human infant carries this process to a level of contrasts and variety of functions not available to nonhuman primates.

CHAPTER THREE

Communicative Gestures

What Is a Gesture?

Gesture is a common term used to describe anything from simple motor acts, such as catching and returning a ball (e.g., Rome-Flanders & Ricard, 1992) to vocal sounds (Lock, 1980; Vihman, 1991). A typical dictionary definition refers only to a "movement of the body, head, arms, hands, or face expressive of an idea or an emotion" (Barnhart, 1948, p. 509). Despite the extended use of the term *gesture* beyond this definition, in developmental research the term is often taken to mean only gestures that express an idea – that is, symbolic gestures. This restricted focus follows the influential work of Werner and Kaplan (1963), who originally made a distinction between expressive and depictive gestures. The boundary between the two types is often difficult to draw. Expressive movements are viewed as reactive or coactive patterns "directly involved in pragmatic commerce with objects" (Werner & Kaplan, 1963, p. 85). For example, an infant may react to the sound of music with a bodily rocking motion but later may use this motion to *request* music when it is *not* playing, a depictive gesture. A depictive or symbolic gesture, in the view of both Werner and Kaplan (1963) and of Piaget (1962), requires some distance (in time, space, and content) between the movement and that to which it refers. Such distancing is similar to the property of displacement in language described by Hockett (1958).

Another problematic distinction involves anticipatory movements versus gestures. Werner and Kaplan (1963) presented the example of a 13-month-old lifting his legs before reaching the stairs. This could be either a motor pattern preparatory to climbing the stairs or a gesture depicting the stairs (in Piaget's terms, a recognitory gesture).

Anticipatory movements are quite likely the ontogenetic origin of gestures. For example, a nursing infant lying on a bed began by 6 months to turn her head directly away from the breast after a period of time. After several repetitions, it became clear that this was a signal that she was ready to be nursed on the other side. Is this a gesture? Most researchers would agree that anticipatory actions arise from repeated activity and lack conscious intentionality. The issue of what is a gesture is, thus, bound up with the problem of intentionality.

Ekman and Friesen (1969) made a distinction between gestures in adults that may be unintentionally informative to the observer and those which are consciously intended to communicate a message. The first type can be illustrated by the way a person crosses her legs during an interview, and the second by someone shrugging her shoulders in response to a question. The distinction between these two types, again, becomes very fuzzy if we consider what happens when people become aware of previously unconscious nonverbal behavior and modify it intentionally – for example, by changing the way they are sitting. Gestures that may be originally unintentional often are expressive of emotional states (fear, anxiety, excitement) and appear to have their roots in nonhuman species. We assume, then, that perhaps they are of a lower order; hence the emphasis in developmental research on symbolic gestures or at least on communicative gestures with a clear intent (pointing, showing, request-reaching). In the work of Bates and her colleagues (Bates, 1979; Caselli, 1990), these intentionally communicative gestures are called deictic gestures because they draw attention to people or objects and their location. Symbolic gestures are called referential gestures by this group because, like words, they represent actions or objects. For a deictic gesture to be viewed as intentionally communicative, these researchers have required that the gesture involve eye contact with the partner. This criterion, however, is often difficult to meet, as infants make assumptions about the attentional focus of their partners, particularly their mothers and particularly in naturalistic contexts (see also Lock, Young, Service, & Chandler, 1990). Furthermore, in an experimental context, infants who were left alone hardly pointed at all to a doll display compared with when their mother was present (Franco & Butterworth, 1991). This finding implies that a responsive social partner is needed for pointing and that truly noncommunicative pointing is in fact quite rare.

In this chapter, I focus on communicative gestures, and in the next chapter I discuss depictive or symbolic gestures, along with symbolic

play. Symbolic gestures often originate in symbolic play (Werner &
Kaplan, 1963; Zinober & Martlew, 1985), so it is fitting that they
should be examined together. Although my colleagues and I have
recorded eye contact when it occurred with the gestures in our inventory, we have not considered it to be a necessary criterion for a gesture
to be called communicative. The description of infant communicative
gestures in our research followed an ethological approach in which the
use of clearly defined behavioral inventories in observation was emphasized. The gestural inventory that we have used (Blake & Dolgoy,
1993; Blake, McConnell, Horton, & Benson, 1992; Blake, Olshansky,
Vitale, & Macdonald, 1997) is given in Table 3–1. We believe that this
is close to an exhaustive inventory of bodily movements that communicate functional meaning to the observer in infants between 9 months
and 2 years of age. To avoid including simple actions on objects that
are clearly not communicative, the inventory specifies that for most
gestures, the hands of the infant neither contain an object nor make
contact with an object. The exceptions are for those gestures that

Table 3–1. Categories of Communicative Gestures

Comment
> *Point:* Involves the extended arm and index finger and lightly or tightly
> curled other fingers. No contact with object. Directed at person, object, or
> event.
> *Point in book:* Same as above except that the point is to a book. Can have
> contact with the book.
> *Show:* Holds up object to another, usually with bent elbow. Object remains
> in infant's possession.
> *Bye-bye:* Waving of arm or hand.
> *Head nod/shake:* To indicate yes or no. The shake must be with positive
> affect; otherwise, it belongs in *Protest/rejection.*

Object exchange
> *Offer:* Infant holds out object to another, usually with arm extended and
> palm up. Object remains in infant's possession; otherwise a *Give.* Not a
> request to do something with the object.
> *Give:* Infant hands object to another. Object changes hands. *Not* a request
> to do something with the object.
> *Take:* Infant reaches out for object in another's possession and obtains it.
> Object changes hands. Also coded when infant accepts object given by
> another.

Request

Reach: Arm is extended, palm is usually down, hand is open, and fingers are straight. Usually continued until request is granted. Coded only for something out of reach. Reaching that culminates in the infant's grasping something on his/her own is not coded.

Point: Same form as *Point (Comment)*, but context appears to be that of request.

Up: One or both arms are raised toward another or merely moved away from the body to allow room for another's hands to pick up the infant. Includes reach to adult if results in being picked up.

Down: If held in adult's arms, infant leans away from adult and toward ground. If in a lap or seat, leans or stiffens/straightens body so he/she tends to slide down.

Seek assistance: Infant exhibits effort in his/her actions and affect is often negative. Must have eye contact with adult.

Give/offer: As above, but the infant wants adult to do something with object.

Takes hand: Infant takes hold of part of another's body, usually the hand, and either guides it to an object or leads the person somewhere to do something (e.g., open a door).

Protest/Rejection

Turn away: Infant turns head or body away from another's actual or approaching physical contact.

Push/pull away: Infant uses hand or arm to push away another person or an object that the person is offering. Infant attempts to remove self (hand, foot, etc.) from the hold of another.

Resist bodily: Includes kick, stiffening of body.

Hit: Open hand is struck against object being offered or another person.

Head shake: Movement of head from side to side with negative affect.

Emotive

Bounce: Bodily movement up and down while either sitting or standing.

Flap/wave arms: Arms sometimes fully extended, sometimes bent at elbow, and moved in an up-and-down or side-to-side direction, often vigorously. No object in hands.

Clasp/clap hands: Open hands brought together.

Source: From Blake, J., McConnell, S., Horton G., & Benson, N. (1992). The gestural repertoire and its evolution over the second year. *Early Development and Parenting, 1,* Appendix, pp. 135–136. Copyright John Wiley & Sons Ltd. Reproduced with permission.

require an object, by definition: give, offer, take, point in book, show, and some rejection gestures. Also, gestures were coded only in a social context; the infant was always interacting with a parent or caretaker. Facial expressions, although properly belonging in the emotive category, are not included. They illustrate well, however, the problem of wandering in and out of conscious intention. Their continuity across species is also well established (Darwin, 1872/1965).

The next section of this chapter examines the degree of phylogenetic continuity in the gestures of our inventory. The ontogenetic origins of some of these gestures in early infancy before 9 months is then discussed, and that discussion is then followed by our findings regarding age of onset of gestures after 9 months and changes in the gestural repertoire between 9 and 15 months in different cultural groups. Finally, I assess the relation of gestural development to early vocabulary acquisition, as well as its long-term impact on receptive vocabulary, communicative competence, and language production at 3 years.

Phylogenetic Origins of Communicative Gestures

Those gestures in our inventory that have also been described in apes, both wild and captive, are listed on Table 3–2 with the relevant sources. The most useful sources for this comparison are Goodall's extensive observations of chimpanzees in the Gombe Stream National Park (Van Lawick-Goodall, 1968; Goodall, 1986), Plooij's (1984) detailed observations of infant chimpanzees in the same area, van Hooff's (1973) observations of chimpanzees in captivity, and Tomasello's (1990) review of chimpanzee gestures in the wild and in captivity. The longitudinal observations of chimpanzee gestures at the Yerkes Regional Primate Research Center by Tomasello and his group (Tomasello, Gust, & Frost, 1989; Tomasello et al., 1997) will be examined in detail. Sporadic information is available on certain selected gestures in other ape populations, the most complete being the development of pointing in a captive orangutan (Miles, 1990) and requests demonstrating cognizance of human agency by a captive gorilla (Gomez, 1990).

The number of gestures in our inventory that have been observed in the Gombe chimpanzees is striking. It is clear from Table 3–2 that chimpanzees in the wild engage in object exchange gestures, request gestures, protest/rejection gestures, and in most of the emotive gestures. It is important to note, however, that although give–take

Table 3–2. Gestures in Human Infant Inventory Reported in the Repertoire of Wild and Captive Apes

Human Infant Gesture	Wild Ape and Source	Captive and ex-captive Ape and Source
Point	Finger extension only. Infant chimpanzees (Plooij, 1984)	Chimpanzees (Tomasello, George, Kruger, Farrar, & Evans, 1985) Orangutan (Miles, 1990)
Show		Orangutan (Miles, 1990)
Head nod/ shake	Gorillas (Schaller, 1965)	Chimpanzees (van Hooff, 1973; Tomasello et al., 1997)
Give	Food sharing only – chimpanzees (Van Lawick-Goodall, 1968)	Orangutans (Miles, 1990; Russon, 1995) Chimpanzees (Russon, 1990)
Take	Infant chimpanzees (Plooij, 1984)	
Reach	Chimpanzees (Van Lawick-Goodall, 1968; Plooij, 1984)	
Up	Infant chimpanzees (Plooij, 1984)	Chimpanzees (Berdecio & Nash, 1981, cited in Tomasello, 1990) Gorilla (Gomez, 1990)
Give-request	Infant chimpanzees (Plooij, 1984)	Orangutans (Miles, 1990; Russon, 1995) Bonobos (Savage-Rumbaugh, Shanker, & Taylor, 1998)
Take hand	Infant chimpanzees (Plooij, 1984)	Chimpanzees (Tomasello et al., 1985; 1Gardner & Gardner, 1969) Gorilla (Gomez, 1990) Bonobos (Savage-Rumbaugh et al., 1998)
Turn away	Chimpanzees (Plooij, 1984) Bending away (Goodall, 1986)	
Push/ pull away	Infant chimpanzees (Plooij, 1984)	Chimpanzees (van Hooff, 1973)
Hit	Chimpanzees (Reynolds & Reynolds, 1965; Van Lawick-Goodall, 1968)	Chimpanzees (van Hooff, 1973; Berdecio & Nash, 1981, cited in Tomasello, 1990)
Bounce	Infant chimpanzees (Plooij, 1984)	
Flap/ wave arms	Chimpanzees (Van Lawick-Goodall, 1968)	Chimpanzees (van Hooff, 1973)
Clasp/ clap hands		Chimpanzees (Berdecio & Nash, 1981, cited in Tomasello, 1990; Tomasello et al., 1985, 1997) Bonobos (De Waal, 1988; Myers Thompson, 1994)

exchanges have been seen between a mother chimpanzee and her infant (Plooij, 1984), they are restricted to food sharing in response to a begging infant (Van Lawick-Goodall, 1968).

Plooij (1984) provided some developmental onset data for request gestures in infant chimpanzees. He observed that reaching for things began toward the end of the second month, and these gestures were combined with effort grunts. Food begging, with outstretched cupped hand under the mouth of an eating mother, was not observed until 9 months and was accompanied with intermittent looks at the mother's face. Although reaching and hand begging would appear to be related, Bard (1990) reported that hand begging in orangutans in the Tanjung Puting Reserve in Borneo began at a much older age than in Plooij's chimpanzees (3.5 years) and well after reaching had dropped to a low level. (See Figure 3–1 for an illustration of reaching in an infant orangutan). Hand begging as a request to be carried, done by captive infant

Figure 3–1: An infant female orangutan at Wanariset reaching. Photograph by Anne Russon.

bonobos, has been observed by De Waal (1988). De Waal also reported that only 13% of the observed begging gestures occurred during food-related interactions.

The evolution of the "up" gesture in infant chimpanzees appears to be similar to that in human infants (Plooij, 1978, 1984) as described by Lock (1978), although the functions of the two gestures are somewhat different. Up to about 6 months, the mother chimpanzee raised her infant's arm to groom underneath. After 6 months, the infant raised its arm itself when its mother approached to groom. By 11 months, arm raising in the chimpanzee infant became a request to groom.

Requests expressed by taking the mother's hand began in the context of a chimpanzee mother–infant tickling game (Plooij, 1984). (See also Gardner & Gardner, 1969, for a description of similar behavior in the captive chimpanzee Washoe.) In human infants, we have also seen this gesture emerge in the context of mother–infant games. For example, an infant whose mother made a game out of counting pictures in a book repeatedly requested this game by taking her hand and guiding it to the pictures. More extensive use of this gesture has been reported in captive apes. For example, Muni, a captive gorilla, took his care-taker by the hand to lead him to a forbidden door and then guided his hand toward the latch. This animal can then be said to have under-stood the "agentive properties of subjects" (Gomez, 1990, p. 346). The bonobo Kanzi's mother, Matata, is also reported to often take a human's hand and lead this person in a desired direction (Savage-Rumbaugh, Shanker, & Taylor, 1998). Kanzi put people's hands on a tree when he wanted them to climb with him. Give-request gestures that are similarly cognizant of adult agency are also reported for Kanzi – for example, giving a caretaker a flashlight as a request to be tickled with it.

From 11 months of age, in the context of the tickling game, Plooij also observed infant chimpanzees trying to push away their mother's hands. We have also seen a similar push-away gesture when a game began to overwhelm a human infant – for example, when a father kept pushing a wet cloth into the face of his bathing infant. Push away and hit are probably defensive in origin (Van Lawick-Goodall, 1968). In chimpanzees, as in humans, they then become part of the repertoire of threat gestures but are at the mildest level of aggression (Goodall, 1986).

Other threat gestures used by adult chimpanzees are arm waving and hand flapping (Van Lawick-Goodall, 1968), the latter occurring frequently during female squabbles. Hand flapping (or wrist shaking) has also been observed in captive bonobos (De Waal, 1988) but rarely as a threat gesture. Rather, it seemed to be an impatient invitation or request. It appears that these gestures in chimpanzees and bonobos involve a forward motion, in the direction of another animal. Bonobo arm waving may involve sideways movements, but these movements serve as a sexual invitation from males to females (De Waal, 1988). When human infants wave their arms as an emotive gesture, the arms may be either toward the front or to the side; but when they hand-flap, the arms are typically to the side. Arm waving and hand flapping in human infants express agitation or excitement. Thus, in this case, the form of the gesture is similar across species, but the only similarity of function lies in the arousal state. Blurton Jones (1972, p. 274) suggested that arm waving in young children "reflects a very generalised kind of activation."

Some gestures are notably absent from the observations of wild chimpanzees. First and foremost is the lack of pointing and showing (of objects). As Plooij (1984, p. 126) commented, "searching for examples of pointing in chimpanzees is not very fruitful." Other researchers stress that nonhuman primates, and even other mammals, often exhibit directional indicating with their posture. For example, "chimpanzees that have seen a member of their group orient toward an object which they themselves cannot see will often search the field in the indicated direction," without being accompanied by the signaler (Menzel & Johnson, 1975, p. 16). Schaller (1965, p. 344) also observed that in gorillas, "a dominant male who stands motionless, facing in a certain direction, indicates that he is ready to leave and the other members of the group crowd around him." Such attention orientation in animals may provide part of the substrate for human gestural communication (Hewes, 1973). However, what may be more important in the spontaneous behavior of wild apes as a precursor to human pointing are both finger extension and exploratory poking. Plooij (1984) called the finger extensions he observed in infant chimpanzees' orienting responses, a term that has also been applied to finger extensions in human infants (Thelen & Fogel, 1986). The role of these finger movements in the ontogenesis of pointing in human infants is further addressed in the next section of this chapter.

With regard to the lack of showing gestures, it has been noted that "chimpanzee cultures are not nearly as object oriented as human ones, and they thus have little 'incentive' to go beyond the social aspects of attracting attention" (Plooij, 1978, p. 122). Apes certainly engage in displays to attract a sexual mate or to indicate submission, but they are presenting *themselves* rather than an object. Their displays could perhaps be loosely compared to Bates's (1976) observations of "showing off" behavior in infants, which she viewed as preliminary to showing objects. Because we have not observed this developmental sequence of showing off to showing objects in our longitudinal studies of infants, however, it may be idiosyncratic to only certain infants.

In contrast to wild chimpanzees, pointing, showing, and giving (of nonfood objects) have all been observed in a human-raised orangutan (Miles, 1990). At 26 months of age, Chantek began spontaneously to point to where he wanted to be tickled. This behavior has also been observed in juvenile chimpanzees at the Yerkes Regional Primate Research Center (Tomasello, George, Kruger, Farrar, & Evans, 1985). However, Chantek went on to point to objects in an indicative rather than an imperative manner and to respond to questions about where things were by pointing to their location. He is also said to have followed the human infant progression from pointing for oneself first, to then pointing for others (Bates, 1976; Werner & Kaplan, 1963). Although pointing in Chantek was delayed by comparison to human infants, who typically point by early in the second year, its ontogeny appears to have been similar. His exposure to human culture thus allowed him to go beyond finger extension and poking.

Chantek is also reported to have engaged in showing objects, such as a blade of grass, and in giving objects (not just food) (Miles, 1990). Giving of objects has also been observed in rehabilitant orangutans in Borneo, who receive much exposure to human culture (Russon, 1995). In both reports of orangutan giving, however, it is not clear if the giving is a simple exchange of objects, as it often is between human infants and their partners, or if there is an expectation that the recipient will do something with the object given (what we have called give-request).

Pointing in captive chimpanzees has been documented in studies of signing chimpanzees (who have been taught a similar gesture as a sign) and of non–language-trained chimpanzees. However, in contrast to Chantek, pointing in these apes seems to be exclusively request pointing – that is, it has an imperative and not a declarative function (compare Tomasello & Camaioni, 1997). Leavens, Hopkins, and Bard (1996) documented spontaneous pointing with an extended index finger or with whole-hand extension in three adult chimpanzees who had not been language trained. These gestures were exhibited 99% of the time in the presence of the observer and were directed mostly at food. Index finger extensions were predominantly right-handed (like pointing in 1-year-old human infants; see below). When whole-hand extensions were directed at a nonfood item, instead of at food, they were considered to have a declarative function; but the nonfood item was often the computer that normally delivered food. Leavens and Hopkins (1998) extended this research to a very large number (115) of captive, non–language-trained chimpanzees representing a wide age range. Whole-hand extensions were more common than index-finger extensions, and juvenile chimpanzees emitted fewer of these gestures.

In two language-trained female adult chimpanzees, index finger extensions were found to be fairly equally distributed across hands in one experiment and were predominantly left-handed in another (Krause & Fouts, 1997). As in the previous studies, whole-hand extensions were not considered to be reaching because they were more frequent in the presence of the observer. Furthermore, establishing eye contact with the observer before hand extension was also viewed as precluding reaching. Since reaching as well as pointing can have a communicative function, these criteria are puzzling. They appear to be based on a failure to distinguish between reaching to grasp a proximal object and reaching as a request for another to obtain a distal object. To consider whole-hand extensions, without finger extensions, or finger extensions without arm extensions, as pointing is problematic. In human infants, neither has the indicative function of pointing (with both arm and index finger extension) nor shows a similar developmental change (Franco & Butterworth, 1996; and see next section).

Thus, with the exception of Chantek, a true sharing of experience expressed by pointing, showing, and give-exchange gestures seems not to have been demonstrated even in captive apes. In the human infant, according to Trevarthen and Hubley (1978, p. 184), "a deliberately sought sharing of experiences about events and things is achieved for the first time" at 9 months. They viewed this emergent behavior as an innate common "rule of sharing" that is "regulated by growth to be active at this age" in different cultures and generations (p. 221). This rule of sharing is similar to the *descriptive* communicative function that Thorpe (1978) saw as differentiating animal and human communication systems and also to Halliday's (1975) informative function in human infants' prelinguistic vocalizations. That chimpanzees have some rules of sharing, particularly with regard to food sources, especially meat, is clear from Goodall's (1986) observations. Russon (1990) also reported that the two captive infant chimpanzees whom she observed shared objects. However, the sharing of information between human infants and their partners by the second year goes well beyond such contexts.

In Table 3–2, other gestures that are absent from wild chimpanzees are head nod/shake and clasp/clap hands. In clasp hands, the hands of the same individual are brought together; whereas in some wild chimpanzees, one animal clasps the hand of another. Head shake has been observed in wild gorillas as a submissive gesture by Schaller (1965), while van Hooff (1973) observed it in the play of captive chimpanzees. He also observed head nod (up and down), associated with an excited state. Clasp/clap hands has been reported in captive apes by Berdecio and Nash (1981, cited in Tomasello, 1990), De Waal (1988), Myers Thompson (1994), and Tomasello et al. (1985). Myers Thompson (1994) found that this gesture was used by bonobos to indicate pleasure in grooming. She also made a case for its cultural transmission in that it was found in only two populations of bonobos and traced also to their offspring. Her interviews with human caretakers revealed no recall of using this gesture with the bonobos, but it nevertheless seems likely that this unusual gesture was imitated from humans. De Waal (1988), who reported clapping by the first generation of these bonobos, stated that they were all human raised. He found, however, a wider function beyond pleasure in grooming, as clapping also occurred in nest building or in playing with an object.

Two other gestures that *have* been reported in apes but were not yet in the repertoire of the human infants whom we observed should be noted. One is the beckoning gesture observed by Van-Lawick Goodall (1968) in the Gombe chimpanzees and by van Hooff (1973) in captive chimpanzees. In the wild chimpanzees, this gesture served functions of male courtship and maternal care. The beckoning gesture is said to be similar to a "stretch-over" gesture observed in captive bonobos (De Waal, 1988). Another gesture not observed in our infants is a head tip as a sign of aggression in chimpanzees (Van Lawick-Goodall, 1968; Goodall, 1986) and in gorillas (Schaller, 1965). In humans, the head tip or head toss gesture appears to be culturally transmitted, because it is not used in all cultures and has various interpretations in different regions (Morris, Collett, Marsh, & O'Shaughnessy, 1979). Darwin (1872/1965), however, sees this gesture as having a universal origin in the infant's early rejections of food (perhaps our turn-away gesture).

The issue of cultural transmission of gestures in chimpanzees has been specifically addressed by Tomasello (1990). He concluded that the only culturally transmitted gestures are attention-getting signals (e.g., ground slap as an invitation to play among juvenile chimpanzees), but that these behaviors are not imitated but rather emulated. The distinction between emulation and imitation concerns a focus by the animal on the end result rather than the means to the end or the signal, itself. Imitation is also contrasted with ontogenetic ritualization (Tomasello, 1996). Ritualization involves a sequential process in which a signal is gradually shaped by the social environment, as in the acquisition of the "up" gesture described earlier. In Tomasello's example, the infant chimpanzee's pulling of the mother's arm away from the breast is gradually abbreviated, with the mother's cooperation, into a simple touch to initiate nursing. Tomasello argued that whereas human infants learn their conventional gestures (such as *bye-bye,* but not *up*) via imitation, chimpanzees learn them only through the shaping process of ritualization. Furthermore, the absence of gestural continuity over 4 years of development in chimpanzees in his longitudinal study (Tomasello et al., 1989) and the absence of gestural overlap both within and across generations in his transgenerational study (Tomasello, Call, Nagell, Olguin, & Carpenter, 1994) were viewed as evidence against cultural transmission. Such a process would be expected to produce a more stable (and more universal) repertoire among chimpanzees living together. Conversely, it would produce differences in repertoire between different groups of chimpanzees, whereas a later study revealed quite similar gesture frequencies (Tomasello et al., 1997). Tomasello (1990) also argued that many of the chimpanzee signals are one-way, from young chimpanzees to adults, and therefore could not have been imitated from adults. Finally, Tomasello et al. (1997) tested degree of gestural imitation directly by training two female chimpanzees to produce a novel gesture to obtain food. Although the other chimpanzees observed these gestures many times, they never imitated them.

The case against imitation for many gestures in our inventory is also strong, either because human adults do not use them (for example, hand flapping) or because they use them in a different form (for example, reach-request with palm up in adults versus palm down in infants) (Clark, 1978). Also, individual differences in human infant gestural repertoire abound; not all infants use all of the gestures in our inventory. If longitudinal results spanning 4 years were available on human children (and, unfortunately, they are not), it is likely that stability would be found for only a select few gestures (e.g., pointing, clap hands, bye-bye). These are conventional gestures that appear to be quite modifiable both in form and frequency by experience – that is, they are culturally transmitted. As previously noted, clap hands may be culturally transmitted in bonobos, whereas the other conventional gestures are largely missing in apes. Darwin (1872/1965) would add head nod/shake to the list of human culturally transmitted gestures. Some infant gestures might appear to be unstable across development because they undergo transformations to reappear in a quite subtle form in the older child and adult. For example, it was once suggested to me that bodily resistance behaviors could still be seen in a 21-year-old man being embraced by his mother. This transformational process has yet to be studied, in either infants or apes (see also Tomasello et al., 1989). Finally, I present later in this chapter data showing similarity in gestures across unacquainted groups of infants from different cultures.

This review of the roots of our gestural inventory in nonhuman primates reveals that most of the gestures can be found in apes and, particularly, in chimpanzees, our closest relative (Quiatt & Itani, 1994). Gestures involving sharing of objects, sharing of information, and clear use of others as agents appear to require human rearing. As Call and Tomasello (1994, p. 315) put it, it is possible that "interacting with others in human-like ways during early ontogeny is a necessary component in the development of a human-like capacity to understand others as intentional agents whose attention may be followed into, manipulated, or shared." They found that Chantek, with this type of rearing, was able to comprehend human pointing, to point to a hidden tool needed by a human to get food, and to inhibit pointing when the human could not see the gesture. In contrast, another captive chimpanzee, without the same human exposure as Chantek, was less able to master all these subtleties of pointing.

Some of the gestures exhibited by nonhuman primates without human rearing show formal but not functional continuity with human infant gestures. This is particularly true of gestures in the threat repertoire of adult apes, such as flap/wave arms. The function of these movements in human infants, if they are indeed related to the ape gestures, has clearly undergone transformation phylogenetically. It is also clear, as we will now see, that formal elements of gestures that appear early in human infancy also undergo functional transformation in ontogeny.

Ontogeny of Gestures in Human Infants before 9 Months

The claim has been made by many researchers that the beginnings of gestural form can be seen very early in human infancy (Bower, 1974; Fogel, 1981; Fogel & Hannan, 1985; Hannan, 1987; Thelen & Fogel, 1986). Trevarthen (1977, p. 252) observed that by 2 months, most infants "show hand-waving, index-finger pointing and fingertip-clasping movements near the face while they are animated to make expressive vocalization and prespeech." He called these hand patterns gesticulation, as did Kendon (1993) when referring to gestures accompanying adult speech. These movements in infants are viewed as innate forms that are not imitated but modified through exposure to adult models. Subsequent studies of hand movements in infants between 2 and 4 months of age have found index finger extensions and finger curling to follow or cooccur with vocalizations and mouthing movements (Fogel & Hannan, 1985; Legerstee, Corter, & Kienapple, 1990). In a recent study, index finger extensions were observed to cooccur specifically with "speech like" vocalizations but not with vocalic utterances (Masataka, 1995). Other studies, however, have found that index finger extensions rarely occur with vocalizations (Blake, O'Rourke, & Borzellino, 1994; Hannan, 1987).

Although these index finger extensions have been called pointing by both primatologists and human infant researchers, *prepointing* is a more appropriate term, since these movements are not mapped onto indicative situations during either the first year (Blake, O'Rourke, & Borzellino, 1994) or the second year (Franco & Butterworth, 1996). In young infants (4- and 8-month-olds), index finger extensions were more likely to occur in arousing situations (mother chatting excitedly, a wind-up toy approaching) than in situations in which the mother modeled pointing (to a book, to an unusual toy, out the window) (Blake, O'Rourke, & Borzellino, 1994). At these ages also, index finger extensions tended to be brief and to occur equally in left and right hands (see also Fogel & Hannan, 1985), features that were *not* characteristic of either pointing or prepointing in 12-month-olds. Rönnqvist and von Hofsten (1994) similarly found more finger movements by neonates in the presence of a chatty, entertaining mother than in the presence of a ball of yarn or nothing. Others have also found, with somewhat older infants, that index finger extensions occur more in social contexts with the mother than with objects (Fogel, 1981; Legerstee et al., 1990).

It has been suggested that the functional continuity between index finger extensions and later referential pointing lies in their orienting aspect (Thelen & Fogel, 1986). Finger movements are viewed as orienting responses because of their putative association with a neutral, attentive state. However, the findings described earlier indicate an aroused rather than a neutral state (see also Fogel & Hannan, 1985). Furthermore, index finger extensions are often undirected to the focus of attention, which seems odd for an orienting response. McGuire and Turkewitz (1978) suggest that at 3 months, finger extensions and flexions are reflex responses to stimulus intensity, extensions occurring as an approach response to weak stimuli and flexions as a withdrawal response to strong stimuli. By 5 months, finger movements no longer show a relationship with stimulus intensity. Although these findings are consistent with the other results cited in highlighting the importance of stimulus intensity in eliciting early finger extensions, they are inconsistent in linking extensions to *less* arousing stimuli.

What we can conclude is that extensions of the index finger are an innately available response that is later recruited as a motor component of pointing. They hardly constitute pointing in themselves, and they have quite a different function. Furthermore, they are not recognized as pointing by observers – even mothers (Fogel, 1981). Such recognition is essential for a gesture to communicate.

In contrast, reaching for an object occurs very early, though not at birth. Rönnqvist and von Hofsten (1994) found longer forward arm extensions by neonates in an object condition than in a social condition, but newborns engaged in just as many forward arm extensions when there was nothing in front of them as when there was an object there (Ruff & Halton, 1978). In von Hofsten's (1984) longitudinal study, infants at 1 week also engaged in as many forward extensions with the object absent as present. Forward extensions then decreased at 7 weeks and the hand became fisted. Only at 10 weeks did forward extensions with the object present begin to exceed those with the object absent, and the hand also opened to prepare for grasping. Fogel (1981) also found an increase in reaching for an object in two infants at about 14 weeks. Thus, we can conclude that reaching for an object properly begins between 2.5 and 4 months, although prereaching preparatory movements may occur earlier (Trevarthen & Hubley, 1978). At 4 months, however, attempts to reach and grasp objects are still largely unsuccessful, one third of them missing the object altogether (Blake, O'Rourke, & Borzellino, 1994). Nevertheless, this represents an improvement over 1- to 2-week-olds, who miss contact about 93% of the time (Ruff & Halton, 1978). Further improvement occurs between

4 and 8 months, when misses drop to about 11% (Blake, O'Rourke, & Borzellino, 1994).

Four-month-olds also reach for objects clearly out of reach and, more importantly, vocalize more when reaching for objects out of reach than for those within their grasp (Blake, O'Rourke, & Borzellino, 1994). Trevarthen and Hubley (1978) also reported that the infant they observed made a grunting sound while reaching at this age. Thus, early forms of directed reaching are more continuous in *both* form and function with later forms of request-reaching than index finger extensions are with pointing, even though later forms of reaching are increasingly coordinated with more urgent and conventionalized vocalizations.

Clasp hand gestures also can be seen in early infancy (Fogel, 1981; Trevarthen, 1977), but whether this gesture is exploratory or the expression of an emotional state is unclear. As I discuss in the next section, the onset of clasp hands as a clear emotive gesture is relatively late, so that, like pointing, it may recruit an early form to express a later-developing function.

An area of neglect in the study of early movements is whole-body movement. For example, Fogel (1981) referred to a body-lean movement in a 2-month-old. Such body-strain movements may have more functional continuity with later gestural communication than hand and finger movements, which appear to express fleeting changes in states in young infants. As such, early hand and finger movements may be more related to facial expression than to later hand and arm gestures. For example, spreading out of fingers has been associated with a relaxed facial expression (Fogel & Hannan, 1985) and closing of the hand with a distressed expression (Legerstee, et al., 1990) in 2- to 4-month-olds.

It is important to emphasize the emotive aspect of these early hand movements in human ontogeny, however. If they do indeed provide the roots of later communicative gestures, then emotive gestures should form the primitive base of the communicative gestural system, similar to the emotive signaling system of nonhuman primates. As human infants become increasingly intentionally communicative, we would expect emotive gestures to decrease in importance, whereas gestures that focus on the sharing of objects and information increase in importance. These are the types of gestures that are rarely reported in wild nonhuman primates but that human-reared nonhuman primates are quite capable of imitating, as we have seen. Because these sharing gestures are typically found to emerge in human infants between 9 and 10 months of age, I now move the story of ontogenetic development to 9-month-old infants.

Gestural Development from 9 Months: Order of Onset

Our longitudinal studies of gestures began when the infants were 8 to 9 months old. Seven babies (four English-Canadian and three Parisian-French) were observed intensively from this age until 14 months; two additional babies (one from each culture) were followed from 11 months to 14 months. Two infants in each cultural group were male. These infants were visited biweekly at home and filmed while they interacted freely with a parent or caretaker. Order of appearance of the gestures in the inventory on Table 3–1 can be divided for these infants into early, middle, and late appearing. In the four English-Canadian babies observed from age 8 or 9 months, the following gestures were seen in the first session, between 8:15 and 9:10, in at least three of the infants: take, reach-request, flap/wave arms, and bounce. Thus, some emotive gestures, plus reaching for something out of reach, are gestures already in the repertoire by 9 months. (In fact, as discussed earlier, Blake, O'Rourke, & Borzellino, 1994, observed reaching for a distal object at 4 months.) There might be some objection to including take as a communicative gesture; however, in object exchange, it is the reciprocal of give. It is interesting that take appears before give, indicating that infants seem to learn to give by first accepting what is given (see also Trevarthen & Hubley, 1978).

By 10 months, at least three infants also exhibited show, give, up-/down-request, turn away, push/pull away, and bodily resist. Thus, the first sharing gestures appear at this age, as well as some protest gestures. That showing is the first "declarative" gesture to appear confirms the results of Bates (1976). Offer was delayed relative to give, not appearing in most infants until after 12 months. The onset of pointing in a book was between 10 and 11 months, whereas the emergence of pointing to a distal object was more variable, 8.5 to 13 months. All caretakers modeled pointing in a book but differentially modeled distal pointing. (They were not given any instructions in this study.) One infant observed from 11 months received a great deal of modeling of distal pointing and in turn pointed with great frequency, to such an extent that he used point-request much more than reach-request. Thus, it seems clear, both from human-reared nonhuman primates and from human infants, that modeling of pointing by caretakers can have a pronounced effect on its frequency of use. The onset of distal pointing typically preceded the onset of pointing as a request, although the latter also had a wide range of onset (9 to 14 months). It also had a very low frequency of occurrence in all but the one infant described above. Reaching clearly was the request gesture of choice.

Gestures appearing between 11 and 13 months were two of the request gestures that involved cognizance of the adult as an agent (give/offer request, seek assistance). Take parent's hand was very variable in age of appearance (9 to 13 months) and did not occur at all for one infant. The comment gesture of head nod/shake also appeared between 11 and 13 months or later.

Late-appearing gestures, observed after 1 year in most infants, were the protest gestures of hit and head shake/rejection and the emotive gesture of clasp/clap hands. Bye-bye was seen in two babies by 10 months, in one after 13 months, and not at all in two infants.

An older group of 3 English-Canadian infants, followed from the age of 13 or 14 months, confirmed the late appearance of hit (14 to 16 months), head nod/shake as a comment (17 months), clasp/clap hands (14 to 16 months), bye-bye (17 months), and take parent's hand (13 to 15 months). Some gestures in this older group thus appeared even later than in the younger group and all after the session.

For the Parisian-French infants, a book was provided to encourage point-in-book behavior, and a windup toy was used to elicit give-request gestures (to rewind the toy). Otherwise, the observations were similarly unstructured as for the English-Canadian infants. Point in book was seen early in only one infant, despite the encouragement, the other three not exhibiting this behavior until 13 months. Distal pointing also began at 13 months in most infants but was infrequent in this group. Again, showing occurred somewhat earlier than pointing, between 10 and 12 months, but not at all for one infant.

The age of onset of object exchange, reach-request, and up-/down-request gestures, as well as that of the only protest gesture exhibited by most infants in this group, push/pull away, was similar to that in English-Canadian babies. Gestures involving cognizance of the adult as an agent, primarily give-request in this group, appeared somewhat later. So did most emotive gestures, with the exception of clasp/clap hands, which occurred earlier.

Finally, we can compare these data from small groups followed intensively to a large group (30) of Italian-Canadian infants who were observed only at 9 to 10 months and at 15 months, but not between those ages. This larger sample was more heterogeneous than the smaller samples in terms of parental education, the majority of the infants in both the English-Canadian and French cultures having highly educated parents. The 9- to 10-month observations for the Italian-Canadian infants came from two 15-minute unstructured sessions 2 weeks apart. They are useful in determining if the early onset gestures of the small samples are replicated in a larger, more heterogeneous sample. The gestures that were seen in the majority of these infants at 9 months were show, give-exchange, take, reach-request, up-/down-request, turn away, push/pull away, resist bodily, flap/wave arms, and bounce. This list is similar to the English-Canadian early-onset gestures, with a somewhat more precocious onset of show and give-exchange gestures, as well as of the protest gestures turn away, push/pull away, and resist bodily. Some of these gestures are illustrated in Figures 3–2, 3–3, and 3–4.

The results for order of appearance of gestures are summarized in Table 3–3. In a very large study using the MacArthur Communicative Development Inventory, Fenson et al. (1994) also found that more than half of the parents surveyed reported the gestures show, give, reach-request, and up-request as appearing early – that is, before 10 months. However, they also reported point and bye-bye as occurring early, whereas we found them to be later appearing for most infants. It is clear from our findings that the modal age of appearance is related to the conventionality of the gesture. The most conventional comment gestures, bye-bye and head nod/shake, are typically later in their appearance, as are the more conventional protest/rejection gestures (hit, head shake) and emotive gestures (clasp/clap hands). The late appearance of these gestures is presumably related to an increase in imitative behavior in the second year. Other late-appearing gestures are dependent upon further advances in the understanding of agency: give-request, seek assistance, and take parent's hand. However, even these modally late gestures show some variability across infants in order of appearance, with a few infants displaying the gesture at a much younger age than the others.

Onset of Coordination of Gesture with Vocalization and Gaze

It has been suggested that gestures are used for a period of time before they are coordinated with vocalizations, at least for the gestures give, show, and point (Lock, 1980; Masur, 1983; Murphy, 1978). For the

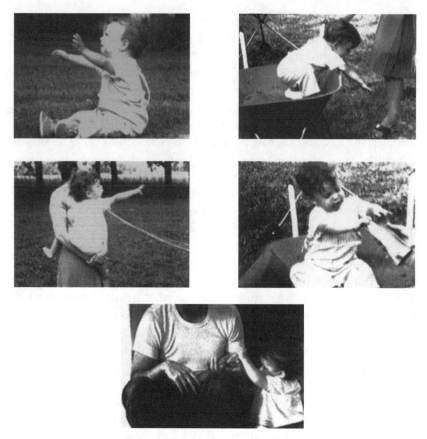

Figure 3–2: A male infant at 15 months gesturing "up" (top left) and reaching out to a tractor (middle left). A male infant at 14 months requesting a piece of wood (top right) and taking a piece of wood from his mother (middle right). A female infant at 14.5 months giving an action figure to her father (bottom). Photographs by E. Maiese and J. Blake.

most part, we have not found this to be true. In our research, gestures were coded as occurring with vocalization if the vocalization occurred within 1 second of the gesture. In the longitudinal study of the younger group of English-Canadian infants, the majority of infants vocalized with the following gestures on the first observation: point, take, reach-request, point-request, seek assistance, push/pull away, hit, resist bodily, flap/wave arms, bounce, and clasp/clap hands. Of these gestures, some (take, reach-request, flap arms, and bounce) were observed in the first session and thus may have occurred earlier without vocalization. Some of the remaining gestures were coordinated with vocalization by

Figure 3–3: A female infant at 15.5 months pointing in a book (top left) and at 12 months pointing at her brother (middle left). A male infant at 16.5 months pointing in a book (top right), leading his mother to the house while reaching out for something (middle right), seeking assistance in opening the car door (bottom left), and clapping hands (bottom right). Photographs by E. Maiese.

some infants on the first observation but not by others. These gestures were show, give-exchange, up-request, give-/offer-request, and turn away. Infants tended not to vocalize at all with head nod and head shake (both as comment and rejection). For both younger and older English-Canadian groups, vocalization was sometimes delayed for the late-appearing gestures, take parent's hand and bye-bye.

For the French infants, the results were quite similar except that vocalization with the following gestures was equally immediate and delayed: take, reach-request, push/pull away, and flap arms. The

Figure 3–4: A male infant at 16 months holding out a cookie.

majority of Italian-Canadian infants coordinated all gestures observed at the first session with vocalization. Although these infants may have used these gestures earlier without vocalization, they were at least coordinating them with vocalization at a relatively early age, 9 months.

Thus, across these groups, most infants vocalized immediately with point, show, reach-request, and most protest and emotive gestures. Masur (1983) was perhaps correct about a delay in the coordination of vocalization with give/offer exchange, but we have found a low fre-

Table 3–3. Order of Onset of Gestures

Early Appearing (9–10 Mo.)	Middle Appearing (11–13 Mo.)	Late Appearing (after 13 Mo.)
Show	Point (distal and in book)	Bye-bye
Give-exchange		Offer-exchange
Take	Point-request	Hit
Reach-request	Give/offer-request	Head shake/rejection
Up-/down-request	Seek assistance	Clasp/clap hands
Turn away		Take parent's hand
Push/pull away		Head nod/shake (comment)
Resist bodily		
Bounce		
Flap/wave arms		

quency of vocalization with this gesture, even in older infants (Blake et al., 1992). More conventional gestures (e.g., head nod and bye-bye) in our infants tended not to be accompanied by vocalizations at all.

I would conclude from these findings that there appears to be a certain automaticity in the pairing of gesture and vocalization. Combining them does not seem to pose a greater demand on the infant's resources such that the infant must be more proficient in his/her use of the gesture before being able to coordinate it with a vocalization. The two modalities go together from the beginning, so to speak, and I return to this point at the end of the chapter.

The same point cannot be made for the coordination of gesture with gaze. Coordination with eye contact from the first appearance of the gesture in the younger English-Canadian group was found for seek assistance, for which eye contact is part of the definition of the gesture; for show, a gesture made while facing another; and for the emotive gestures flap/wave arms and bounce. Eye contact with the following gestures was equally immediate and delayed: point, head nod/shake as a comment, give-/offer-exchange, take, reach-request, point-request, and give-/offer-request. For protest/rejection gestures, eye contact was not found for the majority of infants for any gesture. This was also true for point in book, owing to the position of the infant relative to the caretaker (see also Murphy, 1978) and tended to be true for down-request and take parent's hand for similar reasons.

In the older group of English-Canadian infants, coordination with eye contact in the early sessions was *not* found for the following gestures in the majority of infants: point, point in book, and all protest gestures except head shake. The results for the French infants were again quite similar to those for the younger English-Canadian group except that immediate coordination with eye contact occurred with offer-exchange and give-/offer-request. Also, these infants tended not to coordinate eye contact with emotive gestures as well as with protest gestures.

In contrast, the majority of Italian-Canadian infants coordinated eye contact at the first session at 9 months with all gestures observed, even protest gestures except for resist bodily. These Italian-Canadian infants, then, used eye contact with their gestures more immediately than the other groups. However, their overall *proportional* use of eye contact with their gestures at 9 months was not much greater than that of the other groups (see Table 3–4 below). This indicates that they were quite inconsistent in their coordination of eye contact with gestures, even though they did show such coordination with more gestures at the first session.

Change in the Gestural Repertoire from 9 to 15 Months and in Coordination with Vocalization and Gaze

In Table 3–4, the three groups of infants who were observed at 9 months and again at 14 to 15 months are compared with respect to relative frequencies of gestural categories at these ages. Certain changes in gestural repertoire might be expected to occur across this age period. We have already seen that the onset of more conventional gestures (bye-bye and head/nod shake) tends to occur later, as do gestures that indicate greater awareness of adult agency (take parent's hand). Developmental increases in the relative frequency of gestures that share objects (object exchange) or information (show, point) would also be expected across this period. In contrast, decreases in what might be

Table 3–4. Comparison of Gestural Change in the Groups Observed at 9 and 14 to 15 Months

	English-Canadian (N = 4)		Parisian-French (N = 3)		Italian-Canadian (N = 30)	
	9 Mo. (%)	14 Mo. (%)	9 Mo. (%)	14 Mo. (%)	9 Mo. (%)	15 Mo. (%)
Comment	13.0	21.3	1.9	8.5	9.3	18.4[a]
Point	6.4	14.6	0.6	5.1	2.5	12.0[a]
Show	2.6	4.0	0.4	2.1	2.8	3.3
Exchange	24.5	33.5	21.6	30.1	14.5	27.0[a]
Request	22.1	29.2	49.2	51.7	37.3	22.4[a]
Reach/Point	10.7	8.8	39.5	23.5	14.6	10.5
Agent	2.6	13.8[b]	0.0	14.3	0.7	3.6
Protest	13.4	4.5	4.4	6.2	19.0	19.0
Emotive	26.6	11.6	22.8	3.4[c]	19.8	13.6
With vocalization	67.1	59.1	39.3	40.2	36.1	55.9[d]
With gaze	32.8	39.9	24.0	29.0	37.5	34.2

[a] t's (29) 2.17 to 4.70; $p < .04$ to $p < .001$.
[b] t (3) = 4.46; $p < .02$.
[c] t (2) = 5.20; $p < .04$.
[d] F (1, 28) = 34.51; $p < .0001$.

considered primitive (that is, early onset) request gestures (reach-request, up-/down-request), as well as in protest/rejection and emotive gestures, would be expected. The general gist of these predictions is that gestures found in the natural repertoire of nonhuman primates would be expected to decrease, whereas those that appear to be specific to human culture would be expected to increase during the transition to linguistic communication.

Table 3–4 confirms some of these predictions. The relative frequency of comment gestures increased for all groups between the ages of 9 and 14 to 15 months, and most of this increase is attributable to point gestures (the means combine distal point and point in a book). The increases in comment gestures, and specifically in point gestures, are significant only for the larger Italian-Canadian sample. In contrast, the relative frequency of show gestures increased only slightly. The two Canadian subcultural groups look quite similar in their relative frequencies of these comment gestures; whereas the French group exhibited much less pointing, despite being encouraged to look at a book with their caretakers. Object exchange gestures also increased, relative to other gestures, for all groups, again significantly only for the larger Italian-Canadian sample. For these gestures the English-Canadian and French samples look remarkably similar, but all groups end up with very similar relative frequencies at the older age level. Request gestures, in contrast, appear quite different in importance across the three groups. The French infants exhibited a high proportion of these gestures, which remained stable across the two ages. This stability in overall request gestures, however, masks a considerable change in the types of request gestures used across the period: Reach-/point-request gestures decreased, whereas gestures using the adult as an agent (specifically, give-request and take adult's hand, in this group) increased. Like the French infants, the English-Canadian infants show an increase in the relative frequency of gestures involving cognizance of adult agency (significant for this group) and a small decrease in reach-/point-request gestures. The Italian-Canadian infants show a significant decrease in request gestures, most of this being due to a decrease in up-/down-requests. They show the same pattern as the other groups of a decrease in reach-/point-requests and an increase in gestures cognizant of adult agency, but the relative frequency of the latter is low.

The predicted decrease in protest gestures occurs only for the English-Canadian sample, the French infants exhibiting a very low level throughout and the Italian-Canadian group a high level. The predicted decrease in emotive gestures occurs across all three samples but is significant only for the French sample.

Despite the fact that we found vocalizations occurring with many gestures immediately or soon after their onset, it might nevertheless be expected that gestures would be increasingly coordinated with vocalizations and also with gaze. Table 3–4 shows mixed support for this prediction across groups. For the larger Italian-Canadian sample, the coordination of gestures with vocalizations did significantly increase. For the other two groups, however, this was not the case. For the English-Canadian infants, such coordination of vocalization with gesture was already at a high level at 9 months. For no group did coordination of gesture with gaze significantly increase over this time period, although the small groups show slight increases.

This review of changes across the transition period to language supports predictions about increases in point gestures, object exchange gestures, and request gestures involving adult agency and offers partial support for a predicted increase in coordination of gesture with vocalization. It also provides support for predictions about decreases in primitive request and emotive gestures. It does not support predictions about increases in show gestures or in coordination of gestures with gaze or about decreases in protest.

The increase in point gestures that we found across groups, though not always significant, is consistent with the results of several other studies finding an increase in pointing in the second year (Iverson, Capirci, & Caselli, 1994; Lempers, 1979; Leung & Rheingold, 1981; Murphy & Messer, 1977). Some researchers have found, however, that it decreases again after the middle of the second year (Lock et al., 1990; Petitto, 1987; Zinober & Martlew, 1985). In our sample of older English-Canadian infants followed over the second year, we did not find this to be the case (Blake et al., 1992). An increase in coordination of gestures with vocalization during the second year has also been found in several studies (Lock et al., 1990; Martinsen & Smith, 1989; Masur, 1983; and Zinober & Martlew, 1985). These studies, as well as others (Franco & Butterworth, 1996; Goldin-Meadow & Morford, 1985, for two of three hearing children; Leung & Rheingold, 1981), have found quite high proportions of gestures combined with vocalization. The lower levels of such coordination in our findings are no doubt due to a more stringent time limit for cooccurrence of gesture with vocalization.

In contrast, as in our findings, much lower proportions of gestures coordinated with gaze have been found by most researchers (Leung &

Rheingold, 1981; Lock et al., 1990; Martinsen & Smith, 1989; Masur, 1983; Murphy & Messer, 1977). These findings confirm doubts expressed earlier about eye contact as a criterion for intentional communication. The only aspect of our results that lends some credibility to the validity of eye contact as a measure of intention is that in both Canadian groups, it occurred more frequently with comment and emotive gestures and least with protest. Thus, one could argue that when infants want to share information or affect, they tend to look at the adult. When they reject an overture, they look away. If eye contact is an indicator of intentionality, then its relative absence with protest gestures would have to be interpreted as indicating the involuntary nature of these gestures.

Interrelationships among Gestures

The larger size of the Italian-Canadian sample permitted correlational analyses. These revealed some interesting relationships across ages between types of gestures. The frequency of object exchange gestures at age 9 months was highly related to the frequency of comment gestures at age 15 months ($r = .71$; $p < .0001$), in particular pointing ($r = .69$; $p < . 0001$), as well as the increase in pointing from 9 to 15 months ($r = .70$; $p < .0001$). Thus, infants who engaged in more sharing of objects at an early age tended later to engage in more sharing of information, particularly through pointing.

There were also interesting relationships between gestural categories at the same age level. At 9 months, the frequencies of object exchange gestures and protest gestures were negatively related ($r = -.39$; $p < .05$), whereas those for request and protest gestures, as well as for protest and emotive gestures, were positively related ($r = .76$, $p < .0001$ and $r = .38$, $p < .05$, respectively). At 15 months, request and protest gestures continued to be positively correlated ($r = .46$; $p < .05$). The decrease across ages in request gestures was also correlated with the decrease in protest gestures ($r = .50$; $p < .005$). The increase in object exchange gestures was correlated with the *decrease* in emotive gestures ($r = .38$; $p < .05$). Thus, at both age levels, infants who engaged in more protest gestures also tended to engage in more request gestures. In other words, they were generally more demanding in interactions. Those who decreased their gestures in one category also tended to decrease them in the other. At 9 months, infants who were more gesturally protesting were also more gesturally emotive and less involved in sharing objects.

Those who increased their object-sharing correspondingly decreased their emotive gestures.

These results support the view that protest, emotive, and most request gestures form a "primitive" core of gestures with similar relative frequencies of use for individual infants and similar developmental trends. Use of primitive gestures and change in their use tends to be inversely related to that of object-sharing gestures. Early object sharing appears to be important in the development of pointing.

The patterns of change in the gestural repertoire and of relations among the gestures raise questions about underlying influences for change. Two possible candidates are sex of infant and home environment. There were no gender differences in pointing in this group, but female infants engaged in more showing. Male infants made more up/down request and push/pull gestures, but the decreases in these gestures across age were equivalent for both genders. No gender differences were found in object exchange or emotive gestures. Can individual differences in gestural-frequencies then be attributed to differences in the environments of these infants?

Environmental Influences on the Gestural Repertoire

The environmental factors that were assessed for the larger Italian-Canadian sample were years of maternal education and the level of stimulation in the home. The minimum level of education completed was high school. Fathers' education tended to be at the same level as the mothers' or lower, with very few exceptions. All of these families were two-parent.

During the 15-month visit, the Home Observation for Measurement of the Environment (HOME) scale (Caldwell & Bradley, 1984) was administered. This scale contains six subscales measuring emotional and verbal responsivity of parent, acceptance of child's behavior, organization of physical and temporal environment, provision of appropriate play materials, parent involvement with child, and opportunities for variety in daily stimulation.

As might be expected, scores on the HOME scale tended to be significantly correlated with years of maternal education ($r = .359$; $p < .051$). Scores were negatively related to the frequency of protest gestures at 15 months ($r = -.362$; $p < .05$). Years of maternal education were positively related to the frequency of emotive gestures at 9 months ($r = .39$; $p < .05$) and of point gestures at 9 months ($r = .36$; $p < .05$). These environmental factors, then, are related to two aspects of gestures that appear to be important for language: fewer protest gestures at 15 months and early pointing at 9 months.

Relation of Gestures to Early Vocabulary and Later Language Acquisition

The final and most crucial question concerns the relationship between patterns of gestural change and language acquisition. At 15 months, mothers provided a list of words produced by their infants in both English and Italian. Vocabulary size, composed of words in either language with different meaning, was related to the frequency of object exchange gestures at 15 months ($r = .44$; $p < .05$) and to the increase in object exchange gestures between 9 and 15 months ($r = .38$; $p < .05$), as well as to the frequency of showing gestures at 15 months ($r = .44$; $p < .05$). The absence of a relationship between pointing and early vocabulary is notable, and the relationship with showing gestures may be attributable to sex differences in favor of girls, both for showing and for vocabulary size at 15 months.

Long-term relationships between gestures and later language proficiency were investigated by visiting the children again at 3 years 1 week. At this time, they were given the Peabody Picture Vocabulary Test (PPVT) (Dunn & Dunn, 1981) to measure receptive vocabulary, one form in English and one form in Italian. Because the English scores were higher with one exception, these scores were used except for this one child, for whom the Italian scores were used. The children were also given a game task to measure communicative competence. In the task, they were taught an unfamiliar board game and then were asked to teach it to a puppet. The children's explanations to the puppet were scored on a 30-point scale, according to the level of specificity and accuracy with which the four steps of the game were described to the puppet (see Blake et al., 1997). Finally, a 30-minute sample of the children's spontaneous speech while they played with small toys was both audio- and videorecorded. These samples were transcribed and scored for MLU as described in chapter 1.

The PPVT and game scores were related to each other ($r = .42$; $p < .02$), and MLU was related to PPVT scores ($r = .42$; $p < .02$) but not to game scores. All three language measures were unrelated to vocabulary size at 15 months. The PPVT scores were positively related to years of maternal education ($r = .56$; $p < .001$) and to the frequency of comment gestures at 15 months ($r = .37$; $p < .05$). Game scores were related to the decrease in protest gestures from 9 to 15 months ($r = .56$; $p < .001$). Mean length of utterance was positively related to the frequency of emotive gestures at 9 months ($r = .36$; $p < .05$) and negatively related to the frequency of reach-request gestures at 15 months ($r = -.42$; $p < .05$) (See Blake et al., 1997).

In summary, these results provide some support for the importance of sharing objects in early productive vocabulary acquisition. Both object exchange gestures and vocabulary size at 15 months, it should be noted, were predicted by Bayley Mental Development Indices (MDI) given to the children at 10 months ($r = .46$, $p < .05$ and $r = .59$, $p < .001$, respectively). None of these measures, however, neither object exchange gestures nor early productive vocabulary nor Bayley MDI, showed long-term relationships to later receptive vocabulary, communicative competence, or MLU. Rather, it was the frequency of comment gestures and of reach-request gestures at 15 months and the degree of decrease in protest gestures between 9 and 15 months that revealed long-term relationships with the 3-year-old measures. The developmental pattern, then, is that at 9 months, object exchange gestures are important in that they predict comment gestures, particularly pointing, at 15 months; and comment gestures in turn predict receptive vocabulary at 3 years. It is notable that gesture variables were more important than early vocabulary in predicting later language proficiency. None of the language measures at age 3 was related to vocabulary size at 15 months.

These results are consistent with the long-term relationship found between pointing in the second year and language measures at 24 months by Desrochers, Morissette, and Ricard (1995). However, these researchers found that it was the age of onset of communicative pointing (while looking at the mother) only that was related to both expressive and receptive measures of language. Instead, we found that comment gestures as a whole were related to receptive vocabulary only. This differential relationship between gestures and language comprehension, but not production, confirms the findings of Bates, Thal, Whitesell, Fenson, and Oakes (1989) that gestures reported by parents were more strongly related to language comprehension than to production. However, the gestures in question were the group of so-called deictic gestures, including not only showing and pointing but also giving and reach-request, and the relationships were short term.

Conclusions

Object sharing in the short term and information sharing in the long term, as well as a decline in primitive protest, appear to be the important gestural precursors of the language outcome measures. Fewer primitive request gestures (reach-request) and more request gestures showing cognizance of adult agency also appear to be part of the pattern of gestural change during the transition to language, although the latter did not yield significant relationships with the language outcome measures. Camaioni, Caselli, Longobardi, and Volterra (1991) did find that gestures involving the adult as an agent were related to vocabulary size at 20 months.

Our results also demonstrate that the coordination of gestures with vocalizations tends to increase over the transitional period to language. The degree of coordination at 15 months, however, was unrelated to our language outcome measures. Although such coordination did increase, it was also generally apparent in early observations of gestures. This finding appears to support an interdependence between the two modalities, a view expressed by McNeill and his collaborators with regard to gestures accompanying speech (e.g., Goldin-Meadow, McNeill, & Singleton, 1996; McNeill, 1992). It is also congruent with the findings of Marcos (1991) that gestures and words/vocalizations play complementary roles in the act of requesting. Infants in the middle of their second year were able to emphasize either the gesture or the vocalization in reformulating requests, depending upon the basis for failure to communicate.

The seeming automaticity of the pairing of vocalizations and gestures, as well as the relationships found between gestural change and language outcome measures in our study, do not support a view that gestures and language develop autonomously (Petitto, 1987). Petitto's view is based on a failure to find facilitation of signs for personal pronouns in two deaf infants who used very similar points as a communicative gesture. This very specific kind of relationship is, of course, not demonstrated by our findings. Rather, they show quite general relationships between types of gestures and language outcomes. Such correlational relationships cannot support a strong precursor model, nor do our findings support such a model if it implies that gestures are replaced by words. No such decline in gesturing over the second year was found in our older English-Canadian group (Blake et al., 1992). Certain types of gestures are nevertheless important in mediating the transition to language, both phylogenetically and ontogenetically, namely, those which share objects and information with other humans.

CHAPTER FOUR

Symbolic Gestures and Symbolic Play

In Chapter 3, I made a distinction between communicative and symbolic gestures because the primary function of symbolic gestures is to represent an object or an action rather than to communicate. My distinction is similar to one made by Erting and Volterra (1990) and by Goldin-Meadow and her collaborators (Goldin-Meadow & Morford, 1985; Goldin-Meadow & Mylander, 1984), who used the term *characterizing* or *pantomimic* for symbolic gestures. However, they included in the characterizing category such gestures as holding out the hand to request an object, which we have called reach-request (see chapter 3). Symbolic gestures have also been labeled enactive (Zinober & Martlew, 1985, after Bruner, 1964), referential (e.g., Camaioni et al., 1991; Caselli, 1990), depictive (Werner & Kaplan, 1963), and iconic (McNeill, 1992; Tanner & Byrne, 1996). Iconic gestures refer also to a category of hand movements that accompany speech and are thought to evolve out of infant symbolic gestures (McNeill, 1992); these are called illustrators by Ekman and Friesen (1969).

Because symbolic gestures represent objects, Goldin-Meadow and Mylander (1984) required that they be performed with no object in hand. Most researchers, however, allow objects in the hand that either substitute for prototypical objects (for example, a block for a doll's bottle) or are part of an action involving a missing realistic ingredient (for example, feeding a doll with a spoon but no food).

The distinction between communicative and symbolic gestures is not always a firm one, of course, because symbolic gestures are sometimes communicative, particularly of the infant's desires. An example is an infant performing a twisting motion with its hands to request an adult to open a jar (from Goldin-Meadow & Mylander, 1984). The distinction is useful, nevertheless, because the two general types of gestures appear to have different origins and different developmental trajectories. As argued in chapter 3, many infant communicative gestures have their roots in nonhuman primate communication, and those termed primitive decline as language is acquired. In contrast, symbolic gestures do not appear to have a nonhuman origin unless apes are specifically trained. Even in human infants, they are exceedingly rare in spontaneous behavior compared to the highly frequent communicative gestures. As symbolic play evolves over the preschool years, symbolic gestures used in play increase in frequency. Thus, in this chapter, I review research on symbolic gestures and symbolic play both during infancy and beyond. The focus is on research relating such symbolic behavior to language acquisition.

Theoretical Background

The two major influences on research in this area have been the theories of Werner and Kaplan (1963) and of Piaget (1945/1962). The principal contribution of Werner and Kaplan (1963, p. 84) has been the notion of distancing, or "the increasing differentiation between gestural-motor depiction and the contents depicted" as the infant develops. Distancing can involve decontextualization when a gestural movement is used outside of its typical context, thus becoming somewhat autonomous. When the symbolic gesture becomes differentiated from its content, the gesture becomes "a *representational vehicle,* one of a medium of bodily movements which can be freely used to represent objects even in their absence" (p. 92). An example from Werner & Kaplan (1963) is a child making shoveling movements while looking for a spoon to dig in the sand. This example is symbolic of the object searched for but not yet fully decontextualized.

Distancing and decontextualization form the core of the experimental work on symbolic gestures conducted by Bates and her colleagues (e.g., Bates, Bretherton, Snyder, Shore, & Volterra, 1980). In the situations that they presented to children to elicit symbolic gestures, the form of the experimental object was varied such that its properties were increasingly distant from the real object. For example, the child was asked to eat from a real spoon, a tiny spoon, a schematic spoon, and a wooden cylinder. The culmination of distancing can be said to occur with "empty" gestures, gestures performed with no objects, which tend to emerge during preschool symbolic play. An example from our research is a child outlining the shape of an imaginary stove while calling it a stove (Kushnir & Blake, 1996). It is perhaps this more advanced type of symbolic gesture that Goldin-Meadow and Mylander's (1984) characterizing gestures are intended to describe.

The contribution of Piaget (1945/1962) has been to provide criteria for the emergence of the "true" symbol and to trace its origins in developmental precursors. For Piaget, as for Werner and Kaplan, the true symbol must be distant from its referent and not share many of its properties. However, for Werner and Kaplan (1963, p. 92), "bodily gestures rarely, if ever, attain a level of full autonomy." For Piaget, symbols are *motivated* signifiers, not arbitrary like words. As such, symbols may have some resemblance to that which they signify, but this resemblance can be as vague as a shell representing a cat. Such extreme distancing requires other cues to recognize the symbolic relationship, such as movements or sounds, as in the gesture drawing the outline of the stove described above.

For Piaget, the beginnings of full-blown symbolic play could be seen in the projection of familiar schemes onto new objects. Stuffed animals and dolls are often made to perform these familiar actions. For example, his daughter, Jacqueline, made her duck cry and her bear bite her mother's cheek. Jacqueline also exercised schemes without the usual objects – for example, washing her own hands without soap and feeding her doll by digging a spoon into an empty bowl. Finally, she substituted neutral objects for real objects. For example, she pretended to eat a piece of paper while saying "very nice," and she put a doll to bed, covering it with a postcard that she called a baby blanket. The paper and postcard are "true" ludic symbols in that they bear little resemblance to the real objects that they represent.

Symbolic play was for Piaget and for Werner and Kaplan a manifestation of the symbolic function that lays the foundation for language during the latter half of the second year. Unlike Werner and Kaplan, however, Piaget saw symbolic play as one of several developments that signal the advent of new representational abilities. In chapters 5 and 6, I discuss other developments, foresight in problem solving (means–ends), maintenance of an object concept across invisible displacements, and delayed imitation. Piaget's view of representation is currently the subject of a controversy that is addressed in chapter 6. For now, it can be said that this controversy revolves less around the evolution of the symbolic play than around the other developments included in the symbolic function.

Those who view the development of representation as emerging early in infancy still believe that the emergence of pretense signals new representational abilities, which must then be called metarepresentational. Metarepresentation in pretense is seen as "the beginnings of a capacity to understand cognition itself" (Leslie, 1987, p. 416). For Piaget, the child becomes conscious of pretense in stage 6 of the sensorimotor period, when the ludic symbol is mentally interiorized (Piaget, 1945/1962, p. 100), but consciousness here means inner mental life – that is, representation, and not an ability to *understand* the mind – that is, metarepresentation. There is recent evidence that children in fact do not understand pretense in the way that Leslie claimed they do. Children younger than 5 years were found to interpret pretense as action and not as a representational mental state (Lillard, 1993). For example, they say that a doll that is hopping is pretending to be a rabbit even when they are told that the doll does not know about rabbits.

According to Leslie, in pretend play, the primary representation (namely, perception) is decoupled from its normal action relations and reconstructed in a metarepresentational context. Decoupling appears to be quite similar to Werner and Kaplan's notion of distancing and to Piaget's term *distorting assimilation*. Distorting assimilation is the dissociation of a scheme from immediate accommodation to objective reality. However, keeping both representations (veridical and distorted) in mind simultaneously did not require two levels of representation for Werner and Kaplan and for Piaget, though it did for Leslie. The solution of Harris and Kavanaugh (1993) to the double representation problem was to propose that children attach a flag to the mental representation of the current pretend episode: "The child allows the flagging process to operate only within the context of a particular make-believe episode" (p. 63). Once the episode is completed, the associated flags are no longer effective, although they can be stored for future use. This proposal seems eminently reasonable to me and somewhat reminiscent of the signals that nonhuman primates use to indicate that they are playing.

Symbolic Gestures in Nonhuman Primates

The bulk of the evidence for symbolic gestures in nonhuman primates comes from the sign language projects with captive apes. It is clear that apes can learn a very large number of signs in American Sign Language (ASL) and that they can put them together in simple combinations

(Gardner & Gardner, 1969; Miles, 1990). They can also learn to associate spoken words with lexical symbols and to combine these "lexigrams" (Savage-Rumbaugh, 1990).

Although lack of spontaneity is not characteristic of all the apes trained in ASL (clear exceptions appear to be the female chimpanzee Washoe and the male orangutan Chantek), apes can require prompting and food reinforcement to elicit signs (Terrace, 1979). This may be a result of the training method. Savage-Rumbaugh (1979) made it clear that in their original studies, "naming as a skill divorced from consuming had to be acquired" (p. 9). Autistic children trained in sign language can also show a certain lack of spontaneity in their signing. Oxman and Blake (1980) found that most of the signs of 10 autistic children, after a minimum of 6 months of training, were produced in response to direct questions and prompts from adults.

Because this chapter focuses on symbolic gestures and symbolic play as potential precursors and facilitators of language, the ape language studies are not reviewed here. The signs taught to apes are not comparable to a symbolic foundation for language because they are already a language. Some primatologists would argue that abilities revealed in trained captive apes must be part of the potential repertoire of wild apes (see Cheney & Seyfarth, 1990). Nevertheless, the contrast between the signing of trained apes and the virtual absence of spontaneous symbolic gestures and symbolic play in wild apes is quite striking. Some spontaneous examples of symbolic behavior from "enculturated" apes can be found, however. Miles, Mitchell, and Harper (1996) reported that Chantek imitated "cooking" his cereal by putting it in a pot that he then placed on top of a stove. He also held his thumb and index finger together at his lips and blew through them to represent a balloon. Russon (1996) described a rehabilitant orangutan moving sticks across her hair with a cutting motion to represent scissors. Kanzi pretended to eat imaginary food and fed it to his caretakers (Savage-Rumbaugh et al., 1998). Washoe bathed a doll in a tub, soaping it and then drying it with a towel (Gardner & Gardner, 1969).

Sometimes the same terms used for human symbolic behavior are applied to apes in a different way, which can be misleading. For example, Tanner and Byrne (1996, p.164) defined "iconic" gestures as gestures whose "motion path in space or on another animal's body follows a path of movement or form of an action which is inferred to be desired of another animal by a gesturing animal." Such gestures in a captive lowland gorilla included pulling a hand or pushing it away, tapping as an invitation to a game, head nod, armswing under the genital area, armshake, chestbeat, and knock. Some of these sound familiar, as they form part of our communicative gestural repertoire discussed in chapter 3. The gestural motions are said to be abbreviated, but they are not at all distanced or decontextualized from the action desired of another. Early presymbolic gestures in human infants may also not be decontextualized but rather triggered by an object, what Piaget called recognitory assimilation. An example from our observations given in Table 4–1 from an infant (AD) aged 12:09 is shaking the body to request music. This gesture has presumably evolved from shaking the body while music was being played. It would not be considered fully symbolic until distant in time from music being played or in space from the machine that plays music. A not dissimilar gesture, arm shaking in the gorilla observed by Tanner and Byrne (1996), is said to "represent the gesturer's readiness for motor activation" or to be "a reflection of another's visible activation" (p. 168). This gesture, then, was not at all distanced from at least one of the animals' internal states.

An example of a fully symbolic gesture comes from an older infant (KA), aged 17:12, who was playing at hammering pegs in a board with her mother (Table 4–2). Her mother teasingly held the hammer behind her back and asked her infant where it was. The infant then put her hands behind her own back to represent the hammer behind her mother's back. Tanner and Byrne (1996) might have seen this gesture as comparable to their knock gesture, which appeared to indicate a

Table 4–1. Presymbolic and Symbolic Gestures in Younger Group of English-Canadian Infants

Gesture	Age (Months:Days)
Boys	
AD	
1. Shakes body to request mother to play music.	12:09
2. Makes car noises as pushes toy car.	12:09
3. Makes horse walk at mother's request. Later makes bunny hop.	12:09
4. Pretends to go to sleep by putting head on floor, laughing. Repeats several times.	13:14
	14:18

5. Smacks lips as mother feeds doll, imitating mother.	13:14
6. Moves jaw up and down when mother says, "What does dog do?"	13:14
7. Pretends to feed father with empty hand.	13:29
8. Lifts arm in response to "How big are you?"	13:29
9. Feeds bear with empty spoon in response to father's suggestions that bear is hungry and thirsty. Also feeds father. (Sometimes puts spoon in empty bowl first.)	13:29
	14:18

CA

1. Feeds mother with empty lid.	12:25
2. Claps when mother says, "Pat-a-cake."	13:08
3. Feeds doll after strong modeling.	14:07

Girls

JE

1. Puts telephone to ear and says hi. Repeats. (Mother put it to her ear the first time.)	14:08
2. Rocks doll after mother says, "Rock-a-bye" and as mother sings.	14:08
3. Shakes head in response to father's "The horse goes neigh."	14:08

LA

1. Kisses doll, monkey; hugs and rocks doll after suggestion or modeling.	11:24
	12:08, 13:13
2. Makes blowing sound for matchbox.	11:24
3. Feeds monkey after mother suggests that he is hungry. Later without suggestion.	12:08
	12:29
4. Brushes monkey's hair, doll's hair, with and without suggestion.	12:19
	13:13, 14:02
5. Makes truck sound while pushing truck after modeling by mother. Makes *m-m-m* sounds for vacuum cleaner.	13:13
6. Puts eyeglasses on self, then on monkey.	14:02

AL

1. Puts telephone to ear and babbles. Later says hi.	11:27
	13:19, 14:05
2. Puts doll's hat briefly on her own head, then on mother's head.	12:11
3. Hugs doll.	14:05

Table 4–2. Presymbolic and Symbolic Gestures in Older Group of English-Canadian Infants

Gesture	Age (Months:Days)
Boys	
NI (first observed at 13 months)	
1. Rubs hair with hand in response to mother's question about where brush is. Then rubs mother's hair.	16:19
	17:05
2. Stirs raw potatoes in bowl and offers some to mother to eat. Repeats with peanuts in shells.	17:05
	17:17
3. Slings bag over back and pretends he is going on a trip.	18:00
4. Pretends to shave with covered razor.	18:00
5. Puts a colander on his own head, on mother's head, and on wooden giraffe's head, pretending that it is a hat.	19:00
6. Puts arms out, making engine noises, pretending that he is an airplane.	19:00
NK (first observed at 18 months)	
1. Makes engine noises sitting on top of the videorecorder, riding on a toy, rocking in a chair, and at a picture of a car.	18:21
	19:18
	20:03, 21:26
2. Pokes his finger in a hole in mother's dress, then in a hole in a book cover, then curls his finger to represent a hole.	19:04
3. Makes airplane noises while waving a plug.	19:04
4. Watches tape turn and shakes head from side to side.	20:17
5. Runs around making engine noises, going beep-beep, pretending that he is a car.	21:26
6. Pushes block of wood around, making engine sounds, pretending that it is a car.	21:26
Girls	
KA (first observed at 13 months)	
1. Puts hands behind her own back in response to mother's question about where hammer is. (It is behind mother's back.)	17:12
2. Makes throwing gesture as a request for mother to throw ball.	17:12

CAS (first observed at 15 months)
1. Makes engine sounds as she pushes a toy grasshopper
   around.   16:13

LI (first observed at 18 months)
1. Pretends to drink from an empty cup.   18:00
2. Picks up telephone receiver and says hi.   19:00
3. Pretends briefly to be asleep.   19:00
4. Puts doll to sleep.   20:12
5. Picks up tape case and says bye-bye.   20:26

location where one animal wanted another to go. However, the human infant was trying to represent an *object* that was not visible at the time; thus, the gesture was decontextualized. The knock gesture, in contrast, seems to be a deictic communicative gesture.

Primatologists also use the term *make-believe play* when describing the play-fighting of nonhuman primates (e.g., Liska, 1994). Liska did sound like Piaget when she stated that "a semblance sign shares some quality or property with the entity for which it stands" (p. 238). Her use of the term *ritual semblances* was also quite Piagetian because Piaget (1945/1962) described several ritual games that he viewed as transitional to symbolic play. For example, Jacqueline had a ritual of touching her hair and then hitting the water whenever she was in the bath. Liska viewed rough-and-tumble play in primates as exemplifying ritual semblances in that "playfighting is not real aggression, and its rough-and-tumble aspects are clearly ritualized" (p. 243). She also stressed that play-fighting is often preceded by specific signs that indicate that the fighting is make-believe, most commonly a play face. Play-face expressions also accompany some of the gestures described by Tanner and Byrne (1996). Although such expressions seem similar to the playful (ludic) attitude in symbolic play described by both Piaget and Werner and Kaplan, the symbol is not apparent. It is difficult to see play fighting as a symbolic enactment of real fighting. Rather, it seems more comparable to young children's rough-and-tumble play than to their symbolic play. In humans, interestingly, the latter emerges before the former.

Mitchell (1994) placed pretense in the larger frame of simulating abilities available to primates. "Internal simulation of the external world is a primate adaptation upon which the human mind is based"

(p. 189). Primates are good at simulating their own actions, outside the normal context, often in order to make others respond as they would in the normal context; this he called "deceptive self-pretense" (p. 208). For example, they can lead conspecifics *away* from choice food while deceiving them into thinking that they are being led *to* food. He also admitted, however, that nonhuman primate simulation may simply express an awareness that doing a particular action can influence another to perform a desired action. That nonhuman primates engage in deception and that pretense and deception are both forms of simulation is clear (but see Tomasello & Call, 1997, for a counter claim). However, in human infants, pretense is symbolic; this does not seem to be true of deception.

It is possible to adopt a more general definition of pretend play, such as "the projection of a supposed situation onto an actual one, in the spirit of fun rather than for survival" (Lillard, 1993, p. 349). This definition would probably include play fighting, but it is too general for examining the more specific connections between symbolic development and language acquisition in human ontogeny that now concern us.

Symbolic Gestures in Human Infants

In this section, single symbolic gestures, those which emerge first ontogenetically, are examined in their relation to language acquisition. Linked sequences of symbolic gestures in symbolic play is the topic of the next section.

In an interesting set of studies, Acredolo and Goodwyn (1988, 1990) began by interviewing 38 mothers of infants aged 16 to 18 months, the age of onset of Piaget's symbolic function. Mothers were asked about their infants' use of symbolic gestures – their form, frequency, age of appearance, and manner of acquisition. Mothers reported (retrospectively) that symbolic gestures had emerged during the first half of the second year and had disappeared when a comparable word was acquired. Almost all parents (87%) reported that their infant had had at least one symbolic gesture, with a mean of about four. Thus, it is clear that the frequency of these gestures is low. The majority were either direct imitations (blowing to represent *hot*) or had arisen out of interactive routines, such as being bounced on a parent's knee (bouncing to represent a horse). In a second study, 16 mothers kept weekly diary records of their infants' symbolic gestures and new words between 11 and 20 months. They reported that the majority of symbolic gestures had appeared before their child acquired 25 words, so Acredolo and Goodwyn (1988) have argued that such gestures emerge simultaneously with early language. In both studies, the number of symbolic gestures representing an object was correlated with vocabulary size.

Goodwyn and Acredolo (1993) trained the mothers of 22 infants (aged 11 months or younger) to use with their infants a set of eight target symbolic gestures paired with corresponding words – for example, sniffing for *flower*. Toys, such as plastic flowers, were provided to facilitate daily use of the gestures. Mothers were encouraged to use other symbolic gestures as well. They reported that their children began to use symbolic gestures spontaneously earlier than referential words (11.9 months vs. 12.6 months). In another study (Acredolo & Goodwyn, 1992), infants were assigned to either a sign-plus-label training group or a label-alone training group. At 13 to 15 months, the sign group surpassed the label-alone group in that they had acquired 1 to 1.5 additional gestures per month as compared to words in the second group. It might be argued that some of the trained gestures were closer to recognitory assimilation (i.e., sniffing whenever the child saw a flower) than to a full-fledged symbolic gesture. However, at least two of these gestures ("all gone" and "more") could not have been triggered by objects and furthermore were also used as words in the label training group. The same group differences were found with these two symbols alone, with the gesture-plus-label group outperforming the label group. A slight advantage for gesture was also found by Volterra and Caselli (1985) in comparing two pairs of hearing and deaf children in their acquisition of words versus signs.

Acredolo and Goodwyn (1992) pointed out that the gestural advantage found in their study occurred despite potential confusion in the sign-plus-label group. It was emphasized in chapter 3 that coordination of a gesture with a vocalization seems to be quite automatic and thus not more demanding for the infant than producing either alone. However, in the case of a symbolic gesture plus a word, the same referent is involved, and the two signifiers may not be functioning in a complementary fashion.

Bates et al. (1989) varied the type of label accompanying a modeled symbolic gesture, so that it was sometimes redundant and sometimes not. For each child, aged 13 to 15 months, three target gestures were performed with a block – for example, tilting the block to the lips to represent a cup. Three of these gestures were accompanied by the correct label (*cup*), three such gestures were accompanied by an incorrect label (*plane*) appropriate for a different modeled gesture, and three were accompanied by neutral language (*this*). The effect of incorrect labels was related to the infants' level of comprehension, as reported by parents. Those at a higher level followed the label rather than the gesture in their imitation behavior. Children with higher productive vocabularies imitated more gestures under all labeling conditions. Parental report of infant gestures and direct observations of gestures in free play also were part of the study, but the gestures said to be symbolic in this data set also included presymbolic recognitory gestures. Although Bates, Shore, Bretherton, & McNew (1983) view recognitory gestures as enactive naming, they are clearly not yet decontextualized. This point was in fact underlined by Bates et al. (1980), who found quite different imitation results with an appropriate or featured object versus an inappropriate or unfeatured (decontextualized) object. Gestural imitations by 13-month-olds under these different conditions were not correlated, and imitations with a decontextualized object were more highly correlated with language measures (as reported by parents). Thus, Bates and Snyder (1987) concluded in their review that object substitutions – that is, using a dissimilar object to represent another object – under these experimental conditions is the best predictor of language at 13 months, even though they note that such substitutions are rarely observed naturalistically until the middle of the second year. Imitation of modeled symbolic gestures with a neutral object (object substitution) by late talkers, children between 18 and 32 months of age with low productive vocabularies, was found to be very similar to their younger language-matched counterparts and much lower than their same-age peers (Thal & Bates, 1988). These findings all provide support for a relationship between elicited symbolic gestures and lexical acquisition.

Direct observations of symbolic gestures under naturalistic conditions reveal that they originate within established routines, as reported by Acredolo and Goodwyn's (1988) parents, and become progressively detached from these routines (Caselli, 1990; Zinober & Martlew, 1985). In further support of the simultaneous emergence of symbolic gestures and language, Caselli (1990) found that her son, Luca, began to produce words at the same time as his gestures began to be decontextualized. For 12 children observed at 16 and 20 months, there was a decrease over this period in recognitory gestures (drinking from a toy cup) and an increase in empty-handed gestures replicating the form or movement of the referent (flapping the hands to represent a bird), or truly symbolic gestures (Iverson et al., 1994).

From their observations of deaf children of hearing parents, 1 to 4 years of age, who were not exposed to conventional sign language, Goldin-Meadow and her colleagues (Goldin-Meadow & Morford, 1985; Goldin-Meadow & Mylander, 1984) reported that these children were particularly adept at inventing gestures to refer to objects and actions. Two of their examples are (1) holding a fist to the mouth while chewing to represent eating and (2) forming a circle with index finger and thumb to represent a round object. Three comparison hearing children observed from the age of 10 to 17 months until 22 to 30 months produced many fewer symbolic gestures, one child producing none, one child producing one gesture to represent the long trunk of an elephant, and the third producing several, such as moving her fist up and down to represent brushing teeth (Goldin-Meadow & Morford, 1985). In the absence of language, then, children will fully exploit the gestural system to express themselves, often going beyond the symbolic gestures of children who are acquiring language normally.

Our Observations of Symbolic Gestures

We observed symbolic gestures in our longitudinal studies of five English-Canadian infants followed from late in the first year until 14 months, four Parisian-French infants followed over the same age period, and five English-Canadian infants followed during the second year. In Table 4–1 are all the gestures of the younger English-Canadian group that could be considered as presymbolic or symbolic, with the ages of the infants at the time of observation. It is clear that there are few truly symbolic gestures in this group. The exceptions are AD pretending to feed his father with an empty hand at 14 months and LA making a blowing sound to represent a matchbox at 12 months. The parents of these two children engaged in the most symbolic play with them. Other gestures appear to be presymbolic gestures of four types: (1) simple recognitory gestures (putting a telephone to the ear and saying hi), (2) those arising out of routines (shaking the body to request music) but not yet decontextualized, (3) sound effects accompanying vehicle movement (*m-m-m* sound for a vacuum cleaner), and (4) use of one's own body to pretend (putting the head on floor laughing, similar to Piaget's well-known example). Early symbolic gestures seen in Table

4–1 involve the animation of dolls or stuffed animals to use as objects of affection or other actions (feeding, brushing, hopping) (level 3 on McCune's 1995 scale; see Table 4–3).

Presymbolic and symbolic gestures for the older group of English-Canadian infants are given in Table 4–2, with ages at the time of observation as well as at the first home observational session. Many of the same types of gestures can be observed as in the younger group, but they have often evolved into a longer scene. For example, with NI, the cooking scenes with raw potatoes and peanuts are not just brief feeding gestures but include searching for the ingredients to put in a bowl, stirring them around for a while, and then offering them to someone to eat. Pretending to go on a trip involved using a real bag but also moving to the door as if leaving. This elaboration is also found for LI with a videotape case. Even vehicle noises are more elaborated (NI's simultaneously putting his arms out to pretend he is an airplane), as well as being more generalized (NK's making these noises while rocking in a chair and while looking at a picture of a car). Most important, these infants showed clear spontaneous object substitution: NI using a colander as a hat and NK using the plug of a cord and a block of wood as a vehicle. KA used empty-handed gestures to represent an action request (to throw the ball) and the location of an object. The representational correspondence between KA placing her hands behind her own back and the position of the hammer behind her mother's back can also be seen in NK's gesture representing a hole in his mother's dress and in a book cover. These are all quite inventive gestures, occurring after 17 months, and clearly on a higher level than those observed in the younger group. Thus, these observations suggest that 17 months may be a minimum age for full-fledged spontaneous symbolic gestures.

The most advanced in lexical acquisition among the younger group was AD, who had about 50 words at 14 months. He exhibited several symbolic gestures, but so did LA, and her word acquisition was much slower. In the older group, KA was the most advanced in lexical acquisition, but she did not exhibit many symbolic gestures. Conversely, NI and NK were quite symbolic in their gestures but were slow in lexical acquisition. Thus, in these two groups of infants, there is no clear relation between symbolic gesturing and vocabulary development. In terms of timing of emergence, some of these infants had no words at the age when their first presymbolic or symbolic gesture was observed (CA, LA, NK, LI), but others had several words (AD, KA).

Some of the symbolic gestures of the four French infants have been reported previously (Blake & Dolgoy, 1993). For these infants, an attempt was made to elicit such gestures by providing specific toys (pots, feeding utensils, a doll, and a teddy bear) and by modeling feeding of the doll or bear. Two of the infants (both female) did perform this activity after modeling, at the ages of 12:17 (12 months 17 days) and 14:14, respectively. At 13:21, one of these infants (FL) also spontaneously hugged the bear and rocked the doll. This same infant at 10:15 shook her head in imitation of the movement of a windup toy and at 12 months shook her body as a request to reactivate this toy. At the same age, she also shook her body to ask her mother to sing, whereas at 13:07, she used a hand gesture extracted from a "marionette" song routine to request this specific song. One of the male infants (PI) at 12:23 fed his mother with an empty spoon upon her request but refused to feed the doll and bear, even as late as 14 months. At this age, he made a waving gesture with his arm when his mother suggested playing a game that involved pushing arms back and forth. The other male infant also did not perform symbolic feeding after modeling at 14 months.

In this French group, there was some support for the relationship of symbolic gestures to language, because FL was the most advanced in both. The other female infant used no words over the observation period. The two male infants used very few words.

In a study of elicited symbolic gestures, Blake and Quartaro (unpublished data, 1983) gave a symbolic play task to 14 day care children, speaking only English and ranging in age from 18 to 36 months (mean, 27.8). In this task, the children were presented with three sets of toys in succession. These were a cup and a pitcher, a doll and a bed with a blanket, and a doll and a bottle. First the real toys were presented, and then a neutral object or objects were substituted in each set: (1) a block for the cup, (2) a block for the doll and a paper towel for the blanket, and (3) a block for the bottle. With each set of toys, the experimenter first waited for the child to perform a symbolic action, such as pour from the empty pitcher into the empty cup. If nothing occurred, then the experimenter suggested an appropriate action. If again nothing occurred, then the experimenter modeled a symbolic action. The children received a score of 3 for spontaneous performance of an appropriate action, a score of 2 for performing it after a suggestion, and a score of 1 for performing it after modeling. For extended symbolic play and/or symbolic verbalization, the child received an additional .5, whereas for applying the action only to herself (the infant drinking from the toy bottle herself, instead of giving it to doll), .5 was deducted. Scores on this task were then correlated with the children's MLU obtained from two spontaneous speech samples. The correlations were moderate but not significant given the small sample size. For performance with real toys and MLU, the correlation was $r = .38$, $p > .05$, whereas for performance with neutral objects and MLU, it was $r = .40$, $p > .05$. As might be expected, the correlations with age were significant: for performance with real toys, $r = .53$, $p < .05$; for performance with neutral toys, $r = .59$, $p < .05$. In fact, the last correlation would have been higher except for a noticeable U-shaped relation with age in willingness to accept the neutral object. The youngest children (18 to 21 months) were quite compliant in following the experimenter's suggestions about the block and towel, and the 3-year-olds carried out elaborate play with the neutral objects. The 2-year-olds, however, often refused to incorporate the neutral objects into their activity and asked for the real objects. The order of presentation of the toy sets, with real toys always presented before neutral objects, might have contributed to this reluctance to accept substitutes. However, the observation does highlight an interesting developmental trend that is not unique to this study. Bretherton, O'Connell, Shore, and Bates (1984) also found an increase in verbal protest to object substitution between 20 and 28 months. They reason that such protest is "likely to be pronounced when an ability has just been mastered, but not when it has become firmly established" (p. 295). The willingness to accept neutral objects among 3-year-olds shows that the decontextualization process continues to develop over the preschool years, as does the complexity of symbolic play. These developments are described in the next section.

Symbolic Play

The distinction being made here between symbolic gestures and symbolic play is somewhat arbitrary because symbolic gestures, as noted above, can occur in a symbolic play context. Their relationship to language acquisition, which is my focus, is different, however. Single symbolic gestures, as we have seen, tend to emerge simultaneously with early words. These gestures then evolve into connected sequences of pretending with a theme topic, what is being defined here as symbolic play. Symbolic play develops over a long time period and both enhances language acquisition and benefits from it in a complex inter-active relationship (see also Bretherton & Bates, 1984). At the same time, as we shall see, it is possible to engage in quite complex symbolic play nonverbally.

McCune (1995) (see also McCune-Nicolich, 1977, 1981b) has pro-vided a framework for research on the evolution of symbolic play based on Piagetian notions but with clear definitions of different levels in symbolic development. This framework clearly distinguishes and also links presymbolic gestures, symbolic gestures, and symbolic play. Her levels are outlined in Table 4–3. At the first presymbolic level are

Table 4–3. McCune's (1995) Levels of Representational Play

Sensorimotor period

1. *Presymbolic play schemes:* The child recognizes the function of an object by use (e.g., touching a comb to hair, touching a cup to lips, rubbing a sponge on the floor, or pushing a toy car).

2. *Self-pretend (autosymbolic schemes):* The child pretends at self-related activities, such as eating, drinking, sleeping, or grooming, while showing by elaborations such as sound effects, affect, and gesture an awareness of the pre-tend aspects of the behavior.

Symbolic stage

3. *Other-pretend (decentered symbolic play):* The child extends pretending beyond the self by (a) pretending at others' activities (e.g., cooking, reading) or (b) having others enact pretend schemes (e.g., feed doll, groom mother).

4. *Combinatorial pretend:* Several schemes are related in sequence: level 4.1 – a single scheme is enacted with several agents (e.g., feed mother, then doll); level 4.2 – different schemes are played in sequence (e.g., feed doll, groom doll); and level 4.3 – different schemes are played in order (e.g., place doll in car, roll car).

5. *Hierarchical pretend:* Level 5.1 – a single act exhibits hierarchical struc-ture in one of the following ways: (a) A plan is apparent before the enactment as the child verbalizes, searches for materials, or engages in other preparation; (b) one object is substituted for another with evidence that the child is aware of the multiple meanings expressed; (c) a doll is treated as if it could act inde-pendently (e.g., placing food in the hand rather than the mouth or moving its legs as it walks along). Level 5.2 – An act meeting the above criteria is part of a play sequence as described in level 4.

Source: From McCune, L. (1995). A normative study of representational play at the transition to language. *Developmental Psychology; 31*, Appendix A, p. 206. Copyright 1995 by the American Psychological Association. Reprinted with permis-sion of the author and of the American Psychological Association.

the recognitory gestures described above, which acknowledge the function of an object (puts telephone to ear). At the next level, routine activities are playfully applied to the self in the absence of some usual props (eats from an empty spoon). At the third level, symbolic gestures are applied to other people/toys (feeds bear with an empty spoon) or the child adopts the actions of other people (sweeps floor). This level is the actual beginning of the symbolic stages. It is illustrated in Figure 4–1. At the fourth level, combinations of symbolic schemes appear, what I have called symbolic play. This level is illustrated in Figure 4–2. Finally, at the fifth level, planning is manifested in an announced intention or search for a particular object, an object is substituted for another, or a doll or animal is treated as an agent. These actions might be called metarepresentational by Leslie (1987) because they reveal an awareness on the part of the child that an object has two existences, its "real" function and its pretend one. For McCune, they are called hierarchical because the actions are controlled by internal mental processes, or representational intention.

Bates (1979) proposed a reversal of levels 4 and 5, with object substitution preceding combinatorial symbolic play. This reversed order is consistent with our view that single symbolic gestures precede more elaborate symbolic play. However, the order probably depends on whether the play is elicited or spontaneous, object substitution being much less frequent in naturalistic observation and thus appearing often

Figure 4–1: A 17-month-old boy offering his mother some food on an empty dish (level 3 on McCune scale).

Figure 4–2: A 29-month-old girl putting her new doll to sleep (level 4 on McCune scale).

later than combinatorial symbolic play. Planned or announced object substitution clearly must be at a higher level than simple combinations.

In a large observational cross-sectional study of 40 infants between the ages of 7.5 and 21 months, Belsky and Most (1981) adopted Bates's (1979) order but added two higher steps: object substitution as part of a sequence and double object substitution. The results were found to satisfy the requirements of a Guttman scale, but only 3 infants showed double object substitution. Despite the scalability findings, the order of sequenced play versus object substitution is still unclear, because one 15-month-old showed the second without the first, and the remainder of the infants demonstrated both or neither. Also, scores for sequences with subsitution were added to sequenced play, so the two levels were confounded.

Interesting relationships between symbolic play and language milestones have been revealed using the McCune scale. For five female infants observed longitudinally by McCune-Nicolich and Bruskin (1982), level 4 combinatorial play occurred either at the session before or during the same session as the first word combinations (between the ages of 18 and 23 months). Ogura (1991) also found a cooccurrence between level 4 combinatorial play and word combinations, but the latter were nonproductive. A relationship between combinatorial play and multiword usage was also confirmed in an elicited symbolic play task (Shore, 1986), but particularly for combinatorial play with counterconventional objects.

Productive word combinations have been linked with level 5 planned play. In McCune-Nicolich and Bruskin (1982), level 5 play signaled positional patterns in word combinations (for example, *it's* plus *X*) based on Braine (1976), as well as a dramatic increase in different types of word combinations. Productivity of word combinations and an increase in positional patterns also followed the emergence of level 5 play for Ogura's (1991) four children.

McCune (1995) provided additional longitudinal and cross-sectional findings in support of relations between symbolic play and language developments. The onset of lexical development (a minimum of five spontaneous observed words) was associated with play at least at level 2 in the cross-sectional sample of children who were not yet combining words (72 children). Nine children were followed longitudinally, but two of them passed all play levels before showing any language milestones. For the remaining 7 children, lexical onset occurred between 0 and 5 months after the onset of level 2 or level 3 play. In contrast, other researchers have found a relationship between level 1 play and naming (Bates et al., 1983; Ogura, 1991). This difference in results is likely due to a criterion difference for lexical onset, because for McCune (1995) there had to be five words directly observed in multiple occurrences and not just reported by a parent/caretaker. In support of McCune (1995), Smolak and Levine's (1984) cross-sectional study determined that level 3 play was the minimum level achieved by children showing *representational* language – that is, words referring to absent objects or past events. This type of word use is more advanced than simple lexical onset and more likely to coincide with multiple occurrences of a word, McCune's criterion.

McCune (1995) replicated the original findings of McCune-Nicolich and Bruskin (1982) that level 4 play was associated with the onset of word combinations in 41 children of the cross-sectional sample, those who had achieved lexical onset but were not yet using predominantly multiword utterances. The children followed longitudinally first produced multiword combinations between 0 and 6 months after demonstrating independent level 4 play. Finally, level 5 play was associated with a predominance of multiword utterances in those 48 children of the cross-sectional sample who used more than five single words. The children followed longitudinally showed spurts in MLU (in words) subsequent to the onset of level 5 play. Although these findings are said to support a view that specific transitions in play are basic to language milestones requiring the same underlying mental representation, McCune points to other variables that must also be considered. For example, articulatory control may act as a "rate-limiting factor . . . that leads to a greater lag between representational play and language in some children" (McCune, 1995, p. 204). Her 2 children who exhibited all the play levels before any language milestone exemplify this lag. (See below for more discussion of symbolic play in language-delayed children.)

The relation between play and language has been explored further in a series of recent studies conducted by Tamis-LeMonda and Bornstein and their associates. These researchers often use the play scale of Belsky and Most (1981), which includes manipulative, functional, and relational play, as well as presymbolic and symbolic play. Thus, unlike the previous studies reviewed, specific levels of symbolic play are not related to language milestones. The target age groups have been typically 13-month-olds and/or 20-month-olds. Vibbert and Bornstein (1989) found that the highest play level was strongly related in 13-month-olds to a noun comprehension index based on the Reynell Developmental Language Scales (Reynell, 1981) and on a maternal interview modeled after the one used by Bates, Bretherton, and Snyder (1988). Mean play level was related to *flexible* language comprehension (across contexts), based on maternal interview, again in 13-month-olds (Tamis-LeMonda & Bornstein, 1990). In this same sample of children, a play index based on symbolic play only was related to flexible receptive vocabulary at 13 months and to semantic diversity at 20 months. Semantic diversity is a measure of the number of different semantic categories expressed. This symbolic play index was not related to productive vocabulary size at either age or to MLU based on the five longest utterances at 20 months

(Tamis-LeMonda & Bornstein, 1994). In another sample of 13-month-olds, a greater number of different symbolic actions (scheme diversity) was associated with a larger receptive vocabulary between 10 and 12 months and a larger productive vocabulary between 11 and 14 months, based on monthly maternal reports (Tamis-LeMonda, Kahana-Kalman, Damast, Baumwell, & Bornstein, 1992). By 17 months, symbolic play and vocabulary measures were no longer related in these children. A composite play index including nonsymbolic play was related at 13 months to a composite language index across both comprehension and production, based on the Reynell scores and maternal interview; at 20 months, the two indices were not related (Bornstein, Vibbert, Tal, & O'Donnell, 1992). Similarly, at 20 months, the same composite language index was not related to child-initiated symbolic play, but children with greater language ability engaged in more symbolic play that was mother-initiated (Bornstein, Haynes, O'Reilly, & Painter, 1996). These tended to be girls, since girls had higher language scores than boys, and mothers of girls engaged in more symbolic play than did mothers of boys. However, mothers' play did not influence children's solitary symbolic play.

Although this series of studies cannot clarify the relationship between developmental changes in particular levels of symbolic play and language because of the global nature of the play variables used, the quantitative measures can be considered a complement to the qualitative measures reviewed above. The findings obtained with these measure are interesting because they reveal stronger associations with language comprehension than with language production. This contrasts with the focus on production in the studies emphasizing qualitative level of symbolic play.

The research of the Tamis-LeMonda and Bornstein group is also directed at revealing cultural influences on children's symbolic play. For example, Tamis-LeMonda, Bornstein, Cyphers, Toda, and Ogino (1992) found that Japanese mothers of 13-month-olds demonstrated and solicited more other-directed symbolic play than did American mothers, who tended to focus more on nonsymbolic (functional) play. Japanese infants used more self- and other-directed symbolic play than did American infants. However, only in the American infants, and not in the Japanese, was the frequency of symbolic play related to flexible receptive vocabulary. Such findings on cultural variation in the relationship between symbolic play and language set important limits on our view of the importance of symbolic play in language acquisition.

After infancy, many children reach ceiling on the McCune scale, so that other measures must be used to tap the more sophisticated symbolic play abilities of children older than 24 months. Bretherton et al. (1984; see also Bretherton & Bates, 1984; and Shore, O'Connell, & Bates, 1984) developed a symbolic play task involving three scenarios: having breakfast, giving dolly a bath, and making a mother bear put a baby bear to bed. After a brief period of spontaneous play with a set of objects, a scenario for that set was modeled three times, once with only realistic objects, once with a neutral object (block) substituted for one real object, and once with a counterconventional object substituted for one of the real objects (e.g., a comb for a spoon). Several quantitative measures were applied to the observations: number of symbolic schemes (actions), number of *different* symbolic schemes (scheme diversity), average sequence length (i.e., mean number of connected schemes), and longest sequence length. Scheme diversity, sequence length, and longest sequence were found to increase significantly between the ages of 20 and 28 months in children followed longitudinally. Play at 20 months had the same number of schemes but was more repetitive than play at 28 months. Scheme frequency, scheme diversity, and sequence length all increased after modeling with the realistic toys but decreased with the substitute objects. At 20 months, only three children treated the doll as an active recipient in the bath scenario (by talking to it), whereas at 28 months, the majority of children did so. More importantly, only one child at 20 months used a bear as an agent, whereas almost all of the children did so at 28 months. Thus, only at 28 months were the children "able to reproduce a script in which two toy figures engaged in reciprocal interaction" (Bretherton et al., 1984, p. 291). At 20 months, the *longest* sequence of different symbolic schemes (2.36) averaged across children was similar to their *longest* utterance in morphemes on average (2.55); and the *mean* sequence length (1.28) was similar to the *mean* length of utterance in morphemes, or MLU (1.13). Furthermore, MLU was predicted by the longest sequence of different schemes, but only with the neutral and counterconventional objects. By 28 months, the longest utterance in morphemes (6.83) exceeded the longest sequence in symbolic play (3.46), which was then more similar to the longest sequence in content words (3.13) (Shore et al., 1984).

Corrigan (1982) also found that there was a relationship between the complexity of symbolic play and the complexity of sentences produced by children between the ages of 19 and 28 months, but this time in imitation. Most children who imitated play behaviors requiring only a single symbolic substitution produced imitated sentences with only a single clause (a prototypical animate subject plus inanimate object sentence). Children who were able to imitate two substitutions in play were typically able to imitate two or three animate or inanimate components in language, but it was the 28-month-olds who tended to reproduce three components. Thus, again, the language measure at 28 months began to outstrip the symbolic play measure.

These findings of a close relationship between quantitative indices of play and language at 20 months but not at 28 months are similar to the relationship between memory span and MLU that I discuss in chapter 7, namely, that it holds only for children at the early stages of syntax. As children master syntax, attentive processing of each morphemic unit is no longer required – that is, the critical unit of language changes (Blake, Austin, Cannon, Lisus, & Vaughan, 1994).

Our Research on Symbolic Play

In a study reported in Chiasson (1987), we gave 2-year-olds a symbolic play task that was an elaborated adaptation of the bath and bedtime scenarios described above (Bretherton et al., 1984) but with a different task sequence and somewhat different toys. To enable observation of spontaneous symbolic play, we gave the child, for the first 5 minutes, a doll with a dress on and several neutral toys (blocks, paper towel, facial tissues, shoebox). This neutral set included one realistic toy (doll in dress) because Fein (1975) found that children were more likely to substitute neutral objects for real objects if there were some real toys available to provide contextual support. For the next 5 minutes, the child was given a full set of realistic toys: a doll with a dress, a bottle, a washcloth and a cloth towel, a pillow, a mattress, a blanket, and a bathtub. The observer then enacted a story with these realistic toys about the doll's being given a bath and put to bed, and she asked the child to tell her the story. Finally, the first set of toys with the neutral objects was presented again for 5 minutes. This sequence allowed us to observe spontaneous symbolic play with neutral objects before the child was aware that realistic objects for these neutral objects were available and to compare it with spontaneous play with realistic objects. We then observed elicited play after modeling with realistic objects and the effects of such modeling on subsequent play with neutral objects. The toy sets and task sequence are presented in Table 4–4.

Table 4–4. Task Sequence for Bath and Bedtime Scenario

1. The child is given a realistic doll in a dress with neutral toys for 5 minutes.
   Neutral toys: shoebox and lid, tissues, cylindrical block, paper towel, rectangular block
2. The child is given a doll with real toys for 5 minutes.
   Real toys: bathtub, washcloth, plastic bottle, towel, pillow, mattresss, blanket
3. The investigator says, "Now I am going to tell you a story about a dolly taking a bath. Listen. Then you tell me the story.
   'Time for dolly to take a bath. Let's take off her clothes. Now we put her in the bathtub. Now we are washing her. Let's pour some shampoo and wash her hair. Time to dry her off. Give her a good-night kiss. Put the dolly to bed [covers her]. Night-night, dolly [pats her back].'
   "Now you tell me the story about dolly taking a bath." The investigator gives the child the dressed doll. The child is given 5 minutes or until she/he finishes the story.
4. The child is given neutral toys and the doll again for 5 minutes.

This symbolic play task was given to 21 children, 11 girls and 10 boys, ranging in age from 19 to 30 months (mean, 26.4 months), who had not participated in our previous symbolic gesture task. The children all had mental ages, as assessed by the Merrill–Palmer scales (Stutsman, 1948), that were higher than their chronological ages. They all attended a university day care center, where the task was administered. Only English was spoken in their homes. Performance on the symbolic play task was videotaped and scored according to McCune-Nicolich's qualitative levels as well as the quantitative measures developed by Bretherton et al. (1984), Bretherton and Bates (1984), and Shore et al. (1984). These were number of schemes, number of different schemes (scheme diversity), number of sequences (related schemes), greatest number of different schemes in a sequence (longest sequence), number of symbolic verbalizations (including sound effects), and number of object substitutions (either of neutral objects, of counterconventional objects, or of a substance created out of nothing). Interrater reliabilities on all these measures were at .80 or above, except that for longest sequence, which was .73.

The quantitative measures were all higher with the realistic toys, as might be expected, with the obvious exception of number of object substitutions, and generally tended to be higher after modeling. They were collapsed across the task sequence for comparison with the other measures.

McCune's levels were highly correlated with all of the quantitative measures (r = .59 or higher; p < .01), though somewhat less so for longest sequence (r = .49; p < .05). The only exception was the correlation with symbolic verbalizations (r = .42; p > .05).

Spontaneous speech samples were also recorded from the children while they played freely with a different set of toys for 20 minutes. The number of utterances obtained from each child ranged from 79 to 255, with a mean of 143. The speech samples were scored for MLU and semantic complexity. The semantic complexity measure is described in Blake and Quartaro (1990) and is similar to the propositional measure outlined in Bretherton and Bates (1984) except that it is based on case grammar (Fillmore, 1968). It yields a measure of the average number of semantic categories that a child can combine in a sentence (see Table 7–1). The rules for determining MLU have also been described in Blake and Quartaro (1990) and reported in Blake et al. (1993). They are an extension of those used by Brown (1973) and were also used for the speech samples of the Italian-Canadian children reported in chapters 1 and 3. The MLU was positively but not significantly related to McCune's level of symbolic play (r = .33; p > .05), but the correlations between MLU and the quantitative measures of symbolic play were lower, ranging from r = .02 with number of sequences to r = .28 for both longest sequence and symbolic verbalizations. That the last two correlations were higher agrees with the findings of Bretherton and Bates (1984). The results for semantic complexity were quite similar: a moderate but nonsignificant correlation with qualitative level of symbolic play (r = .36; p > .05) as well as with longest sequence (r = .37; p > .05), but this time the correlation with object substitution was moderate (r = .26; p > .05) and the correlation with symbolic verbalizations was low. Interestingly, longest sequence was significantly correlated with IQ (r = .50; p < .05); IQ was not correlated with any other symbolic play or language measure. The findings of this study concerning the relationship of both qualitative and quantitative measures of symbolic play to language complexity were suggestive but not overwhelming. The small sample size may have precluded significant results.

In a published study, Kushnir and Blake (1996) gave preschool (3- to 5-year-old) language-impaired and matched language-normal children the same bath and bed scenario and task sequence outlined in Table 4–4, as well as a longer adaptation of another scenario from

Bretherton et al. (1984) about a big bear feeding a little bear lunch. Performance on this task by 14 specifically language-impaired (SLI) children was compared to their normal-language (NL) peers matched within 3 months of both chronological age and nonverbal mental age, as measured by the Arthur Adaptation of the Leiter International Performance Scale (Arthur, 1952). A spontaneous speech sample was also recorded from the children and scored for MLU and semantic complexity as in the previous study. The Reynell Developmental Language Scales (Reynell, 1981) were also given to all children, and SLI children were at least 1 standard deviation below the mean on the expressive scale. Their mean delay was 14.6 months, whereas NL children were above their chronological age on the expressive scale. The NL children did tend to outperform the SLI children on scheme diversity, on creating objects out of nothing, and on symbolic verbalizations, whereas the SLI children used more symbolic sounds. None of these group differences was significant, however. The only significant difference was a greater effect of modeling on the subsequent use of a toy as an agent among NL children (i.e., making the big bear feed the little bear). It is important to note that where possible, symbolic actions were coded nonverbally in this study. Nevertheless, across the groups, the proportion of different schemes in symbolic play was significantly related to MLU, Reynell expressive scores, and Reynell receptive score (r's = .40 to .42; $p < .05$), whereas average sequence length was correlated with Reynell receptive scores ($r = .43$; $p < .05$). Thus although these measures did not significantly differentiate the groups, they were related to language performance. Thal and Bates (1988) also found that nine "late talkers" between 18 and 32 months of age did not differ from their NL peers in a symbolic play task that involved modeling of similar scenarios. The specific measures on which the late talkers were similar to their age-matched peers were number of different schemes imitated in the correct order, longest sequence of different schemes, and scheme diversity.

The results of Kushnir and Blake (1996) and Thal and Bates (1988) differ from findings showing slower development of symbolic play among children who are atypical in their language acquisition. Skarakis-Doyle and Prutting (1982) found that three SLI children did not reach level 5 of McCune's play scale until 35 months, almost a year later than NL children. The SLI children were also deficient in number of schemes and scheme diversity. Terrell and Schwartz (1988) reported that SLI children between 3 and 4 years engaged in more nonsymbolic play and tended to show less object substitution than did their NL peers. Some researchers have compared SLI children with language-matched (LM) children rather than age-matched controls. This can be done only for older SLI children because the younger LM children must be at an appropriate age for symbolic play tasks. A comparison of 5- to 8-year-old SLI children with their LM controls, who were 2 years 9 months, showed that the SLI children were less advanced in symbolic play (Roth & Clark, 1987). A problem with some of these studies, however, is that the SLI children, although selected to be of normal nonverbal intelligence, may still have a lower nonverbal IQ than controls. Thus, it is important to match individually on mental age at least for comparison with NL peers.

Spencer (1996) compared ten 2-year-old deaf children of deaf parents, ten deaf children of hearing parents, and ten hearing children of hearing parents using McCune's scale. Deaf children spent more time in symbolic play than did hearing children. The most linguistically advanced children, who produced more than 200 words/signs and frequently combined them, exhibited more level 5 play. This latter group comprised five hearing children and two deaf children of deaf parents. Thus, deaf children of hearing parents were disadvantaged in both language and symbolic play.

Ungerer and Sigman (1984) defined symbolic play acts as object substitution, use of a doll as an agent, and creation of objects out of nothing. They tested both preterm infants and full-term infants at 13.5 and 22 months, close to the ages targeted by the Tamis-LeMonda and Bornstein group. Symbolic acts were first modeled to the children, and then the children were observed in free play with a set of toys. There were no differences between the two groups of infants. For both groups combined, the number of different symbolic play acts at 22 months was moderately but significantly correlated with measures of a language developmental quotient (DQ) and of expressive and receptive language at the same age. A somewhat higher predictive correlation was found between symbolic play at 13.5 months and language DQ at 22 months. Given the sophistication of the operational definition of symbolic play acts, it seems surprising that there were very many at 13.5 months. In contrast, Russell and Russnaik (1981) found that both the amount and the complexity of symbolic play at ages 12 to 14 months and 20 to 22 months were unrelated to MLU, longest utterance, or vocabulary diversity at the older age.

Conclusions

This review of both early and recent research relating symbolic gestures and symbolic play to language makes it abundantly clear how variable the findings are. The most consistent results appear to be those showing simultaneous emergence of single symbolic gestures and single words, of sequenced symbolic play and word combinations, and of planned play and varied word combinations. Measures of language comprehension have also been related to a composite index of play and to length of symbolic play sequence.

At the beginning of syntax, the complexity of play and productive language is similar, as is the complexity of imitated object substitution and sentence imitation. Subsequently, language begins to outstrip symbolic play in complexity.

Studies of atypical children show that symbolic play can be done nonverbally, though such measures as creating objects out of nothing are made clearer to the observer through verbalization. Thus, on these measures, SLI children may appear to be deficient. On measures such as longest symbolic play sequence, however, language-delayed children are often quite similar to their peers.

In conclusion, symbolic gestures can be considered a precursor to language onset in that they signal the readiness of the child to adopt referential words. The ability to combine symbolic actions is also a precursor to word combinations, but this relationship may be mediated by processing capacity, to be discussed in chapter 7. More sophisticated aspects of symbolic play interact with language abilities, both affecting and being affected by developing language. The original nonverbal nature of symbolic play is transformed into a more verbally expressive fantasy even before dramatic play with peers begins.

CHAPTER FIVE

Tool Use and Object Concept

Tool use has been associated with language development both in evolution and in infancy. In evolution, the necessity to communicate with others regarding the use and construction of tools is considered to be among the most important forces propelling selection for verbal communication. The historical importance of tool use specifically in the extractive foraging of encased foods, such as nuts and tubers in the ground, and in food sharing, particularly of meat, has been emphasized. "The shift to primary dependence on extractive foraging with tools, and the attendant food sharing that characterized hominid differentiation, favored canalization of language-learning abilities and resulted in a strong propensity to acquire protolanguage" (Parker & Gibson, 1979, p. 374). Furthermore, language and manual dexterity are thought to be controlled by the same neural structures in the left hemisphere, namely, Broca's area and connected neural circuits (See Figure 1–2) (Greenfield, 1991).

Tool use in human infants is seen as underlying children's understanding of their ability to control the environment, including the intentional use of language to influence people (Siegel, 1981). An important prelinguistic milestone is achieved when infants extend their understanding of object tool use to the use of human agents as instruments (Bates, 1979). This instrumental use of persons has also been found in apes (Köhler, 1927; Gomez, 1990) and is sometimes called social tool use (Bard, 1990). Social tool use, or the understanding of adult agency, is addressed in chapter 3, so I do not discuss it further in this chapter.

Arguments against the relevance of object tool use in the evolution of language include the fact that studies of current tool use and tool making among apprentices indicate that it is essentially a nonverbal process (Wynn, 1993). Marshack (1979, p. 395) argued that "tool making and tool use are not learned through language, and the skills of the hunt are learned by example and participation, not by linguistic description. . ." Understanding of these tasks is often idiosyncratic, whereas "language is shared in a much more thorough and specific way" (Wynn, 1993, p. 401). A response to these arguments might be that it is risky to generalize from modern-day tool-using practices to those of hominids. It seems unlikely, however, that hominids would be verbal in demonstrating these tasks and modern apprentices would learn them nonverbally.

A standard definition of tool use among animal researchers is that it is "the external deployment of an unattached environmental object to alter more efficiently the form, position, or condition of another object. . ." (Beck, 1980, p. 11, cited in McGrew, 1993). Developmental studies of tool use in human infants generally adopt a Piagetian approach (Piaget, 1952), which focuses on the type of means used to achieve an end. The goal-directedness invoked in the operational definitions used in both animal and developmental research makes tool use more specific than simply relating two objects. Object relations that involve problem solving, such as nesting cups, however, have some resemblance to means–ends behaviors. Furthermore, using an object as a tool appears predicated on having an underlying concept of what an object is and how it behaves in the environment.

In this chapter I first review evidence for tool use among apes in the wild and experimental evidence for both tool use and object concept among captive apes and some species of monkeys. Interestingly, as Piagetian theory and methodology have fallen in favor among many developmental psychologists (see chapter 6), they have risen in popularity among comparative developmental researchers. According to Parker (1990, p. 30), "the Piagetian framework is better at identifying species differences than are traditional learning tasks." These researchers have adopted traditional Piagetian methods for examining the development of tool use and of the object concept, such as the Uzgiris–Hunt (1975) scales (see Tables 5–1 and 5–2). In Tables 5–1 and 5–2 are presented only those items related to Piagetian stage 5 (items 6 through 10 in Table 5–1; items 8 and 9 in Table 5–2) and Piagetian stage 6 (items 11 and 12 in Table 5–1; items 10 and 14 in Table 5–2, with item 15 being transitional to the preoperational period). Stage 6 items are directed at foresight, planning, and mental imagery, all aspects of the mental representation that defines stage 6.

Table 5–1. Selected Advanced Items from the Uzgiris–Hunt (1975) Scale II: The Development of Means for Obtaining Desired Environmental Events

6. Use of the relationship of support

 Place an object on the center of a support (e.g., a pillow) beyond the infant's reach. Can demonstrate that the object will move when the support does.

 Pass: Infant pulls the support and obtains the object.

7. Understanding of the relationship of support

 Hold object above the support.

 Pass: The infant does not pull the support but points, reaches, or looks at the object.

8. Use of string horizontally

 Tie one end of string to an object and put other end close to infant's hand. Can demonstrate.

 Pass: Infant obtains object by pulling the string.

9. Use of string vertically

 Lower object tied onto string to the floor, extending other end of string to infant's hand. Can demonstrate.

 Pass: Infant obtains object by pulling the string.

10. Use of stick as means

 Place object out of reach and place a stick near the infant. Can demonstrate.

 Pass: Infant obtains object by means of the stick.

11. Foresight in the problem of the necklace and the container

 Present to the infant a long necklace and a tall, narrow container. Can place necklace in container out of sight of infant and show final arrangement to infant. Then go back to original presentation.

 Pass: Infant adopts a method that takes account of the unsteadiness of the container, such as rolling the necklace up first.

12. Foresight in the problem of the solid ring

 Spread rings in front of infant, including a solid ring. Demonstrate stacking one ring on a rod. Encourage infant to stack remaining rings.

 Pass: Infant sets aside the solid ring without attempting to stack it.

Source: From Uzgiris, I.C., & Hunt, J. McV. (1975) *Assessment in infancy: Ordinal scales of psychological development* Chicago: University of Illinois Press. Reprinted with permission of J. A. Hunt.

Primatologists have also related these developments to more general characteristics of Piagetian stages – that is, primary, secondary, and tertiary circular reactions. Although some of their definitions of circular reactions might be criticized, the overall research effort allows a direct comparison with findings on human infants. In the

Table 5–2. Selected Advanced Items from the Uzgiris–Hunt (1975) Scale I: The Development of Visual Pursuit and the Permanence of Objects

---

8. Finding an object after successive visible displacements

   Hide the object successively under each of the three screens by moving the hand holding the toy in a path from left to right or from right to left so that the object becomes hidden under one of the screens, then reappears in the space between the screens, and then again becomes hidden as the hand passes under another screen.

   Pass: Infant searches directly under the last screen under which the object disappeared.

9. Finding an object under three superimposed screens

   Cover the object with one screen, then with a second, and then with a third.

   Pass: Infant removes all screens and finds the object.

10. Finding an object following one invisible displacement with a single screen

    While the infant watches, put the object in a box and hide the box under the screen. Turn the box over, leaving the object hidden, and show the infant the empty box.

    Pass: Searches for object under the screen where the box disappeared.

14. Finding an object following a series of invisible displacements with three screens

    While the infant watches, place the object in the palm of one hand and hide it. Move the hand under the first, second, and third screens without opening the hand between screens. Leave object under last screen and show the infant your empty hand. Repeat always in same direction.

    Pass: The infant searches in the same order as followed by hand or searches directly under last screen to find object.

15. Finding an object by searching in reverse of the order of hiding

    After #14, repeat the same task but leave object under the first screen, continuing the movement to the second and third screens.

    Pass: The infant searches systematically backward from last to first screen.

Source: From Uzgiris, I.C., & Hunt, J.McV. (1975). *Assessment in infancy: Ordinal scales of psychological development.* Chicago: University of Illinois Press. Reprinted with permission of J. A. Hunt.

second part of this chapter, I review those studies which directly relate the performance of human infants on tool use and object permanence tasks to their communicative development. Finally, I briefly discuss the relationship between object constructions and language acquisition.

Tool Use in Wild Apes

It is well known that Goodall's observations of the chimpanzees at Gombe (Goodall, 1965, 1986) were the first to reveal that wild chimpanzees spontaneously use one kind of tool, such as a grass stem, to fish for termites in mounds and another kind of tool, such as a stout stick, to enlarge the opening of bees' nests to get honey. Her observations also revealed that chimpanzees often select tools when the mound or nest is out of sight and modify some tools before use. Clearly, then, there is planning in chimpanzee tool use and possibly also mental imagery. Tools also vary with the season. Dry season termiting calls for a different type of tool than does wet season termiting, when the termites are closer to the surface. When the Gombe chimpanzees were being provisioned, they would also fashion a stick to fit into the openings of boxes to obtain bananas. These chimpanzees also used leaves as tools to wipe themselves and as an absorbent sponge for collecting rainwater in tree hollows. Finally, according to Goodall, they threw objects in threat displays but rarely hit their targets. Significantly, Goodall has not seen changes in tool-using behaviors across the generations that she has observed at Gombe.

Tool use is found in all three geographical races of chimpanzees in eastern, central western, and far western Africa, but there is no universal pattern (McGrew, 1993). The distribution of types of tool use in chimpanzees across study sites in Africa is shown in Figure 5–1. Most tool use occurs in subsistence activities, especially those involving insects and nuts. Tool use in nut cracking is restricted to the chimpanzees of Liberia, the Ivory Coast, Guinea and Sierra Leone (McGrew, 1992), even though the same nuts are found in other forests (Boesch, 1993). Chimpanzees in the Tai forest of the Ivory Coast use hammers to crack five hard-shelled nuts but ignore the palm nut (McGrew, 1992). Chimpanzees at Gombe and Lope eat the outer pulp of the oil palm but discard the nut, whereas chimpanzees at Bossou (Guinea) use a tool to get at this nut (McGrew, 1992; Sugiyama, 1993). Chimpanzees in the Nimba Mountains, 10 kilometers from Bossou, have not yet been observed using stones as tools (Matsuzawa & Yamakoshi, 1996). Bossou chimpanzees also use twigs to obtain safari ants, but there is no evidence of ant dipping in Nimba even though safari ants exist there (Matsuzawa & Yamakoshi, 1996). Similarly, ant dipping for driver ants is found in Gombe chimpanzees and for wood-boring ants in Mahale K chimpanzees, but the reverse is not true

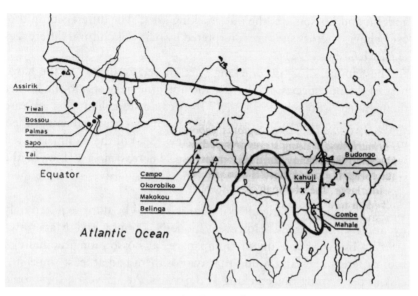

Figure 5–1: Distribution of study sites and main types of tool behavior: —, approximate boundary of *Pan troglodytes* distribution; △, termite tunnel probing using flexible tensile stalks; ▲, termite mound digging using hard sticks; ●, nut cracking using stone or wood hammer; X, none of the three main types of tool behavior. From Sugiyama, Y. (1993). Local variation of tools and tool use among wild chimpanzee populations. Figure 10.1. In A. Berthelet & J. Chavaillon (Eds.), *The use of tools by human and nonhuman primates: A Fyssen Foundation symposium.* Oxford: Clarendon Press. Reprinted with permission of Oxford University Press.

though both types of ants are found in both locations (Tomasello, 1990). Tai chimpanzees mostly use their hands to eat driver and safari ants, but females have been observed to use sticks (Boesch & Boesch, 1993). Tai chimpanzees also use their hands to eat five species of termites, none of which is the species for which Gombe chimpanzees fish with tools (Boesch & Boesch, 1993). Bossou chimpanzees use leaves to sponge water from holes in trees, like Gombe chimpanzees, but they eat termites by hand. They do use long wands to catch Dorylus ants in underground nests (Sugiyama, 1993). Chimpanzees at Campo (southwest Cameroon) use a hard, straight stick, rather than a flexible stalk as at Gombe, to fish for termites (Sugiyama, 1993). Sugiyama (1993, p. 183) concluded: "Gombe and Mahale are 'the termite tunnel probing area,' Campo and Okorobiko are 'the termite mound digging area,' and Tai and Bossou are 'the nut-cracking area.' The differences in tool use behavior across sites are interpreted by many as cultural differences (e.g., McGrew, 1992).

The hammers for nut cracking "are chosen according to the hardness of the nut species: the harder the nuts, the heavier and the harder the hammer" (Boesch, 1993, p. 173). Because stone hammers are rare in the forest, chimpanzees transport them or they may remember their locations (see chapter 7). At Tai, very few (8%) of the hammers, even wooden ones, are fashioned before use, whereas most (91%) of the stick tools are modified, usually by removing the leaves to make them smoother (Boesch & Boesch, 1993).

Nut cracking is a difficult skill that is said to be fully acquired only by adult chimpanzees. However, Inoue-Nakamura and Matsuzawa (1997) observed three infant chimpanzees at Bossou longitudinally at four different ages and found that two of them had at least some success in performing nut cracking at 3.5 years. At 1.5 years, they could easily put a nut on a stone. By comparison, termite fishing seems to be acquired by 3 years (McGrew, 1992) and ant dipping somewhat later, presumably because of the possibility of painful bites (Tomasello, 1990).

Mothers apparently attempt to foster acquisition of nut cracking in their offspring by leaving a tool and intact nuts on an anvil (Boesch, 1993). Two cases of active teaching have been observed: One mother repositioned a nut for her son and another very slowly rotated the position of a hammer for her daughter (Boesch, 1993). These are the only examples of pedagogy in the acquisition of tool use in the wild. Inoue-Nakamura and Matsuzawa (1997) reported that their chimpanzee infants increasingly watched adult conspecifics (not necessarily their own mothers) as they grew older, even after they had begun to crack nuts themselves. The adult chimpanzees that they watched did not show any active teaching to the infants, however, nor did they give the infants any feedback. They did provide them with free access to stones and nuts, and infants continued to steal kernels from their mothers even after they were successful at nut cracking. Gombe mothers also sometimes allowed their infants to take termites from their fishing tools (McGrew, 1992).

Extensive observations of wild bonobos (earlier known as pygmy chimpanzees) are fairly recent (e.g., Ingmanson, 1996). Their most illustrious use of tools involves rain hats. At Wamba, half of the adult bonobos used rain hats, and no individuals younger than 10 years did so successfully (Ingmanson, 1996). Notably, the use of rain hats was found to run in families. Offspring of mothers that used rain hats were all observed to use them, whereas offspring of mothers that did not use rain hats also did not. According to Ingmanson, however, no active teaching by mothers was ever observed. Although not strictly speaking tool use, branch dragging was also observed in bonobos to initiate group movement, to indicate direction, and to keep straggling group members together. These functions appear similar to the social functions of vocalizations for other apes reviewed in chapter 2. Bonobos at Wamba do not appear to use tools for food extraction. Although they dig in the ground for mushrooms, the ground is soft and they can extract them by hand.

Mountain gorillas in the wild also do not use tools in foraging, perhaps because of their great strength and largely herbivorous diet (Schaller, 1965). The fecal samples of lowland gorillas in Gabon reveal that they, like chimpanzees, eat termites (Tutin & Fernandez, 1983). They appear to eat them by hand, as there are no signs of tools.

Wild orangutans eat termites, bees, ants, and hard-shelled fruits, but they are able to open hard gourds and prickly durian fruits with their hands and teeth without tools (Lethmate, 1982; MacKinnon, 1974; Parker & Gibson, 1977). Galdikas (1982) reported that they open very hard nuts (*Mezzettia leptopoda*) with their molars while pressing their cheeks against a tree so that the nut will not pop out. Like chimpanzees, orangutans throw objects (branches) as part of an agonistic display toward humans or other animals (Galdikas, 1982; MacKinnon, 1974). Like bonobos, they also put branches or leaves over their heads and backs to make umbrellas (MacKinnon, 1974) (Figure 5–2). Otherwise, it is said that "wild orang-utans do not exhibit tool-using and tool-making behaviors that even remotely resemble the sophisticated technological skills found among wild chimpanzee populations" (Galdikas, 1982, p. 28). This statement may have to be revised in the light of recent evidence that orangutans in Sumatra at the Suaq Balimbing Research Station use tools to extract insects or honey from tree holes and seeds from hard-husked fruit (Fox, Sitompul, & van Schaik, 1999). All tools were made from branches that were modified by removing the bark and leaves and by chewing or splitting the tip. The tool was typically held in the teeth during use. Orangutans also engage in much manipulation of vegetative material, particularly for locomotion (Bard, 1993). Technically, this cannot be classified as tool use because such material is attached to the substrate (branches to

Figure 5–2: A rehabilitant juvenile orangutan at Sepilok in Sabah with a leaf hat. Photograph by Anne Russon.

trees, for example). In contrast to the observations of some great apes in certain natural habitats, all great apes have been found to use tools in captivity.

Tool Use in Captive and Ex-captive Apes and Monkeys

Ex-captive orangutans who are being rehabilitated for return to the wild exhibit much tool use, even though in Tanjung Puting (Borneo) they have never been observed using tools to exploit wild foods (Galdikas, 1982). In the camp, Galdikas reported that they had been observed to use sticks as rakes to pull out objects from fires, as ladders to climb up to high windows, as potential keys to open doors, and as tools to open fruit. They used coconut shells as containers for liquids and vegetation, and they sponged with cloths and plastic bags. They also dragged logs and vines to the river to form a bridge for crossing over the water. Figure 5–3 shows an example of a juvenile male orangutan at Wanariset inventing a tool to use in a game.

According to Lethmate's (1982) review of the tool-using skills of captive orangutans, orangutans are also able to (1) stack boxes in order to reach suspended food, (2) use a hammer to open tough-skinned

Figure 5–3: A juvenile male orangutan at Wanariset making a hoop from a garden hose, which he then would go through. Photograph by Anne Russon.

fruit, (3) use vegetable materials to wipe dirt from their body parts, (4) fashion tools (e.g., by stripping leaves), and (5) combine tools (e.g., by joining sticks to make a tool longer). They also exhibit insightful problem solving. One 3-year-old orangutan was presented with a long tool and a transparent plastic tube baited with sweets. After some failed attempts, he moved away with the tool, then looked back, suddenly approached the tube again, and inserted the tool correctly. Another orangutan, 5 years old, had learned to use a combined stick and tube to reach some food outside his cage; he was given three tools to put together to reach a more distant reward. He persisted instead with a double tool until he put the tube on his finger. He then ran back to the edge of the cage and used this combined tool (finger, tube, and stick) to obtain the reward. Because, in these situations, it is difficult to clearly distinguish the role of trial and error from insight, Lethmate put the first orangutan in an experimental situation. He was presented with several boxes, including a key box and a box containing food. A key for the food box could be obtained by pressing down on a trapdoor of the key box. All box contents were visible and were changed from trial to trial. The orangutan, trained previously to find the right tool to open a box, achieved a 78% success rate across 400 trials in this task. Response latency was very short (mean of 6.5 seconds), apparently indicating immediate solution.

Four nursery-reared orangutans observed longitudinally were able to get honey out of a narrow-mouthed jar with a stick at 3 to 4 years of age (Chevalier-Skolnikoff, 1983). Problem solving involving mental representation (Piagetian stage 6) was exhibited by only two adults that selected the correct tool on the first try in this honey-jar task, without trial and error. At a younger age (2 years), however, these orangutans did show planning with a different type of problem. They aligned the wheels of their cage before moving it in a desired direction. One orangutan was also able to use a string to obtain a bottle attached to the end of it before 2 years of age.

Mathieu and her colleagues (Mathieu, Bouchard, Granger, & Herscovitch, 1976; Mathieu, Daudelin, Dagenais, & Décarie, 1980) were apparently the first to administer formal Piagetian tasks to captive apes. Mathieu et al. (1980) gave a series of tasks to two house-reared chimpanzees, a female aged 1:10 and a male aged 2:6. The tasks involved (1) pulling a horizontal string to obtain a piece of food tied to the other end, (2) pulling a towel or cardboard with food placed on the other end, (3) using a rake to obtain food, and (4) looking for a rake that the experimenter had hidden 2 minutes earlier and then trying to obtain food with it. The first three tasks are said to be at the same level (stage 5, but see discussion of the rake task below) and are standard Piagetian tasks used with infants. These three tasks correspond to items 8, 6, and 10 in Table 5–1. The last task is unique and was intended to measure representation. The criterion for passing each task was two of three trials correct. The stage 5 tasks were passed by both chimpanzees and the last task – a representational one – was passed only by the older chimpanzee.

Two younger chimpanzees in their first year, a male and a female, were tested using the Uzgiris–Hunt Means–Ends Scale monthly from the age of 12 weeks (Hallock & Worobey, 1984). Unfortunately, details of the specific tasks passed are not given; but the male is said to have achieved stage 5 by 1 year of age, whereas the female did not. It is notable that the male was human reared whereas the female was mother reared until age 6 months and had no access to toys except during testing. Both animals were perceived as "slowing down" at age 12 months by comparison with human infants.

Chantek, a captive orangutan, passed all the relevant items (Tables 5–1 and 5–2) on the Uzgiris–Hunt (1975) scales by 4:7 years (Miles, 1990). He also showed evidence of stage 6 tool-use sequences involving up to 22 problem-solving steps.

Chevalier-Skolnikoff (1983) reported that gorillas passed formal tool-use tasks, such as raking in an out-of-reach object, at 3 to 4 years of age, similar to the age at which she reported that orangutans can get honey out of a jar with a stick and to Chantek's age of success in completing the Uzgiris–Hunt scales. Gorillas, however, did not show insightful problem solving until adulthood, similar to what she reported for orangutans. Chevalier-Skolnikoff (1983) also did not observe skilled tool use in captive chimpanzees until 4 years of age, later than the age found by both Mathieu et al. (1980) and Hallock and Worobey (1984) but close to the ages of the other apes and the age at which successful nut cracking and termite fishing is found in wild chimpanzees.

Antinucci (1989, 1990) and his collaborators observed a female lowland gorilla at the Rome zoo from birth until 15 months and then tested her periodically thereafter. At 19 months she was tested on the support problem (task 2 of Mathieu et al., 1980). The particular task used in this study (Spinozzi & Poti, 1989) was modeled after one originally used by Köhler (1927) with chimpanzees and involved presenting the gorilla with a piece of candy placed on the end of one of two strips of cloth. She always pulled the correct cloth, but when the candy was placed either beside the cloth or in front of it, she sometimes erroneously pulled the cloth nevertheless. The gorilla was also given a stick task in which the stick was placed perpendicular to the bars of the animal's cage and a reward was put out of reach, 5 centimeters to the right or left of the stick. At 24 months, she began to establish systematic

contact between the stick and the reward but had difficulty bringing
the reward within reach, largely because it was displaced with too
much force. When she was about 3 years of age, the gorilla invented
her own tool, throwing the edge of her blanket outside her cage over
the reward and pulling it in successfully. Köhler's (1927, p.33) chimpanzee also tried to use a blanket as a tool but was unsuccessful. That
the gorilla in this case suddenly went to look for her blanket appears
indicative of insightful planning – that is, stage 6 behavior. Cebus monkeys were also found to be successful on the support problem, and they
persevered to obtain the reward successfully on the stick task (Natale,
1989).

Another comparative study of tool use included chimpanzees, bonobos, an orangutan, and capuchin monkeys (Visalberghi, Fragaszy, &
Savage-Rumbaugh, 1995). Similar to Lethmate's (1982) task with
orangutans, the task in this comparative study involved a transparent
tube baited in the center with a food treat. In this case, however, the
subjects were presented with different types of tools: a straight stick; a
bundle of three sticks, which had to be unwrapped to obtain an individual stick; and an H-shaped stick, which had to be modified before
insertion. The six capuchin monkeys solved all the problems quickly
but made errors. The apes, except for the youngest (a 3-year-old
bonobo and a 3.5-year-old chimpanzee), easily solved the first two
problems with the straight stick and the bundle of sticks. With the H-
shaped stick, they made errors similar to those of the capuchins (inserting the stick without removing the transverse sticks). The errors
persisted for the monkeys but not for the apes, indicating to the
researchers that the apes acquired a fuller comprehension of the task
than did the capuchins.

Visalberghi and Limongelli (1996) directly compared children to
chimpanzees and capuchin monkeys on the transparent tube problem
with a straight stick. Children under 2 years, chimpanzees under 5
years, and most capuchin monkeys used a trial-and-error approach.
Children and chimpanzees older than these respective ages inserted the
stick into the tube on the first trial. Modeling improved the performance of 15- and 18-month-old children, but not 12-month-old children. Chimpanzees did not benefit from modeling until they were 3 to
4 years of age. A trap-tube task, which required that a stick be inserted
into one specific end to avoid pushing the treat into a trap, was solved
by children older than 3 years, by two of five chimpanzees aged 11 and
13 years, and *not at all* by capuchin monkeys. The successful children

and chimpanzees seemed to evaluate the situation mentally first and selected the correct side immediately.

Tool use in captive chimpanzees and 2-year-old children was also compared by Nagell, Olguin, and Tomasello (1993). The task was to obtain a piece of food or a toy through bars or a fence using a rake. The spokes of the rake were sufficiently far apart that it was more efficient to use this tool on its back edge. For each species, three groups were formed: a no-model group, a partial-model group for which the raking in of the desired object was demonstrated, and a full-model group for which both flipping over the rake to its back edge and the raking in procedure were demonstrated (a two-step process). Although chimpanzees and children were equally successful on this task, only children were said to have truly imitated the model. Chimpanzees, instead, were purported to have "relied on their own individually created strategies in attempting to emulate the results of the model" (p. 180). This conclusion was based on the finding that children in the full-model group imitated the flipping action more than did children in the partial-model group, whereas this difference was not found for chimpanzees. In fact, however, the proportion of tool-use trials in which the back edge of the rake was used was equivalent for both species in the full-model condition. There was also an increase in edge use across trials for both species, although it began earlier and peaked higher for children. The difference between species is that successful chimpanzees in the partial-model condition used the back edge *more* than successful chimpanzees who saw this as part of their demonstration, whereas children in the partial-model condition very rarely used the edge. Support for any difference in imitation of tool use, then, lies in the lack of exploration of the tool by children who did not see modeling of a novel use of a rake (flipping to the back edge). Tomasello and Call (1997), however, interpret the results as indicating that chimpanzees used the same method regardless of the model, whereas children copied the precise method modeled.

Circular Reactions

Piagetian stages are also defined by the presence of primary, secondary, and tertiary circular reactions. Primary circular reactions are repeated actions involving only the infant's own body – for example, bringing the hand to the mouth. Secondary and tertiary circular reactions are repeated actions on outside objects, the difference between them being that tertiary involve more variations in the actions and appear more experimental. In practice, they are often very difficult to distinguish, and animal researchers have applied quite different criteria for these behaviors than those of researchers studying infants, particularly for tertiary circular reactions.

Secondary circular reactions are attempts to reproduce interesting environmental events, which Piaget (1952) viewed as characteristic of stage 3 in human infants (4 to 8 months). Chevalier-Skolnikoff (1983) gave several examples of these in the orangutans that she observed, the best of which are repeatedly rocking the body to make a noisemaker ring and repeatedly batting a hanging object and watching it swing.

Tertiary circular reactions are characteristic of stage 5 (12 to 18 months) because they focus on discovery and experimentation. Some of Chevalier-Skolnikoff's examples appear questionable in this regard: dangling a rope over the face and catching its end in the mouth and putting objects repeatedly into a bucket. These might easily be secondary circular reactions. Better examples of tertiary circular reactions might be balancing a bucket on the head after several tries and twirling a rope while hitting the ground with it on each rotation.

Antinucci (1989, 1990) and his collaborators reported limited secondary circular reactions in their gorilla and no tertiary circular reactions. Spinozzi and Natale (1989) observed this gorilla at 1 year, however, banging a rattle against different surfaces (the floor, walls, and bars of the cage) and at 14 months pushing objects repeatedly with her muzzle. These actions appear to be secondary circular reactions. Gibson (1993) also reported that the home-reared chimpanzees that she observed rarely exhibited either secondary or tertiary reactions.

The apparent rarity of tertiary circular reactions among these apes is problematic because the beginning of mental representation in Piagetian stage 6 "results from the interiorization of tertiary circular reactions and from active experimentation of novelty" (Doré & Dumas, 1987, p. 221). As Piaget (1952, p. 324) himself put it, the groping or trial and error of stage 5 becomes "internalized and proceeds by means of representation instead of depending exclusively on external and immediate activity."

Conclusions

Use of a detached tool in foraging for encased foods, in sponging liquids, and in aggressive displays is prevalent among modern-day wild chimpanzees. A broader definition of tool use that would allow a tool to be attached to a substrate – for example, using branches for locomotion or building nests – would admit greater tool use among other species, particularly orangutans. It is possible that object manipulation and construction, and not tool use per se, is the critical ability, as Galdikas (1982) suggested. (See also the last section of this chapter.) In the wild, it is clear that tool use is neither directly taught nor genetically determined, given the variations across regions. Rather, it is indirectly fostered, similar to current-day human tool learning, but with less feedback.

Captive apes have little difficulty with standard Piagetian means–ends tasks, though they may solve the more advanced tasks at somewhat older ages. They are usually better at tool tasks than are the monkey species that have been tested. The relative absence of advanced circular reactions may simply reflect an impoverished environment relevant to these behaviors. Alternatively, it may be that apes attain cognitive levels implying mental representation by processes different from those in human infants. More information on exploratory behaviors in wild apes is needed.

Object Concept in Apes and Monkeys

The development of the object concept in Piagetian theory involves the acquisition of an understanding that objects are independent in their identity and movements through space and time, "an independent body in motion which is capable of multiple displacements" (Piaget, 1937/1954, p. 93). Piagetian methods require that understanding of objects be assessed through direct action – that is, through a search for them. Researchers have recently criticized the age limits that such action requirements entail and instead have promoted passive methods appropriate for very young infants. The relevance of these methods for studying the development of the object concept is particularly important for the issue of representation, and I discuss this issue in the next chapter.

In the studies of object concept in apes, procedures have been adapted (sometimes loosely) from Piagetian tasks. Researchers have claimed to show that apes demonstrate both stage 5 and stage 6 object concept abilities whereas monkeys show only stage 5. In traditional Piagetian methodology, for example, the Uzgiris–Hunt Scale I (1975) (see Table 5–2), stage 5 of the object concept scale is assessed by a visible displacements task (item 8) and stage 6 by an invisible displacements task (items 10 and 14). In the former, an object is hidden under (or behind) a screen, then removed and shown to the infant, and then hidden again under another screen. This procedure is usually repeated and the object is left under (behind) a third screen. In the latter, the same displacements occur, but the object is hidden either in a container or in the experimenter's hand so that it is not visible to the infant. After the second displacement, the object is surreptitiously dropped under or behind the third screen, and the empty container or hand is shown to the subject. The visible displacements task is said to measure the infant's ability to follow an object's movements from one location to another and to recognize that it has a permanent existence or identity throughout these movements. The invisible displacements task measures similar abilities but further requires mental imagery of the object throughout the movements because it is not shown to the infant between hidings. In the visible displacements task, the infant must directly search in the *last* hiding place to pass the trial, according to Uzgiris–Hunt Scale I. In the invisible displacements task, the infant may pass either by searching in the last hiding place or by searching the hiding places in sequence – that is, by recreating the whole sequence of hidings. In a final "trick" task, the experimenter surreptitiously drops the object under the first screen and continues the displacements under the remaining screens. This task can be solved only by a sequential search in reverse.

Mathieu et al. (1976) compared two monkeys (*Lagothrica flavicauda* and *Cebus capucinus*) with a 5-year-old zoo chimpanzee on object permanence tests. The object hidden was a star-shaped wooden object that the animals had been trained to exchange for food. The apparatus contained three boxes that the animals had also been trained to push so that they would rotate upward. The animals underwent 60 trials each of visible and invisible displacements, with direction of movement counterbalanced. Oddly, the object was not always left under the last hiding place, but its hiding place was counterbalanced. In addition, the invisible displacements were screened, and the animal was shown the unscreened display after each displacement – that is, with the object present or absent. These are two variants from the usual procedure used with human infants. The *C. capucinus* monkey and the chimpanzee performed almost perfectly on both types of tasks, pushing the box in which the object was hidden and giving the star to the experimenter in exchange for food. There were many trials, but these animals were correct on both early and late trials. The *Lagothrica* monkey made many errors.

Natale (1989) administered a visible displacements task with two and three screens to the gorilla in the Rome zoo, described above. The gorilla was 18 months old, and two cebus monkeys were also tested. Both species made some residual errors (going to the screen that had been correct on the previous trial); these are characteristic of stage 4. On the vast majority of trials they were correct, however, going directly to the screen where the object had last been hidden. Natale, Antinucci, Spinozzi, and Poti (1986) compared the same gorilla and a Japanese macaque, both at 22 months of age, on an invisible displacements task with several variations. First, they hid a candy under a small block, moved this block under one of two identical large blocks, surreptitiously left the candy under the large block, and then moved the small block back. They then changed the blocks in color and size on each trial and incorporated "false" trials, similar to the "trick" task outlined above, in which they kept the candy under the original small block. Unlike the trick procedure, however, the small block was never moved but rather the large block was simply lifted. Last, they varied trials in which the small block remained next to the large block where the candy was hidden with trials in which it was next to the other large block (without the candy), which was, in turn, next to the large block with the candy. As with the Uzgiris–Hunt (1975) scales, the animals could search directly under the correct large block or sequentially – that is, under the small block first and then under the correct large block. Both animals performed similarly on the first task using a majority of direct responses – that is, searching directly under the correct large block. The gorilla switched to sequential responding on the second task variant ("false" trials), whereas the macaque did so when it was given a long series with false trials. The gorilla, unlike the macaque, never made an error on false trials and was also more correct than the macaque on the final "nonlinear" trials where it had to skip over the adjacent large block to pick up the correct large block. The performance of three crab-eating macaques and two cebus monkeys on the last version of this task was random. The researchers concluded that only the gorilla was able to representationally reconstruct the invisible displacements sequence.

A recent study compared a sample of seven orangutans with a sample of nine squirrel monkeys on visible and invisible displacements tasks (de Blois, Novak, & Bond, 1998). Both species performed above chance on visible displacements tasks, but only the orangutans did so on a single invisible hiding task. On an invisible displacements task with two screens, the orangutans were above chance when the object (treat) was hidden in a cup instead of a hand. No invisible displacements task with three screens was administered. Again, as in the study above with the gorilla, only the orangutans and not the monkeys were able to mentally represent the unperceivable object.

Conclusions

There appears to be much less interest in object concept than in tool use among primate researchers, so there is not much evidence on which to base a conclusion that great apes attain a representational level (stage 6) and monkeys do not. The single gorilla, the single chimpanzee, and the several orangutans in the studies reviewed did, however, generally outperform monkeys (with the exception of *C. capucinus*) on invisible displacements tasks. More data are needed on the great apes as well as on the lesser apes (compare de Blois et al., 1998); but at this point it appears that if tool use and object permanence are essential precursors of language, these abilities are present in apes at the highest representational level. I now address the question of the degree to which these abilities are indeed directly related to communicative development.

Early Findings in Favor of a Relationship between Tool Use and Communication in Human Infants

It was Bates and her colleagues (Bates, 1979) who first provided empirical data on the relationship between measures of communication and Piagetian measures of tool use (means–ends), as well as measures of object concept. It was Bloom (1973), however, who first suggested that a stable representation of objects was essential for attaching verbal labels to them. Bates (1979) administered the Uzgiris–Hunt (1975) scales to a sample of American and Italian infants and correlated performance on these scales to measures of gesture and language.

Between the ages of 9 and 13 months, object concept was not found to be correlated with many of the gesture or language measures. Performance on this scale at age 9 months, however, did predict observed giving at 10 to 13 months and nonreferential word use at 13 months. In contrast, means–ends performance was said to be a good predictor of many of the gesture and language measures. Specifically, means–ends performance at age 9 months predicted observed showing, pointing, giving, and referential words at later ages. In a follow-up study of 11 children at age 17 to 19 months, most infants were found to have reached ceiling on the Uzgiris–Hunt (1975) scales. Means–ends and object concept scores at the end of the first year were both found to be randomly related to language measures at the age of follow-up.

Performance on means–ends tasks across the first year (at 4, 8, and 12 months) was found to predict both receptive and expressive language on the Reynell Developmental Language Scales at age 2 years for a very large sample of children (Siegel, 1981). Thus, it may well be that the failure of Bates (1979) to find long-term relationships stemmed from the small size of the sample. In addition, Siegel (1981) also found long-term predictive relationships from object permanence performance at ages 12 and 18 months but only for expressive language at 2 years. In a more recent study by this group (Miller & Siegel, 1989), with, again, a very large sample (309 children), scores on *both* means–ends and object permanence at age 8 months were found to discriminate between language-delayed and non–language-delayed children on the Reynell Expressive Scale at 3 years of age. By age 12 months, only object permanence scores discriminated the groups on expressive language at 3 years.

In contrast to these positive predictions from means–ends performance to later language abilities, performance on a rake task at age 13.5 months was negatively correlated with later receptive language as measured by the Receptive and Expressive Emergent Language Scale (REEL) at 22 months (Ungerer & Sigman, 1984). It could be argued, however, that age 13.5 months is too young for stable performance on a rake task; and in another study, Sigman and Ungerer (1984) did find that use of a rake to obtain a toy hidden in a tube was related to a concurrent clinical assessment of expressive language in older children aged 16 to 25 months.

Concurrent relationships between means–ends performance and language were also established by Snyder (1978). She compared 15 language-delayed 2-year-olds with 15 normally developing children matched on MLU whose mean age was about 15 months. All children were at stage 6 on object permanence tasks, as measured by the Uzgiris–Hunt (1975) scales. The language-delayed children attained only stage 5 in means–ends tasks, whereas the NL children attained stage 6. The scores on the means–ends scale were, in fact, the single

cognitive predictor that accounted for most of the variance in performance on declarative and imperative tasks. The declarative task
involved a repeated action in which the object of the action was suddenly changed; the children were expected to indicate the new object in
some way. Language-delayed children differed from NL children primarily in their failure to *label* the new object. In the imperative task, a
desired object was made inaccessible; language-delayed children tended
to request it nonverbally (gesturally) rather than verbally as did their
NL counterparts. Thus, in this study, means–ends solutions involving
foresight (tasks 11 and 12 in Table 5–1) rather than trial and error
were related concurrently to the ability to label in a communicative
task.

Specific training on means–ends tasks in very young infants (aged 7
to 11 months) was not found to affect the infants' use of imperative or
declarative performatives, however (Steckol & Leonard, 1981). This is
not surprising because the training did not affect means–ends performance, either.

Methodological Problems in Means–Ends and Object Permanence Tasks

It is clear that the early findings relating means–ends and object permanence tasks to language measures are very mixed. Some of the
mixed results are due to variants in methodology and in assignment of
task difficulty. For example, in Bates (1979), it was claimed that the
stick task was passed at a young age, but Bates and Snyder (1987)
stated that infants often do not pass the stick task until as much as a
year after passing the string tasks. Using a rake instead of a stick sim-
plifies the task (Uzgiris, 1987), but the majority of infants still do not
pass this task until after age 15 months (Blake & Dolgoy, 1993;
Holloway, 1986), and the average age may be as old as 22 months
(Uzgiris, 1987). Thus, Piaget's (1952) observations of his own infants
notwithstanding, the stick task does not appear to be characteristic of
stage 5 behaviors. Gopnik and Meltzoff (1984) grouped the stick task
with stage 6 tasks because of their findings regarding a lack of ordinal
sequence between these tasks.

There are also methodological inconsistencies in object permanence
tasks across studies that may account for some of the mixed results
(Corrigan, 1979). The major variants involve the number of displacements, direction of displacements, number of screens, distinctiveness of

screens, definition of systematic search (direct versus sequential), and number of correct trials required. Task difficulty increases with the number of displacements and the number of screens and decreases with the degree of distinctiveness of screens. The last variation, number of correct trials required to pass the task, is crucial because a single correct trial, the criterion used by Bates (1979), does not guarantee that the child can search correctly across trials varying in displacement direction. A displacement task that does not vary direction is easier than one that does (Corrigan, 1981), even for children who are in their third year. In fact, the instructions for the Uzgiris–Hunt (1975) scale specify that the displacements should always go in the same direction (right to left or left to right) on a set of trials, so that following these instructions would facilitate passing the task. Furthermore, in Corrigan's 1981 study, only direct search under the last screen was credited, whereas the instructions for the Uzgiris–Hunt (1975) scales state that in the invisible displacements task, either direct or sequential search is acceptable.

Corrigan (1981) investigated practice effects and found that performance improved with practice on invisible displacement trials for up to 12 trials for 24-month-olds, with somewhat less effect for 18-month-olds. Holloway, Blake, and Pascual-Leone (1987) gave infants who failed a displacements task (visible or invisible) 3 training trials in which the mother helped the infant to obtain the object. Five additional trials without help were then given, with a passing criterion of 3 of 5 correct. This procedure represents an extreme of practice, and it did have effects, though surprisingly limited. None of the ten 6-month-olds passed anything beyond the partial hiding task (finding an object with part of it visible), usually passed by infants of this age. Half of ten 10-month-olds passed the visible displacements task, but only 2 passed invisible displacements. Nine of the ten 15-month-olds passed invisible displacements. This study was not designed to assess the effects of training, and thus a no-training group was not included. The results do appear to show, however, that practice can accelerate performance in infants who are close to the expected age of mastery of an object permanence task, but not in infants who are distant from that age.

Following the Uzgiris–Hunt (1975) scale means that the tasks are presented in order of difficulty. Interestingly, the object permanence tasks still do form a scale of increasing difficulty even if the tasks are presented following a Latin square design (Kramer, Hill, & Cohen, 1975). In addition, *changes* in performance across three testing sessions over a 6-month period were found to be consistent with an ordinal scale in the majority of cases. In a longitudinal study of 12 children over the first and second years, both the object permanence and the means–ends scales were found to fit a cumulative scaling model starting with task 5 or 6 (total hidings in object permanence scale, use of support in means–ends scale) (Uzgiris, 1987).

Results Relating Object Permanence Tasks to More Specific Aspects of Language Acquisition

The methodological variations in object permanence tasks described above become somewhat less problematic when researchers relate specific tasks to specific aspects of language. For example, Smolak (1982) reported that infants who passed at least the visible displacements task with three screens and/or the task of finding an object under three superimposed screens (tasks 8 and 9 in Table 5–2) had begun to talk, according to their mothers' report. Solving a single invisible hiding task (task 10 in Table 5–2) was related to infants' use of representational language (to refer to past events and absent objects) (Smolak & Levine, 1984) and to use of sentences (Smolak, 1982). This task should perhaps be regarded as tapping the very onset of stage 6, whereas task 15, a trick procedure requiring a reversed sequential search, measures more advanced representational ability (imaging the whole sequence) that is transitional to preoperational thinking (compare Corrigan, 1978). Success on the latter task has been found to correspond to the first use of relational words (*all gone, more* when referring to an absent object) and a vocabulary spurt in three children followed longitudinally (Corrigan, 1978). In contrast, McCune-Nicolich (1981a) found that relational words, and especially *all gone* and *more,* were acquired prior to success on this more advanced representational task, in five girls followed longitudinally. These children had all passed the single invisible hiding task at the beginning of the study and so could be considered to be at least at the onset of stage 6. Tomasello and Farrar (1984, 1986) reasoned that relational words involving visible dynamic movement of objects should depend on passing the visible displacements task whereas relational words involving invisible dynamics should depend on solving the invisible displacements task. They judged such words as *move, uh-oh, up,* and *stuck* as falling into the first group and *all gone* and *more* (as in the previous studies), as well as *find* and *another,* as belonging to the second group. An intensive longitudinal study of six infants between the ages of 12 and 18 months revealed that the first group of words began to emerge after success on the visible displacements task and the second after success on either a single invisible hiding task or a three-screen invisible displacements task (task 14 in Table 5–2). Tomasello and Farrar (1986) further found that only children with more advanced representational abilities, as measured by the "trick" procedure (task 15 in Table 5–2), could learn a nonsense word referring to an invisible movement. Those who passed no invisible task could learn a nonsense word referring to a visible movement only.

The Specificity Hypothesis

Bates (1979) suggested that it would be wise to adopt a "task-specific" approach in which target skills from different domains are related, rather than a general approach to cognition–language relationships. To a certain extent, the studies summarized in the preceding section do relate quite specific cognitive and language skills, although there is still the underlying notion that the shift into representational abilities signaled by success on invisible displacements tasks is critical. In addition, the language category investigated is still somewhat general – for example, representational or relational words. The skill-specific notion has been taken to its limits by Gopnik and her collaborators (Gopnik, 1984; Gopnik & Meltzoff, 1984, 1986; Gopnik, Choi, & Baumberger, 1996). These researchers claimed to have found relationships between particular target words and particular sensorimotor tasks, namely, between disappearance words and invisible displacements tasks and between success–failure words and means–ends tasks. In Gopnik's 1984 longitudinal study, use of the word *gone* was said to emerge simultaneously with passing invisible displacements tasks. However, two of the five children studied already used *gone* in the first session, so its emergence in relation to cognitive tasks is unknown. Performance on means–ends tasks was *not* apparently related to the production of *gone,* nor was the use of other terms (e.g., *more*) related to solution of the object concept tasks. However, again, two children used *more* in the first session, and the other three never used the term. A further analysis of data from this sample (Gopnik & Meltzoff, 1984) revealed that use of success–failure words (*no, uh-oh, there*) for four of the five children occurred in the session *after* the vertical string means–ends task was passed whereas the fifth child already used three of these terms in the first session. It is argued that success–failure words showed no relationship to object concept tasks, but in fact, four of the five children were at least at the onset of stage 6 in object permanence when these words emerged. In a larger cross-sectional study, children were found to produce *gone* following simple onset of stage 6 (passing a single invisible hiding with three screens), somewhat earlier than in the Gopnik (1984) study. As in the longitudinal study, passing the vertical string means–ends task appeared critical to the emergence of success–failure words.

Gopnik and Meltzoff (1986) reported results again from both a cross-sectional study of 18-month-olds and a longitudinal study that included the previous sample plus additional subjects. The results of the cross-sectional study do not provide support for a specificity hypothesis relating performance on invisible displacements tasks to disappearance words and performance on means–ends tasks to success–failure words. Disappearance words and ability to pass an invisible hiding task were both shown by 14 of 15 children, but 12 of these children also passed the vertical string task. Similarly, only 2 of the 21 children who used success–failure words passed the vertical string task without passing the invisible hiding task. In the longitudinal study, two important changes from the previous studies were made: Children had to pass a cognitive task in two successive sessions, and parents reported disappearance and success–failure words only if they occurred in three different contexts. Thus, the criteria for acquiring both abilities being related were made more strict. Passing an invisible hiding task *and* the vertical string task preceded or coincided with the use of disappearance words for all but 4 of the 17 children who used such words. Two of these children used disappearance words *before* passing an invisible hiding task and two *before* passing the vertical string task. The vertical string task was solved by all but 1 child before or coincidentally with their first use of success–failure words, whereas only 14 of 19 children passed an invisible hiding task before using such words. The specificity hypothesis is thus better supported for success–failure words and means–ends tasks than for disappearance words and invisible hiding tasks. The authors, in fact, suggested that in this study the emergence of the target words was closer in time to solving more advanced tasks – that is, the invisible *displacements* task and the stick or foresight tasks (though not necessarily *following* such solutions). This new relationship might, of course, have been due to the more stringent criteria adopted in this study. The strongest case for specificity in this set of studies seems to be the pattern of correlations obtained in the last study between age of passing the advanced object permanence versus means–ends tasks and age of emergence of target relational words. The correlations are much higher between invisible displacements and disappearance words and between advanced means–ends tasks and success–failure words than between these respective word categories and the other type of cognitive task.

Finally, in a longitudinal study of 11 Korean-speaking children of immigrants to the United States (Gopnik et al., 1996), the performance of 8 of the 10 children using disappearance words supported specificity: Such words emerged closer in time to solution of object permanence tasks than to the solution of means–ends tasks. For only 5 of the 11 children using success–failure words was their emergence closer to the solution of means–ends tasks than of object permanence tasks. These findings are then the reverse of the previous study.

Support for skill-specific relationships thus seems quite weak. Clearly, a Piagetian at heart would not find very satisfying the notion that performance on a task such as invisible displacements, purported to measure a change from sensorimotor functioning on the plane of action to the plane of mental representation, is related only to a verbal expression of disappearance. Much more satisfying is the evidence in favor of a relationship with a category of representational or referential words that name objects out of context or across contexts, or with words that express different general relations to objects.

Our Research Relating Piagetian Tasks to Communication

A general problem in relating language milestones to performance on Piagetian tasks is that variability across children is far greater in the former than it is in the latter (see also Bloom, Lifter, & Broughton, 1985). Typical infants tend to pass Piagetian tasks at quite similar ages, whereas onset age of referential words, for example, is highly variable. For this reason, we decided to examine longitudinally the relation between performance on specific Piagetian tasks and communicative gestures in infants between the ages of 9 and 14 months. The rationale for this research is that sensorimotor cognitive achievements, as Dale (1980) suggested, might be expected to relate more closely to pragmatic communicative abilities than to language.

Four French infants, two male and two female, were visited biweekly at home from the age of 9 or 10 months until 14 months

(Blake & Dolgoy, 1993). The critical object permanence tasks administered were visible displacements and invisible displacements, both with three screens and with varied directions of displacement. Criterion for passing both was two clearly successful trials without aid. The critical means–ends tasks given were use of a support, the horizontal string task, the vertical string task, and the rake task. The means–ends tasks were demonstrated by the observer, who also helped the infant if he or she did not immediately perform the task. At each session, a few tasks were administered, in order, until the infant met the criterion on each.

The results were that pointing in a book occurred reliably (i.e., more than once) shortly after passing the horizontal string task for three of the four infants, who demonstrated a link between these abilities at quite different ages (10:28/11:13, 11:17/12:27, and 12:21/13:25, respectively). The fourth infant rarely pointed. Reliable demonstration of showing also followed success on the horizontal string task, as well as on the visible displacements task, for two infants. The other two infants did not exhibit much showing. Gestures involving cognizance of adult agency (give-request and take adult's hand) also occurred after passing the horizontal string task for three infants. Give-request specifically to wind up the toy provided by the observer occurred either in the same session as passing visible displacements or shortly afterward for three infants. Thus, two Piagetian stage 5 tasks, visible displacements in object permanence and the horizontal string means–ends task, appeared to be critical, though not always sufficient, for the acquisition of indicative gestures and of more sophisticated request gestures involving understanding of adult agency. Because the related abilities emerged at different ages for different infants, age alone was not the critical factor. Also, it is clear that in contrast to some language abilities discussed above, the emergence of pragmatic gestures is not dependent upon stage 6 representational tasks. None of these infants passed the rake task (which we consider to be stage 6), and the two male infants did not pass invisible displacements.

Object Constructions

A number of researchers have argued that object constructions are related to language (Bloom, 1993; Greenfield, 1991; Langer, 1986, 1993, 1996). Object constructions are configurations that are built either spontaneously or imitatively. They involve relating objects to each other rather than notions of object permanence as discussed above. However, like object concepts, object constructions involve understanding about movements of objects in space.

Greenfield (1991) considered that hierarchical object constructions are homologous to grammatical constructions and suggested that both are controlled by Broca's area. She cited evidence from Roland (1985) that Broca's area is implicated both in grammatical, descriptive speech and in motor sequencing. Early in development, the many short-range connections from an undifferentiated Broca's area are said to make it cross-modal. With development, the system becomes modularized, as Broca's area creates two separate networks with the prefrontal cortex. In an earlier cross-sectional study of children between 1 and 3 years of age, Greenfield, Nelson, and Saltzman (1972) found that the children first nested cups using a pairing strategy (one cup into or on top of another), then progressed to a pot strategy (two cups placed in sequence into or onto a third cup), and then finally used a "subassembly" strategy (one cup placed into a second, with both then moved into a third). The last strategy is seen as hierarchical because two cups are combined to form a higher-order unit, which is then combined with another unit to make a final structure. The vast majority of children used one of these strategies more than half of the time, thus making them appear to be internal rules. The progression from the pairing strategy at age 1 year to the pot strategy at 20 months to the subassembly strategy at 3 years is seen as comparable to early progress in word combinations from simple sentences (actor, action, acted upon) to compound sentences to relative clauses in which the acted upon becomes the actor of the next clause. It seems clear, however, that early constraints in both domains are related to underlying processing limitations before both abilities become more automatized (see chapter 7 and also Bloom, 1991), an interpretation with which Greenfield might agree (see Greenfield et al., 1972, p. 309).

Langer (1986, 1993, 1996) makes a distinction between first-order linear cognitions, which operate directly on objects, and second-order hierarchical cognitions, which are mapped onto each other. First-order cognitions are one-way (using a block to push an object repeatedly), whereas second-order cognitions can be two-way (using a tool to both move and stop an object). "Second-order structures are integrative constructions" that evolve in the second year out of the coordination of first-order structures (Langer, 1986, p. 19). Such combinations are reproduced until they become rule-governed routines. "The features of

pragmatic propositions (arbitrariness, substitution, and conventional-
ization, etc.) that mark the symbolic medium of routines are generalized or transferred to the medium of language" (Langer, 1986, p. 387).
Langer's observations revealed that more complex object constructions
(four- and five-object) increase between the ages of 12 and 15 months,
and object substitutions within compositions increase between the ages
of 15 and 18 months. Langer believes that first-order cognitions are
necessary for signaling and that second-order operations, involving
composing, decomposing, matching, commuting, and substituting, are
the basis for the rewriting rules of grammar. He hypothesized that
because chimpanzees develop only rudimentary second-order cognitions, they are limited to acquiring only protogrammatical language
(Langer, 1996).

Bloom (1993; see also Lifter & Bloom, 1989) reported longitudinal
data on 14 infants, most of whom were followed from 9 months of age
until they produced simple sentences. The results that concern us here
are the observations of object play in which the children either took
apart objects (separated two nested cups) or related them (put two cups
together). Object constructions began between the ages of 9 and 11
months before the onset of speech. At the time of emergence of first
words, there was an increase in constructions with thematic relations
between objects as opposed to simple separations. According to
Bloom, the infant now "could think about the objects as separate entities and appreciated the reversibility of actions with them" (Bloom,
1993, p. 223) – that is, the infant could construct after separating.
Before the emergence of first words, these infants also began to solve
an invisible hiding task (with a single screen).

Over a 5-month period, the children progressed from constructions
with generic relationships based on containment or support (putting
beads into a box) to increasingly specific relations based on particular
properties of individual objects (putting beads on a string). Increase in
the second type of construction was associated with a vocabulary
spurt, and this was not simply a function of age. The sequence of developments in object knowledge and in language, and the associations
between them, were similar across children even though the achievements in both domains occurred at widely different ages. For the
majority of the children, the vocabulary spurt also roughly coincided
with solution of the invisible displacements task. Clustering with these
abilities for some children was also spontaneous search for objects outside the perceptual field to make novel constructions.

These researchers all stressed the importance of object constructions in the transition to language. However, they viewed the relationship between domains quite differently. Greenfield and Langer both drew analogies between rule-governed behavior in object constructions and the grammatical rules of language. Greenfield, however, viewed the resemblance as due to control by the same underlying neural substrate (Broca's area) and limited to early childhood. Langer (1986) viewed conceptualization and symbolization as developing independently but believed that "conceptual development could be a necessary but not sufficient condition for language development during infancy" (p. 394). Both Langer and Bloom stressed the reversible (nonlinear) nature of object constructions. Whereas Langer saw these as basic to grammar, however, Bloom stressed reciprocity. Despite the serial appearance of the cognition–language relationships in Bloom's longitudinal study described above, Bloom et al. (1985) argued that word learning may itself contribute to the child's continuing development of knowledge about objects.

Conclusions

Early findings relating Piagetian tasks to language abilities were interpreted as favoring a closer relationship with means–ends than with object permanence abilities (Bates & Snyder, 1987). This review, I believe, shows quite equivalent relationships to language for both types of tasks. Although the results across studies are mixed, often due to varying degrees of facilitation in methods and differences in critera for success, it seems that there are some suggestive correspondences. Success on visible displacements and horizontal string tasks is linked to the emergence of important communicative gestures, both indicative (pointing in a book and showing) and request gestures involving cognizance of adult agency. Success on a single invisible hiding corresponds to the emergence of relational and representational words. Success on more advanced invisible displacements is related to a vocabulary spurt. Greater specificity in these relationships is not warranted by the weak and inconsistent results across the studies of Gopnik and her collaborators.

The intensive longitudinal studies reviewed provide support for relationships that are more than correlational, although prerequisite relationships are, of course, difficult to establish with observational methodology. However, the timing between success on a critical sensorimotor task and the emergence of a gesture or language milestone does have the appearance of a such a relationship. The fact that they sometimes emerge simultaneously makes a definitive prerequisite view tenuous. Tomasello and Farrar (1986) saw the combined results of their longitudinal observational study and their experimental study as providing strong support for a prerequisite view that sensorimotor abilities precede and provide the necessary foundation for certain language abilities. "The sensory-motor scheme is prior to its symbolization, both logically and psychologically" (Tomasello & Farrar, 1984, p. 490). This view contrasts with the homologous view put forth by Bates (1979), in which she argued that cognition and language are related to an underlying structure and emerge in parallel. She also claimed that Piaget favored such a parallel view, but most would interpret Piaget as espousing a prerequisite view. Like Tomasello and Farrar (1984), Langer (1986) believes that cognition provides the foundation for both syntax and semantics. Bloom, however, does not subscribe to either a prerequisite or a parallel view, despite her earlier suggestion that object permanence is basic to labeling objects. "The developmental relation between early cognition and language is most probably neither parallel nor serial but, rather, interdependent or *overlapping* as children's cognition and language mutually inform and transform one another in the course of development from 1 to 3 years of age" (Bloom et al., 1985, p. 149). Similarly, Gopnik and Meltzoff's (1997) position on the cognition-language relationship is that there is a bidirectional interaction; neither semantic nor cognitive development precedes the other but they emerge simultaneously. It does appear unlikely, however, that the relationship is similar to the reciprocal relationship that exists between symbolic play and language. Although Bloom (1993) argued that children learn about objects from language, it seems clear that nonverbal sensorimotor knowledge is prior. This controversy is further discussed in the next chapter.

CHAPTER SIX

Representation in Human Infants

The development of mental representation in infants is controversial first of all for methodological reasons. Piaget's methodology focused on revealing the infant's developing knowledge as functional adaptation, demonstrable in action. He preferred to rely on unambiguous criteria for making inferences about the infant's underlying understanding. For example, intentional, goal-directed behavior was assumed only if the infant removed an obstacle to reach a goal. It is not that Piaget considered intentional behavior to be absent before the age that infants are capable of this action (about 9 months) but that it is not clearly demonstrable. Nativist infant researchers insist that methods requiring such actions on the part of infants preclude the discovery of sophisticated knowledge in very young infants who cannot yet perform the criterial actions. They claim, in fact, that the frontal cortex of young infants may not yet be mature enough to allow the sequencing of two actions, such as the removal of an obstacle to reach a goal (Diamond, 1991). These researchers adopt, instead, passive methods in which very young infants demonstrate their underlying knowledge by preferential looking at one stimulus longer than another. The challenge of this methodology is to design stimulus situations that can elicit looking responses related unambiguously to differences in stimuli.

Evidence from Preferential-Looking Paradigms

Spelke and her associates (Spelke, 1991; Spelke, Breinlinger, Macomber, & Jacobson, 1992) presented a series of situations to very young infants (aged 2 to 4 months) to test their representational knowledge of objects. In the first situation, infants repeatedly viewed a ball falling behind a screen and revealed on the floor when the screen was raised. After habituating to this display, the infants were shown a display in which the ball fell behind the screen and then was revealed, on alternate trials, either on a new upper surface or below the new upper surface on the floor. Control infants saw the ball only in its final resting place on the upper surface or on the floor, without seeing it fall. On the first test trial, experimental infants looked longer at the impossible display, showing the ball below the upper surface on the floor, than at the possible display of the ball on the new upper surface, and longer at the former display than control infants. In the second situation, a ball moved similarly but horizontally behind a screen and then was revealed at rest against a barrier. After the infants had habituated to this display, a second barrier was added and the infants saw, alternately, the ball next to this additional barrier or beyond it at the original barrier (impossible event). Again, in the first test trial, infants looked longer at the impossible event than at the possible event and longer at the impossible event than did controls, who had not seen the horizontal movement of the ball. Finally, infants were shown a ball falling behind a screen through a gap to the floor. The alternate test situations were a small ball or a large ball passing through the gap to the floor despite the fact that the gap was too small for the large ball (impossible event). On all test trials, experimental infants looked longer at the large than at the small ball and longer at the former than did controls. The following inferences are drawn from these findings: (1) that infants of this age mentally represent hidden objects and their hidden motions, (2) that these early representations are similar to those described by Piaget as beginning in the middle of the second year, (3) that young infants infer that objects will continue to move on unobstructed paths (continuity constraint), (4) that young infants assume that no part of an object can jump over or pass through any part of another object (solidity constraint), and (5) that young infants represent the size of a hidden object and infer that it will maintain a constant shape and size. It was considered possible, however, that these representations occur retrospectively rather than prospectively – that is, after the final viewing of the object in its resting place (Spelke et al., 1992). Spelke (1991) concluded that representation and reasoning about the physical world do not depend on manipulations of objects or sensorimotor coordinations, as Piaget maintains, but are present innately. According to Spelke et al. (1992, p. 605), "cognition develops from its own foundations, rather than from a foundation of perception and action."

In situations more specifically directed at hidden objects, Baillargeon, Spelke, and Wasserman (1985) presented infants with a screen that rotated back and forth through a 180-degree arc. A small yellow box with red stars was then placed in back of the screen in full view of the infants, and the screen now moved either 120 degrees until it reached the box (possible event) or 180 degrees as before (impossible event). Infants of 5 to 6 months of age who were habituated to the first display (without the box) looked longer at the impossible than at the possible event but not longer than did control infants, at least on the first trial. Control infants saw the same events but with the box to the side out of the path of the screen. A replication of this study (Baillargeon, 1987) was conducted with the possible event changed to an arc of 112 degrees. The results revealed that six 4- to 5-month-olds (half of the sample), those who saw the impossible event before the possible event in the test trials, did look longer at the impossible event than controls. Controls showed no preference for either the arc of 112 degrees or the arc of 180 degrees. Infants between the ages of 3 and 4 months who were fast habituators also looked longer at the impossible than the possible event, whereas controls of this age showed no preference. Further research (Baillargeon, 1995) demonstrated that 4.5-month-olds could judge whether the stopping point of the screen was consistent with the size of the box if the box were placed beside the screen in the same frontoparallel plane. By 6.5 months, no visible box was needed, apparently indicating that infants of this age could mentally represent the size of the box in its absence.

In another situation, 3- to 4-month-olds were shown a tall and a short carrot with faces, and each carrot moved behind a screen during habituation (Baillargeon & DeVos, 1991). In the test trials, a window was cut in the screen that was higher than the short carrot but not higher than the tall carrot. The infants saw both the short and tall carrots passing behind the screen and *not* appearing in the window. After the first test trial, they looked longer at the impossible event (the tall carrot that did not appear in the window) than at the possible event (the short carrot that did not appear in the window). Infants who had previously been exposed to the presence of *four* carrots (two of each height) showed no preference, however. It was claimed that these infants were able to deduce that the experimenter used one tall carrot to move up to the window and the other to emerge from the other side of the window.

The final situation to be described presented 4-month-old infants with a car rolling down a ramp behind a screen. After habituating to this event, the infants viewed a mouse placed either on top of the ramp or behind it. A car then rolled down the ramp behind the screen to emerge at the bottom. After the first test trial, 4-month-old female infants looked longer at the first – impossible – event (with the mouse on the ramp) than at the second – possible – event (with the mouse behind the ramp); male infants showed no preference. The female infants were not faster habituators than the male infants, however (Baillargeon & DeVos, 1991).

Although some of these results are not clear-cut, they were said to imply that infants represent objects when they move out of sight. Some challenges to this conclusion have been made, however. Using a situation similar to the last one described above but presented on videotape, Lucksinger, Cohen, and Madole (1992) found no preference for the impossible over the possible event in 6.5-month-olds. It could be argued that young infants need three-dimensional displays to show sophisticated responses to occluded objects. Baillargeon (1995), in fact, claimed that infants cannot process pictorial displays until the age of 7 months. However, it could also be argued that the infants were responding to cues in the live event that were not present in the video-taped event (Lucksinger et al., 1992).

A greater challenge perhaps was offered by Bogartz, Shinskey, and Speaker (1997), who suggested that in the carrot situation above (or rabbit in other uncited studies), the salient visual stimulus for the infant is the face and not the height of the stimulus. Because the infant is tracking the face, scanning produces an encounter with the window in the case of the tall carrot/rabbit but not in the case of the short carrot/rabbit. The window is a novel stimulus, not there during habituation, thereby producing longer looking times for the tall carrot/rabbit. An alternative explanation is that the infant during habituation has been led to expect that the carrot/rabbit will reappear at the next edge. If the region of attention to the face is high, as with the tall carrot/rabbit, then the next edge is the window. When no carrot/rabbit appears, this event is discrepant from the habituation event sequence, thereby producing longer looking. Neither of these explanations requires representation of the occluded object. To test these hypotheses, Bogartz et al. (1997) presented only a tall rabbit, which appeared in the window in the possible event and did not appear in the window in the impossible event. Five- to 6.5-month-old infants were habituated either to the full screen (without the window) or to the possible event or to the impossible event and then tested with all three events. Preferential looking was unrelated to the impossibility of the event. None of the three different habituation groups looked longer at the window with no rabbit sequence than at the window with the rabbit sequence. Looking time in the test trials was attributed instead to degree of change in the test condition relative to the habituation condition. However, all habituation groups seemed to look longer at the window with the rabbit sequence, perhaps attracted by the face. The authors concluded that infants' preferential looking in such situations as this one is better explained by attentional, tracking, and scanning processes and by discrepancy from previous displays than by notions that infants of this age can represent occluded objects and can reason inferentially.

A third challenge involves the problem of visual persistence (Haith, 1998). The duration of occlusion in the above experiments is very brief. Mandler (1990) noted that in the rotating screen experiment, infants had to remember the hidden object for only 8 seconds, a time span that might be considered as perceptual rather than representational.

A final problem raised by Müller and Overton (1998) is that we do not know in these situations exactly when the looking time differences occur. It is only at a certain point in the sequence (the last 6 seconds in the rotating screen situation) that the event becomes impossible. It is only from this point, then, that greater looking time can be said to register surprise or at least interest in something unusual.

It does seem well demonstrated that young infants see objects as spatially bounded entities with internal unity. To do this, they use depth and motion information to detect the separation of objects from the background and from each other (Spelke, 1982, 1998). Presumably, they cannot do this until their stereoacuity is well enough developed. Furthermore, these abilities appear to be accomplished by the perceptual system (Mandler, 1998). The issue being addressed here is whether infants can also mentally represent objects when they are not available to the perceptual system. The habituation–dishabituation paradigm, and its reliance on preferential looking, clearly highlights attentional processes and the effects of familiarity versus novelty on these processes, as Bogartz et al. (1997) pointed out. The paradigm was developed to investigate sensory and perceptual abilities, not cognitive ones (Haith, 1998). It is a very different paradigm from object search tasks and can hardly be viewed as measuring the same abilities. According to Haith (1998, p. 172), "there is virtually no evidence that the putative cognitive skill has functional or action consequences." In fact, Spelke (1994) herself argued that *separate* systems of knowledge may underlie infants' reasoning in situations in which they observe objects and in which they act upon them. That preferential looking alone can be said to reflect reasoning about the physical world seems highly doubtful, however.

Two findings with object search that have been widely replicated are quite relevant to this issue. First, 6-month-old infants who easily search for a partially protruding object will *not* search for a fully occluded object (e.g., Holloway, 1986). Second, infants who easily pass a visible displacements task cannot pass an invisible displacements task at the same age (Blake & Dolgoy, 1993). Although I noted in chapter 5 that practice on visible displacements can sometimes facilitate performance on invisible displacements, this is not always the case. For many infants, there is a delay between the two tasks, particularly for a sequential invisible displacements task (task 14 in Table 5–2) relative to a sequential *visible* displacements task (task 8 in Table 5–2). Even Spelke (1994) agreed that performance of older infants on invisible displacements tasks suggests that "knowledge of physical objects undergoes a change between infancy and adulthood" (p. 442). Spelke (1998) also cited evidence showing that limits on sensorimotor coordination cannot explain failures in search tasks. Convincing evidence for the last point is provided by Munakata, McClelland, Johnson, and Siegler (1997), who demonstrated clearly that 7-month-olds have the means–ends skills to succeed on search tasks despite Diamond's (1991) insistence that the immaturity of the frontal cortex prevents this. These 7-month-olds were able to pull a towel or push a button to retrieve a toy (a two-step sequence) when the toy was behind a transparent screen but less so when it was behind an opaque screen. Thus, although preferential looking may involve a rudimentary form of representation, similar to the kind of representation reflected in infant long-term recognition memory, representation in action is a much more complex ability.

Evidence from Delayed-Imitation Paradigms

To further address the issue of representation in infants, I turn to the research on delayed imitation conducted by Meltzoff (1985, 1988a, 1988b). Delayed imitation, particularly of novel actions, is thought to require mental representation because the infant must hold in mind an image of the model's action. Meltzoff (1985) presented 14- and 24-

month-olds with a dumbbell-shaped toy that was pulled apart by the experimenter three times. Infants were then given the reassembled toy either immediately or after a 24-hour delay. Control infants were presented with the toy either without the demonstration or with a demonstration of a different action, a circular movement. Among the 2-year-olds, 70% of the experimental infants performed the target action after a 24-hour delay and 80% immediately, as compared with only 25% of the control infants after the delay and 20% immediately. Among the 14-month-olds, 45% produced the target action after a 24-hour delay and 75% immediately, whereas 8% of the controls produced it after a delay and 20% immediately. Meltzoff stressed the difference between the experimental and control groups in both conditions, but it is important to note that not even half of the experimental 14-month-olds produced the target action after the delay. It is common among developmentalists to consider that a behavior is not age appropriate until more than half of the subjects have mastered it. Meltzoff also stressed the speed with which experimental infants copied the action "without engaging in exploratory manipulations before imitating" (p. 68). This reinforces the impression that the toy provides the occasion for the target action – that is, that it elicits the action, although such elicitation occurred in only 20 to 25 percent of control infants. This simple imitative act is quite different from the examples of constructed imitation cited by Piaget (1945/1962), and a single imitative act can hardly be viewed as reconstructive memory.

Meltzoff (1988a) also exposed 14-month-olds to a model performing six different actions and tested their imitation after a 1-week delay with the same control groups as in the previous study. Of the experimental group, 11 of 12 infants duplicated three or more of the target actions, whereas only 3 of the 24 control infants did so. The most novel action, touching the forehead to the top of a box, was performed only by the experimental infants (8 of 12), and pulling apart a dumbbell toy was also more frequently performed by experimental than by control infants. Pushing a button, shaking an egg, and folding a hinge were done equally often by both groups of infants; making a bear dance was performed by neither group. Thus, two of the six target actions showed delayed imitation, but only one of these (forehead touching) is clearly not in the repertoire of the infants, was never practiced, and cannot be viewed as simple elicitation by the object. Finally, in another experiment, three of these actions, pushing a button, shaking an egg, and folding a hinge, were demonstrated to 9-month-old infants (Meltzoff, 1988b). Following all demonstrations, the infants were given each object to see if they would imitate the observed action. Groups of control infants were given the objects (1) without seeing them previously, (2) after seeing the experimenter simply holding each one, or (3) after seeing the adult manipulate them without performing the target action. Experimental group infants performed more of the target actions immediately than did the controls combined across groups. The results were almost identical after a 24-hour delay. Half of the experimental group infants in both the immediate and 24-hour delay conditions imitated at least two of the three actions, as compared with 8% and 19% of the controls, respectively. However, the mean of the first control group (baseline) was quite close to that of the experimental group in both the immediate and delayed conditions (1.0 vs. 1.5 and 1.2 vs. 1.6, respectively). It is not clear if these groups were significantly different, because all controls were combined for comparison with the experimental group. Thus, it appears that some of the objects, most likely the button and the egg, had demand characteristics that elicited the target actions in controls who had not previously seen the objects. Why the same effects were not found in the other control groups is unclear.

These findings, then, do not provide clear-cut support for delayed imitation among 9-month-olds, because the baseline controls appeared to perform the target actions just as frequently. There is also a question about the form of representation required to reproduce these actions. Is it simply recognition that this is the action I saw associated with this object – that is, recognitory assimilation? (See chapter 4.) Delayed imitation is extremely difficult to identify in the spontaneous behavior of infants unless one is well acquainted with their daily experiences. Thus, most often, it needs to be assessed experimentally. Such an assessment, however, is easily open to the criticism that the object is eliciting the learned action via associative memory rather than symbolic representation. I would conclude that the only clear evidence for delayed imitation in this series of studies is the forehead touching by 14-month-olds and the pulling apart of the dumbbell by the 24-month-olds, the latter not being surprising.

An improvement to delayed imitation of a single action is imitation of a sequence of actions (Mandler & McDonough, 1995), because this paradigm is less subject to simple elicitation or recognitory assimilation. Infants at 11 months were shown 4 two-action sequences, of which two were causally ordered (pushing a button through a slot in a box and then shaking the box) and two were arbitrarily ordered (putting a ring on a bear's arm and then brushing its head). For one of each type of sequence, infants were given the opportunity to imitate immediately (after a 20-second delay). After a 24-hour delay, they were given the opportunity to imitate all sequences, one at a time. The procedure thus differed from Meltzoff's in at least two respects: (1) the infants had a chance to practice some of the actions immediately and did not perform them only after the delay and (2) none of the actions was novel. The results of this study showed that infants performed more actions of both types (causally ordered and arbitrarily ordered) immediately after modeling than during an initial baseline (before modeling). After 24 hours, only imitation of causally ordered actions exceeded baseline performance. However, the mean number of actions imitated was about one in all conditions with the exception of 24-hour recall of arbitrary sequences, for which it was less than one. Thus, infants of this age had difficulty replicating the event sequence in order; and even when they could replicate it, the researchers themselves stated that the causal sequences seemed to be experienced as a single action. At 14 months, these same infants were able to reproduce more of the causal two-action sequences after modeling.

Even at ages 16 and 20 months, infants on average could reproduce immediately only two of the actions (2.5 at 20 months) – that is, one of the two sequences in a three-action modeled event (Mandler, 1990). At 20 months, performance was maintained after 2 weeks, whereas at 16 months, it was not. No differences between 16- and 20-month-old infants were found by Bauer and Dow (1994) in delayed recall after 1 week, however, either in number of actions reproduced or in the number of sequences reproduced, although older infants did tend to sequence actions more correctly. Across this age range, infants reproduced about two actions after 1 week – that is, one correctly ordered sequence, though less for arbitrarily ordered sequences. The sequences were familiar (laying down a teddy bear, covering it up, and reading a story), novel enabling (causally ordered: putting Play-Doh into a garlic press, pressing it to make "spaghetti" come out, cutting "spaghetti"), and novel arbitrary (drawing a picture on the slate, putting on the sticker, and making it stand). Follow-up experiments indicated that these infants could also remember the details of specific events over a 1-week interval – that is, they could select the correct props for the target actions.

Although delayed imitation of event sequences is an interesting method for assessing constructed representations, infants appear not to be able to do the task until well into their second year. Whereas 11.5-month-olds are able to reproduce *immediately* two causally ordered target actions, whether familiar or novel (Bauer & Mandler, 1992), they apparently cannot do this after a delay. Toward the middle of the second year, not only can infants correctly reproduce a sequence of two actions after a delay but they can also remember details about the objects. Thus, there does appear to be a shift in representational abilities at this age.

Evidence from Reaching Paradigms

Another method used to demonstrate representation in action is reaching for an object in the dark. For example, Goubet and Clifton (1998) showed infants between 6 and 7 months of age a lighted display in which a ball dropped noisily through a tube. It then continued through this central tube for one group but descended through a tube on the right or left side for another group, the final descent being noiseless. The infants were then given trials in the dark in which the ball dropped only through the side tubes. Those who had experienced lighted trials with the side tubes reached more into the correct side and made contact with the correct general area more often than did infants who had experienced only the central tube in the light. However, they were not more successful in contacting the ball, the tray it was on, or the table in front of the ball. The researchers concluded that the infants experienced with the side tubes in the light were able to discriminate the ball's direction of falling from brief auditory cues and to coordinate their search with stored information (i.e., their representations) from the lighted display. Their success in this task is attributed to only one simple motor action (reaching) being required, in contrast to object permanence tasks. It seems significant, however, that infants in this study were not more successful in actually contacting the ball than infants of the same age are in total hiding tasks. We have to be content with simple reaching in the general vicinity of the ball as a demonstration of mental representation of its location.

Theories about the Development of Representation

Meltzoff and Moore (1998) claimed that representation is the starting point of infancy and not its culmination. Nevertheless, they do not believe that the infant has object permanence from the beginning, but rather object identity. Object identity seems to be a precursor of object permanence. "An infant can have a representation in mind but not think the object continues to exist in the external surround" (Meltzoff & Moore, 1998, p. 204). For very young infants, evidence for object permanence varies with the measure used, in contrast to the converging results obtained for 9- to 10-month-olds with different measures (manual search, visual search, preferential looking). They conclude that younger infants are behaving according to only object identity, based on spatiotemporal, featural, and functional criteria. Infants compare objects in the perceptual field with those in their steady-state representation using these criteria, and this comparison process appears to be similar to the one outlined by Mandler.

Mandler (1988, 1990, 1998) has proposed that infants engage in perceptual analysis from birth and that such analysis is a symbolic and probably conscious process of active comparison. It involves not primitive recognition but conceptual thought. The results of perceptual analyses are stored in an accessible representational system that is viewed as developing in parallel with the sensorimotor system, rather than being derived from it in the Piagetian manner. The sensorimotor system involves procedural knowledge, whereas the representational system contains declarative knowledge. This distinction is somewhat equivalent to the distinction between implicit and explicit memory. The representational format is that of image-schemas, which are more abstract than images and represent meanings; image-schemas themselves are not conscious. These image-schemas are formed through a selective simplifying perceptual analysis of complex events, focused on what objects do and how they relate to each other. According to Mandler (1998, p. 22), "the claim of a purely sensorimotor form of representation during the first year and a half of life depends on [the] assumption that there is no imagery during this time." She saw some of the findings above on infant recall (for example, Meltzoff, 1988b) as supporting her notions. Apart from the research of Spelke and her collaborators, however, there is little direct evidence of perceptual analysis occurring very early in infancy and none that clearly supports symbolic representation. Mandler (1990) herself, as noted above, stated that the delays in Baillargeon's experiments may be too short to tap memorial processes.

Image-schemas are said to provide the ground for words referring to them, in a similar way to the relation discussed in chapter 5 between object concept and words. They are supposed to serve a symbolic function, although it is not clear what the symbol is and how image-schemas can serve as both symbolic vehicle and ground.

Relevant to Mandler's focus on perceptual analysis is the distinction in Piagetian theory between figurative and operative knowing (Furth, 1969; Gratch, 1975; Müller & Overton, 1998; Pascual-Leone & Johnson, 1999). Operative knowing derives from activity that allows the infant to experience objects in relation to other objects, whereas the figurative aspect provides the content or data. The first is dynamic and the second, static. The simple type of representation invoked in Mandler's theory is content representation and therefore essentially figurative (Pascual-Leone & Johnson, 1999). These figurative schemes act as signals for other schemes that "are related to the content representations either indexically (i.e., via associative learning) or iconically (i.e., via a configural similarity relation produced by innate mechanisms or biases)" (Pascual-Leone & Johnson, 1999, p. 173). With the symbolic function appears the more complex form of representation, the only one that Piaget recognized, which might be called operational representation (Pascual-Leone & Johnson, 1999). In this type of representation, the symbolic schemes are detached from their referents (Müller & Overton, 1998; Pascual-Leone & Johnson, 1999) (see chapter 4).

Another approach to the development of representation that bears some similarity to Mandler's is that of Karmiloff-Smith (1992). Karmiloff-Smith saw her model as a compromise between nativism and constructivism in that she argued for innately specified predispositions or attentional biases but also saw development as a dynamic process of interaction between mind and environment. Like Mandler, Karmiloff-Smith has described development as movement from implicit information in a procedural format to more explicit representation. She has not invoked image-schemas, however, but rather a reiterative process of representational redescription with four levels: implicit (procedural), explicit but not yet consciously accessible, explicit and consciously accessible, and explicit and capable of being analyzed to provide a verbal rule (metacognitive). How a representation can be explicit and not consciously accessible (second level) is not entirely clear. The change from procedural to explicit is reminiscent of the Piagetian movement from sensorimotor to symbolic representation, and Karmiloff-Smith has acknowledged that there may be something special about the 18-month shift in representation. Also, the levels appear to be hierarchical, but the procedural level is always available, as in Piaget's theory.

Karmiloff-Smith also invoked the Piagetian notion of consolidation before movement to the next level. She stressed, however, that, unlike Piagetian theory, her levels are not age-related and do not necessarily apply across domains simultaneously. Furthermore, redescriptions of representations at higher levels are due not to experience but rather to an internal process of pattern analysis. It is difficult, then, to see where the interaction between mind and the environment applies.

Karmiloff-Smith (1992) has presented interesting data on article development over the preschool and elementary school years, supporting a transition from implicit representation to each higher explicit level. Her model, like Mandler's, however, suffers from a lack of direct evidence regarding the earliest transition from implicit to explicit representation in infancy. Thus, it is difficult to use their theories to discount Piagetian notions regarding the transition from sensorimotor, procedural functioning to symbolic representation. Their similar idea that there may be more than one level of representation is useful, however, in terms of accommodating the sets of contradictory data that are available concerning infant representation.

Elman et al. (1996) (including also Karmiloff-Smith) argued against the nativists that representation-specific predispositions "may only be specified at the subcortical level as little more than attention grabbers . . . [whereas] at the cortical level, presentations are not prespecified; at the psychological level representations *emerge* from the complex interactions of brain and environment and brain systems among themselves" (p. 108). Very early learning can be rapid, and this may explain some of the early behaviors thought to be innate.

Conclusions

Different paradigms have been used to examine representation in infants and have yielded results showing considerable variation in the ages at which different tasks can be accomplished. Nelson (1995) has suggested that early novelty preferences revealed by the preferential-looking paradigm may be reflexive or obligatory in nature and mediated only by the hippocampus and not by cortical areas. This view applies primarily to simple visual recognition tasks but also perhaps to more complicated preferential-looking paradigms that involve uncontrolled novelty effects, such as those noted by Bogartz et al. (1997). The transition from this possibly more "primitive" form of memory to "explicit" memory is thought by Nelson to occur after age 8 months, an age that does coincide with the infant's ability to search for a totally hidden object. Delayed imitation or event memory paradigms are said to involve higher cortical structures that do not develop until toward the end of the first year. Even at this age, as we have seen, infants are able to retain only one action in memory to imitate after a delay and not two actions in sequence. It is only in the middle of the second year that they can remember two actions and the sequencing order between them, as long as this order is not arbitrary.

The arguments over representation in infancy can be viewed as taking the extreme forms of a principle-based approach versus an adaptive process approach (Munakata et al., 1997). According to a principle-based approach as espoused by Spelke et al. (1992) and Baillargeon (1995), infants have early access to principles about object knowledge and can reason according to these principles. In contrast, according to an adaptive process approach, knowledge is graded and evolves with experience. The ability to represent hidden objects, in particular, depends on maintaining connections among relevant neurons, and these connections strengthen through experience. Such connections may be strong enough to support longer looking times at "impossible" events at age 7 months but not reaching. Simulation modeling by Munakata et al. (1997) demonstrated that the network came to exhibit knowledge of object permanence through learning to predict the reappearance of an object. It did this through patterns of activation in which representation of the occluded object became gradually similar to representation of the visible object. The simulations are consistent with the possibility that a looking measure might be sensitive to hidden objects relatively early, whereas full development of object representation may take a much longer time. They also showed that reaching behavior can improve through development in the representational system alone.

Whatever one thinks about simulations, the possibility of a graded development of representation seems best able to explain the conflicting data and is particularly well illustrated by the gradual development of delayed enactment in the studies of Bauer and Mandler and their colleagues. Such a gradual developmental process is not in fact inconsistent with Piaget's views on the development of object permanence, although, according to Piaget, full-fledged symbolic representation is not available until well into the second year. The dynamics of a simulation can also be seen as capturing the Piagetian processes of assimilation, accommodation, and equilibration (Elman et al., 1996). A gradual development of representation differs from the levels proposed by Karmiloff-Smith but probably not in an irreconcilable way. An adaptive approach also can accommodate the role of environmental structure. Many "early" abilities are detected only in highly structured experimental settings in which the experimenter is prestructuring the problem for the infant (Bremner, 1994). Because our goal is to explain infant abilities across contexts, adaptation to the natural environment in an interactive framework would seem to be an essential aspect of a theory of representational development.

CHAPTER SEVEN

Memory in Nonhuman Primates and Young Children

"Of all the prerequisites for language, none is more vital, though more easily overlooked than memory; yet language is possible only because of memory . . . [or rather the] *representation* of the objects, actions, or properties stored in memory" (Premack, 1978, p. 877). All researchers agree that recognition memory is a primitive form of memory available to quite simple animals and to very young infants. It is, rather, *recall* memory that is important for language acquisition. Recall is defined as "accessing (bringing to awareness) information about something that is not perceptually present. By definition, recall is a conscious product" (Mandler, 1990, p. 486). In the previous chapter, I focused on the development of representational processes in infancy that are basic to recall. In this chapter, I focus on the relationship between recall memory and language acquisition. I begin by examining memory in nonhuman primates – not only recall memory but also recognition memory involving representation of a sequence or array. These aspects of nonhuman primate recognition memory are included because sequential memory appears to have important implications for children's acquisition of language.

Memory in Monkeys and Apes

Most of the recent research on memory in nonhuman primates involves experiments with captive monkeys, with research on captive apes largely limited to early studies. However, some evidence exists on spatial memory in both wild and captive apes and on delayed imitation in rehabilitant apes.

Spatial Memory

Boesch and Boesch (1984) have claimed that wild Tai chimpanzees choose for nut cracking a stone hammer that is closest to the panda nut tree that they have selected. "The least-distance principle seems to rule the chimpanzees' decision" about which stone to transport (p. 164). In 10 of 16 cases in which the two nearest stones were approximately the same weight, the chimpanzees chose the stone that was closest to the tree. Furthermore, 40% of the transports of the stone to the tree were made with the tree *out of sight*. It was then inferred that the chimpanzees were mentally comparing different stone–tree distances to pick the shortest one. To do this effectively would have required constant updating of stone site maps with reference to newly transported stones and to new trees. A problem with these claims, however, is that there were few direct observations of the transports. The transports were studied indirectly by marking the stones and tracking their movements every 3 days. This method does not allow us to know how direct the chimpanzees' searches actually were. For example, we cannot know about errors – that is, the number of times a chimpanzee went to find a stone that was *not* there.

MacKinnon (1974) also claimed that his observations of orangutans revealed that they proceeded to good fruit trees by very direct routes. This was true even when it was likely to be their first time feeding at those trees that year.

One of the earliest experiments conducted regarding spatial memory in captive primates was performed by Tinklepaugh (1932) with two chimpanzees, an 8-year-old female and a 6-year-old male, and two macaque monkeys, a 9-year-old female cynomologus and a 7-year-old male rhesus. The animals were first trained to sit on a stool while food was placed under one of two containers. The containers were then screened during a delay interval, after which the animals were allowed one choice to obtain the food. Food was then hidden in one of two containers in each room of a series of up to 10 rooms while the animal watched. The animal was then led back to the first room and released. The two chimpanzees chose the correct baited container 92% and 88% of the time, respectively, and they responded just as accurately when they did not revisit the rooms in order. The monkeys were somewhat less accurate: 78% and 80% correct choices, respectively, for a 5-room series. The pairs of containers were then arranged in a circle, with the animal seated on a stool in the center; and one of each pair was baited

in turn. With 16 pairs of containers, the chimpanzees were both correct about 78% of the time, with no difference in accuracy whether
they went in serial order or not. The monkeys' performance was almost
as high with 3 pairs but dropped to a little above chance with 8 pairs.
With 16 pairs, human adults' performance was mostly above chance,
whereas performance for two children (ages not given) was only
slightly above chance. With a delay of 24 hours, the chimpanzees' performance dropped to chance levels.

More recently, mental mapping of an outdoor enclosure in captive
chimpanzees has been investigated by Menzel and his collaborators
(Menzel, 1973; Menzel, Premack, & Woodruff, 1978). Menzel
(1973) tested six chimpanzees, 5 to 7 years of age, by carrying one
animal at a time while hiding pieces of fruit in 18 locations. All animals were then allowed to search, the other five serving as controls
for visual and odor cues. Each test animal was found to search in
accordance with a least-distance principle, running unerringly and in
a direct line to the hidden food. In only a few instances did an animal
recheck a place that it had already emptied of food. To determine if
the animals were following memory cues alone and not just discover-
ing the food by chance, two food piles were hidden on the far left and
two on the far right of the field. In 26 of 28 trials, the chimpanzees
went to the two piles on one side first and then to the two on the
other side. When three pieces of food were hidden on one side and
two on the other, the animals went first to the side with the greater
amount of food in a majority of trials.

Menzel et al. (1978) further tested four 3-year-old chimpanzees in
pairs in an outdoor enclosure. A familiar caretaker carrying fruit hid
himself in the enclosure under several different conditions: (1) both
animals of the pair viewed the hiding through a window; (2) one animal of the pair viewed the hiding through a window; (3) both animals
viewed the hiding on television; (4) one animal viewed the hiding on
television; (5) neither animal viewed the hiding (control). The animals'
ability to find the caretaker for television trials was intermediate to
their ability to do so under direct viewing and under control conditions. The animals were thus able to use a two-dimensional depiction
to locate the desired caretaker and food better than when given no
information but not as well as with a three-dimensional veridical view.
Two Guinea baboons, 7 years of age, were also tested in a similar task
under direct versus television view (Vauclair, 1996). With direct viewing, the animals performed at a high level, whether or not they viewed

the hiding binocularly or monocularly. Viewing the hiding on television greatly decreased the number of correct trials, from 80% to 33%.

Spatial foraging skills were examined in two captive 12-year-old yellow-nosed monkeys, one male and one female (MacDonald & Wilkie, 1990). Eight yellow plastic cups containing food were placed at various sites in an indoor enclosure. The monkeys were first allowed to explore the sites and remove the food. The male then participated in a series of trials in which half of the sites were first baited and then emptied by the animal; then the other half of the sites (win-shift rule) were baited after a delay of 3 to 15 minutes. Both monkeys then participated in a series of trials in which the same four sites were baited on the search and re-search phases (win-stay rule), with a delay of 3 to 60 minutes before the re-search phase. During the win-shift series, the male monkey was almost always correct on his first four choices after the second trial of re-search, regardless of the delay. Similarly, both monkeys needed only four or five choices during the win-stay series to empty all sites, even after a 60-minute delay. Patterns of search during the re-search phase of this series minimized travel distance for both monkeys. MacDonald (1994) used a similar win-stay procedure with a 20-year-old captive male gorilla. During the first phase of the procedure, 4 of 8 sites in an outdoor enclosure were baited and the gorilla explored the sites. After a delay of 24 to 48 hours, the same four sites were again baited. The mean number of sites visited by the gorilla across 12 re-search trials was 5.5. There was no evidence of a least-distance strategy, but the gorilla always ended his search after finding the fourth baited site. A 1-year-old male gorilla was given a similar task, with three of six food sites baited on each trial and a delay of only 10 minutes between the search and the re-search phases. The mean number of sites visited was 4.5 across 15 trials, but this juvenile gorilla showed no evidence of stopping after finding the third baited site.

The spatial memory of common marmosets was investigated in a simulated laboratory foraging task (MacDonald, Pang, & Gibeault, 1994). With eight sites baited, three adult and one juvenile marmoset avoided revisiting sites that they had already depleted. In a win-stay procedure, an adult female marmoset visited a mean number of 5.6 of 8 sites to obtain four food items, and it tended to minimize the distance traveled by visiting adjacent correct sites. In a win-shift procedure, the same adult female and an adult male performed less well, visiting almost all the sites on every trial before retrieving the four food items.

An arboreal foraging task with elevated food sites was given to one adult female orangutan and two subadult male orangutans in a zoo indoor enclosure (MacDonald & Agnes, 1999). In the first task, all three orangutans visited all eight food sites and revisited very few across trials. In a win-stay task, the number of correct choices in the first four choices was above chance for two of the orangutans. When one site was overbaited, only one orangutan (of two in this task) chose the overbaited site first.

Spatial memory capacity in foraging tasks can then be quite spectacular in nonhuman primates (and in many other species; see Roberts, 1998), although not errorless. It appears to be superior to human spatial memory in such tasks when the number of food sites is large. If an animal has to travel to good food sites while avoiding predators and competitors, it makes sense that it would have an effective mental map of its habitat and of the locations of food, water, and predators (Roberts, 1998). Such maps seem to be superior in great apes as compared to monkeys, and they appear to take some years to develop, although this conclusion requires more comparative developmental research.

Sequential Memory

Several studies have compared the sequential memory of monkeys and humans using serial probe recognition (SPR) tasks. In these tasks, a "list" of stimuli is shown sequentially to the subject. A probe stimulus is then presented, and the subject has to decide whether the probe is the same as a stimulus on the original list or different from all the original stimuli. For nonhuman primates, this decision is usually indicated by pushing a lever to the left or to the right. If the subject's decision is correct, a tone sounds and a reward is delivered. If it is incorrect, the subject is plunged from darkness into illumination for a brief period. Although this is a recognition task, the findings are sometimes compared to results obtained from humans on serial *recall* of lists (as well as on similar SPR tasks). In recall tasks, humans and older children typically show primacy and recency effects in that they recall better the first and last set of items in a list. Primacy effects have usually been attributed to better rehearsal of the first items.

An early study compared a male 4-year-old rhesus monkey and an adult human female on a SPR task (Sands & Wright, 1980). With a 10-item list, both subjects, but especially the monkey, showed the U-shaped function demonstrating primacy and recency effects. With a 20-item list, only the monkey showed both primacy and recency effects, the human showing only a recency effect. A second study (Sands & Wright, 1982) revealed that on same trials (in which the probe was the same as a list item), reaction time (RT) for the same monkey as in the previous study and an adult human female increased monotonically as a function of list length. On different trials, the monkey and the human also showed increasing RTs with increasing list length unless the different item was changed on each trial. These results are thought to be consistent with serial scanning of the list of items in memory. Wright, Santiago, Sands, Kendrick, and Cook (1985) compared rhesus monkeys and adult humans on a SPR task with four-item lists presented with varying delay intervals before the probe item. No primacy effect was found for either species at zero-second delay, but it emerged at intermediate delays, along with a recency effect that then disappeared at longer delays. The timing of these changes was somewhat different across species, but the pattern of changes was similar.

In a different measure of sequential memory, nonhuman primates were trained in a serial learning task in which they reproduced a given order of stimuli in the face of their varying positions in an array. D'Amato and Colombo (1988) presented five female cebus monkeys with five forms to which they learned to respond in the order *ABCDE*. They were then tested on all possible test pairs and triplets. That is, they were shown two stimuli – for example, *BD* – to which they had to respond in the sequence *B* before *D*. If their previous learning had been based solely on associations between adjacent items, then they should have had difficulty with subsets containing nonadjacent items (Terrace & McGonigle, 1994). Instead, their performance was above 80% correct on all pairs except *DE* and all triplets except *CDE*. These results are interpreted as indicating that "the monkeys developed an internal representation of the ABCDE sequence, which later guided their behavior on the pairwise and triplet tests" (D'Amato & Colombo, 1988, p. 134). This interpretation is further supported by the increase found in RT when the first item of the pair or triplet tested was later in the *ABCDE* sequence. The RT to the second item also increased with the number of missing items separating the pairs tested. Neither of these increases in RT has been found in pigeons (Terrace, 1993), but both have been found in 4-year-old children (Terrace & McGonigle, 1994). Terrace (1993, p. 166) concluded that monkeys (and presumably also children) "appear to be capable of forming a template of the entire sequence, one that defines the ordinal position of each item."

In what appears to be the only study of free recall in nonhuman primates, Buchanan, Gill, and Braggio (1981) gave Lana, a chimpanzee familiar with the invented language Yerkish, lists drawn from Yerkish symbols. The symbols of a list were presented sequentially, one word at a time, and Lana recalled by pushing the appropriate keys on her keyboard. Lana showed primacy and recency effects on lists of four to eight items, and, like practiced humans, she also tended to recall the last item first.

The findings with regard to primacy effects in nonhuman primates cast doubt on their attribution to rehearsal. It may be instead that the first and last items in a list stand out and therefore are better encoded (Roberts, 1998). Wright and Rivera (1997) preferred an interference account to this distinctiveness explanation, in part because there are two processes (retroactive and proactive inhibition) that can be invoked to explain the differential effects on primacy and recency that are obtained. Dissipation of retroactive interference with a delay could allow the primacy effect to appear, whereas the slow growth of proactive interference would eventually eliminate the recency effect. Although it is possible that rehearsal accounts for the primacy effect in humans and not in nonhuman primates, the notion that primacy is due to similar processes across species is more attractive, given that human and nonhuman primates show similar changes in primacy effects. However, the fact that monkeys do not benefit from longer intervals between items in a list, whereas humans do, does support a conclusion that humans are rehearsing and monkeys are not (Roberts, 1998).

The primacy effect in monkeys' list memory has been criticized as an artifact of subject self-initiation of list presentation. This procedure is believed to create heightened attention to the first stimulus (Gaffan, 1994). However, when such list-initiation responses have been eliminated, primacy effects have still been found, both in visual memory (Castro & Larsen, 1992) and in auditory memory (Wright & Rivera, 1997).

Monkeys apparently have much greater difficulty with auditory than with visual tasks, even though they have sensitive hearing (Wright & Rivera, 1997). In a rare study using auditory stimuli (D'Amato & Colombo, 1985), only four of eight cebus monkeys succeeded in a task in which they pushed a lever if a second stimulus matched the first and withheld this response if the two stimuli did not match. These monkeys had little difficulty with a 3-second delay interval between stimuli and showed transfer to new acoustic stimuli. Nevertheless, the fact that half of the monkeys could not perform this task is evidence that matching in the auditory modality is more difficult than in the visual modality.

In an unusual study of auditory memory for lists, Wright and Rivera (1997) trained two male rhesus monkeys extensively in an auditory same–different task and then presented them with "lists" of different sound effects in a SPR task. After the probe was heard, the monkeys touched the right speaker to indicate a match or the left speaker to indicate a nonmatch. Lists of 4, 6, 8, and 10 sounds all yielded primacy and recency effects (a significant quadratic component) for match trials. For all list sizes, performance on the first serial position was significantly more accurate than that on a middle position.

Thus, sequential memory in nonhuman primates appears to be qualitatively similar to that in humans, even to the extent of showing a primacy effect. Most of this work is on monkeys, however, so we know relatively little about apes. Furthermore, it should be emphasized that the monkeys receive very extensive training over many days before they can perform these tasks. Finally, despite good hearing, auditory sequential memory tasks seem to be much more difficult than visual sequential memory tasks for these monkeys. As we shall see in the final section of this chapter, the reverse appears to be true for young children.

Delayed Imitation

Spontaneous delayed imitation of human behavior among rehabilitant orangutans in Borneo has been recorded by Russon (1996). The kind of imitation observed involves complex acts, similar to those noted by Piaget in his infants (Piaget, 1945/1962), rather than the simple acts often used in experimental studies of human infants (see chapter 6). The fact that it is human behavior that is imitated by these orangutans means that it is necessarily novel for the animal and not simply species-appropriate behavior. A clear example is an adolescent female brushing her teeth back and forth on both sides and then spitting over a railing. She had been given the toothbrush and toothpaste, just as human infants are also provided with the objects in experimental delayed-imitation tasks. The ape's technique was identical to what she had observed in humans (Figure 7–1). Other examples from Russon (1996) involved lighting a cigarette butt with a burning stick, shampooing hair in appropriate steps, applying insect repellant to foot and shin, and bailing water from a dugout canoe by rocking it. Figure 7–2 shows an adult female imitating sawing. Most of these imitations were reduced versions of the original complex behavior; all were either

Figure 7–1: Davida, a female juvenile orangutan, brushing her teeth at Tanjung Puting. Photograph by Anne Russon.

the first enactment observed or a self-repetition. Although rehearsal is often disallowed in experimental studies (Meltzoff, 1988a, 1988b) to distinguish clearly between imitation and learning, it is unlikely that one-trial learning is sufficient to explain complex delayed imitation (Mandler & McDonough, 1995). Also, the more complex the behavior, the more varied the reenactments were, supporting the view that the orangutans were reconstructing their imitations from fragments (Russon, 1996). These reenactments actually make a strong case, then, for the high cognitive level of recall memory in this species.

It seems clear that this species of great ape does imitate novel and complex behavior after a delay under naturalistic conditions. It would be useful to have studies of spontaneous delayed imitation in other species, both apes and monkeys. More studies of delayed imitation are also needed under conditions comparable to the experimental studies of human infants reviewed in chapter 6. Whiten (1998) has conducted

Figure 7–2. Supinah, an adult female orangutan, sawing wood at Tanjung Puting. Photograph by Anne Russon.

an experimental study of imitation of action sequences in chimpanzees somewhat similar to those conducted with infants by Bauer and Mandler and their colleagues. Four chimpanzees each saw a different arbitrary sequence of three actions performed to open an "artificial fruit" to remove food baits. Although the delay was too short (2 minutes) to view performance as delayed imitation, the chimpanzees did tend to imitate the sequential organization of the actions they observed, especially by the third trial. The experimental study of imitation of tool use in chimpanzees compared with children, conducted by Nagell et al. (1993), was discussed in chapter 5. The results were interpreted as showing that only children imitate fully the means demonstrated, though neither those data nor Whiten's data support this conclusion.

Russon (1999) has maintained that flexible tool use, which is "instrumental behavior that aims for specific ecological outcomes," is acquired only partly through imitation and that such imitation is selective. Selective imitation leads great apes to focus on relational arrangements of tools and objects or the organizational structure, that is, the program level (Byrne & Russon, 1998; Russon, 1999). For example, in her imitation of fuel siphoning (see Figure 7–3), Siswoyo matched the

Figure 7–3. Siswoyo, an adult female orangutan, siphoning fuel at Tanjung Puting. Photograph by Anne Russon.

manipulations of unscrewing and removing lids of containers, placing the containers near the fuel drum, inserting one end of the siphon into the drum, sucking the other end, and inserting this end into the container. She ignored some timing details and also the essential detail that the fuel drum was empty (Russon, 1999). Although children also imitate selectively – for example, when they assimilate adult behavior into their own symbolic play structure – they can also mimic very closely if desired or required. This is presumably a reflection of our mimetic culture (see chapter 8).

Memory and Language Acquisition in Children

It was proposed many years ago that the production of complex sentences in young children was constrained by a limited programming or memory span (Brown & Bellugi, 1964). Case and his colleagues (Case & Kurland, 1980; Daneman & Case, 1981) did find that memory based on word span was related to the complexity of sentences that kindergarten children could imitate and to the complexity of nonwords that 2- to 6-year-olds could learn to produce or comprehend. It is recent programmatic research by Gathercole and Baddeley and their associates, however, that has clarified the contribution of memory to language acquisition. They highlighted the critical role of a phonological storage in the learning of new words. The "function of the phonological loop is to provide temporary storage of unfamiliar forms while more permanent memory representations are being constructed" (Baddeley, Gathercole, & Papagno, 1998, p. 159). The phonological store may also serve as an output buffer in which the intended utterance is held until the articulatory program can be applied. Its role in language production would then diminish as such processes become automated. The measure that these researchers have developed to tap the phonological store is a nonword repetition task, particularly one containing stimuli that have been rated as having low wordlikeness. In a longitudinal study, Gathercole (1995) found that performance on such a task at age 4 years was related to vocabulary knowledge at both 4 and 5 years, with nonverbal (puzzle-solving) ability partialed out. Vocabulary knowledge refers to a combined measure based on receptive vocabulary and word definition. The reverse relationship was not significant – that is, vocabulary knowledge at age 4 years was not associated with repetition accuracy for low wordlike items at 5 years, although it was associated with repetition accuracy for high wordlike but nonword items. Performance on high wordlike items is thought to be affected by stored lexical knowledge. Between 4 and 5 years of age in this study, there was a greater increase in repetition accuracy for high than for low wordlike items, owing, perhaps, to an increasing ability to use a lexical mediation strategy.

Adams and Gathercole (1995) related a combined phonological memory score, based on both digit span and nonword repetition, to measures of productive vocabulary, sentence length, and syntax from the spontaneous speech samples of 3-year-old children. Children with high phonological memory scores produced a larger set of word types, longer sentences in terms of MLU in morphemes, and sentences with greater syntactic complexity as compared to children with low memory scores, with nonverbal ability (puzzle solving) scores covaried. Thus, syntax and morphology, as well as vocabulary, were found to be associated with phonological memory. According to Speidel (1993), the ability to hold phonological sequences in short-term memory is essential in order to acquire a corpus of patterns from which to learn syntactic rules. However, in Adams and Gathercole's study, relationships between memory and syntax disappeared when articulation rate was partialed out.

For 5-year-olds, in contrast, articulation rate was not a significant contributor, over and above age, nonverbal cognitive ability, and vocabulary knowledge, to sentence length in a narrative. Neither was a combined memory score based on word span and digit span, although nonword repetition scores did account for a small but significant amount of additional variance (3.5%) (Adams & Gathercole, 1996).

Finally, Gathercole, Hitch, Service, and Martin (1997) examined directly the relationship between memory and the learning of new words in a word–nonword paired associate task, as well as the recall of new words and definitions from a story. In 5.5-year-olds, digit span and nonword repetition scores were correlated with word–nonword associative learning and with recall of new (nonsense) words; only nonword repetition was correlated with recall of new word definitions. Correlations with nonword repetition disappeared, however, when vocabulary knowledge scores were partialed out because these two measures were highly correlated. This was not true of correlations with digit span. The authors concluded that digit span may be a purer measure of memory capacity than nonword repetition because the phonological loop and the processes of learning the sound structure of new words operate in a highly reciprocal manner. Thus, by 5 years of age, according to this study and to the one by Gathercole (1995), vocabulary knowledge becomes "the pacemaker in the relationship between nonword repetition and vocabulary acquisition" (Gathercole & Baddeley, 1993, p. 51).

This series of studies shows a relationship between memory and both vocabulary acquisition and sentence production in children between 3 and 5 years of age. In fact, Gathercole (1995) made a case for the causal contribution of phonological memory to vocabulary acquisition. The rationale for the specifically phonological nature of the memory storage lies in the fact that *non*word repetition must tap primarily phonological forms of representation. To the degree that digit span also predicts the same language measures, however, the term *phonological memory* may be too restrictive.

Bowey (1996) argued that it is phonological processing or phonological sensitivity, and not memory, that accounts for the relationship between nonword repetition accuracy and vocabulary acquisition. She gave a very large sample of 5.5-year-olds several tasks: a sound identity task, in which they selected the picture depicting a word with the same final sound as a given word; a rhyme oddity task in which they selected the word that did *not* rhyme with two other rhyming words; the nonword repetition task; a digit span task; a receptive vocabulary measure (the PPVT); and a test of morphology. The two measures of phonological sensitivity, sound identity and rhyme oddity, each con- tributed significantly to variance in receptive vocabulary after age ar.d nonverbal ability (block design) were controlled. Only digit span accounted for further variance beyond that accounted for by all these variables; nonword repetition did not. When these two memory scores were entered before the phonological sensitivity scores, the measures of phonological sensitivity still accounted for further additional variance. For the morphology test scores, only sound identity and digit span accounted for additional variance above that contributed by age and nonverbal ability. Bowey concluded that phonological sensitivity is as strongly associated with the language measures as phonological mem- ory. She further argued that digit span is a better measure of phono- logical memory than nonword repetition. Both phonological sensitivity and phonological memory are said to "reflect a latent phonological processing ability, possibly the clarity of underlying phonological rep- resentations of speech," and thus they explain "overlapping propor- tions of variance in receptive language" (Bowey, 1996, p. 75). This argument highlights a basic difficulty in separating processing from memory components in any domain. Although it is possible to devise a perceptual measure that does not tap memory, it is quite difficult to devise a pure measure of memory that does not include a perceptual or processing component. Thus, phonological memory measures would inevitably tap also phonological sensitivity and share a great deal of variance with such measures, more so than the reverse. Gathercole and Baddely (1997) further criticized Bowey's conclusions about the non- word repetition task on methodological grounds.

Much of the research directed at the relationship between memory and language focuses on children with SLI. This particular disability is of interest because although children with SLI are thought to have a language deficit without a deficit in nonverbal intelligence, some researchers believe, nevertheless, that they *do* have a deficit in process- ing and memory abilities. Children with SLI do have difficulty with the temporal processing of brief, rapidly sequenced events in both the audi- tory and visual modalities until about age 7 or 8 years, when the diffi- culty persists only for auditory stimuli (Stark & Tallal, 1988).

Furthermore, performance of 6-year-old SLI children on a nonverbal sequencing test predicted their comprehension of semantically reversible SVO (subject–verb–object) sentences, in which the order of these constituents in speech was crucial to understanding. It did not predict their comprehension of other types of sentences (Curtiss & Tallal, 1991). Children with SLI were four times slower than their non-impaired peers in the sequential scanning of digits in memory in a Sternberg-type task (Sininger, Klatzky, & Kirchner, 1989). This task is similar to the SPR task discussed in the nonhuman primate section of this chapter. Subjects are presented with a sequence of stimuli and then a probe that they judge to be same or different with respect to the items in the original list. Thus, processing of stimulus sequences is clearly implicated in this impairment.

Memory for item location can also be deficient in SLI children. They underperformed NL children in a task in which a probe card was matched to its facedown counterpart (Raine, Hulme, Chadderton, & Bailey, 1991). They were also less able than their peers to reproduce the locations of targets in an array after an 8-second delay (Wyke & Asso, 1979).

Many studies of the memory abilities of SLI children have involved repetition tasks with sentences, words, and nonwords. Menyuk and Looney (1976) found that SLI children between 4 and 8 years of age made more errors in sentence imitation tasks than did non-SLI children between 4 and 5 years, particularly on longer sentences (four and five words) and on negative and interrogative sentences. Repetition of lists of unrelated words has also revealed differences between SLI and non-SLI children. Gathercole and Baddeley (1990) gave lists of words to six SLI children between 7 and 9 years of age who then put pictures depicting the words in the same sequential order in which they had heard the words (a subtest of the Goldman–Fristoe–Woodcock Auditory Skills Test Battery). The SLI children differed from the norms for this test by a mean of 32 months. When phonologically similar and phonologically dissimilar lists of words were presented to these children using a similar procedure, they did not differ from NL controls in terms of their performance on dissimilar lists, at least up to five words in length. One comparison group was matched to the SLI children on the Raven's Progressive Coloured Matrices, and these children were 1 year younger than the SLI children. A second comparison group was matched on receptive vocabulary and reading scores, and they were 2 years younger than the SLI group. All groups did worse on phonologically similar lists than on dissimilar lists, and this finding is interpreted as indicating that SLI children also encode items phonologically.

Van der Lely and Howard (1993) also found comparable effects of phonological similarity across SLI children and matched controls but no differences in word span, whether the response was verbal or non-verbal (pointing to pictures). The sample of SLI children was again small (six), although van der Lely and Howard (1993) matched their SLI children to three different comparison groups on the basis of three different language measures. Nevertheless, with only six SLI children, their ability to detect true differences in this study was reduced, given that the spans of the SLI children were lower but not significantly lower than those of controls (see also Gathercole & Baddeley, 1995).

Gathercole and Baddeley (1990) also found that SLI children were significantly poorer in nonword repetition than were controls, particularly for three- and four-syllable nonwords. They did not differ from their peers in rate of articulation nor in correct discrimination of CVC word pairs and nonword pairs differing in one phoneme. These findings are interpreted as ruling out an explanation of the memory deficit in SLI children in terms of either speed of articulation or phonological processing. In a slightly older group of language-disordered children with central auditory processing difficulties, phoneme discrimination for nonword pairs, but not for word pairs, was comparable to that for LM controls (James, van Steenbrugge, & Chiveralls, 1994). Articulation rate and the effect of phonological similarity were found again to be similar across groups. The language-disordered group showed poorer repetition of nonwords, but again, only for three- and four-syllable nonwords. The researchers interpret their results as showing that these language-disordered children have a reduced capacity in phonological memory storage and poor phonological processing. Their phoneme discrimination is comparable to that of LM controls, however, at least for nonwords.

The nonword repetition difference for three- and four-syllable nonwords was replicated by Montgomery (1995) in a comparison between SLI children and younger LM children, with receptive vocabulary covaried. Again, this difference in nonword repetition was not attributable to differences in articulation rate or in phonological encoding. However, SLI children showed poorer discrimination of four-syllable nonword pairs than controls. Thus, these results imply that SLI children have both a perceptual processing and a memory problem, although their discrimination of stimuli simpler than four-syllable pairs seems unaffected. All of these researchers have underlined the point made earlier that the distinction between perceptual and memory processes is not always well defined in current models of memory.

Our Research on Memory and Language

Our research on the relationship between memory and language was directed first at determining the types of memory that are related to language abilities in normally developing children. The first type of memory investigated was memory for spatial position in which we used a position probe task based on a task developed by Atkinson, Hansen, and Bernbach (1964) and similar to the task described above used by Raine et al. (1991). In our task, animal pictures were presented one at a time and then placed facedown in a horizontal row. Above this row, in the center, a probe card was then placed faceup, and the child was asked to find the matching facedown card. Test trials began with a sequence of two animal pictures, and the sequence was increased by one picture as long as the child performed above chance. Memory span was the longest sequence for which at least half of the trials were correct. This task was given to 27 children, 10 boys and 17 girls, ranging in age from 18 to 44 months. A speech sample was also recorded while the child played with a set of small toys provided by the experimenter; these children spoke only English at home. The MLU in morphemes was determined on the speech samples, and our rules for MLU involved a precision and extension of the sketchy rules outlined in Brown (1973). The changes particularly resulted in the crediting of more irregular forms, thus making MLU a more suitable measure for older preschool children (see Blake & Quartaro, 1990; Blake et al., 1993). A measure of semantic complexity was also applied to the speech samples. This measure was derived primarily from case grammar as described in Fillmore (1968) and determined the number of semantic categories related in an utterance (Table 7–1). Unlike Fillmore, we distinguished *dative, genitive,* and *experiencer* to reflect their apparently separate functions in child language (Brown, 1973). We considered it important to include modifiers also in a measure of the complexity of young children's language These were taken from Ramer (1977), except that *demonstrative* she called *explicit deixis.* We added the *purposive* category.

This measure of semantic complexity was highly correlated with MLU ($r = .88$; $p < .001$). Memory spans on the position probe task

Table 7–1. Semantic Categories with Examples from Child Language

---

Agentive: *I* put it.
Locative: The lady sit on the *table*.
Instrumental: I can't hold it with the *handle*.
Essive: This is a *train*.
Comitative: I go with *Mommy*.
Objective: Throw *ball*.
Benefactive: I put it for *you*.
Factitive: *They*'re made out of paper.
Temporal: I'm gonna see her *next week*.
Dative: Talk to your *mom* about it.
Genitive: *I* have that toy.
Experiencer: The *lady* want a cracker.
Attributive: *little* boys
Quantitative: *two* bags
Recurrence: *another* car
Manner: Put it the *right way*.
Demonstrative: Don't chase *that* bird away.
Purposive: This is *for baking*.

---

were moderately but significantly related to the language measures ($r = .37$, $p < .05$ for MLU and $r = .39$, $p < .05$ for semantic complexity), but these correlations were not independent of age.

The second type of memory investigated was memory for a visual array. The same sample of children was shown an array of objects, the array was screened, and one object was removed. The screen was then lifted, and the child was asked to name the missing object. A smaller set of objects was used for children who could not label all the objects in a pretest. Trials began with two-object arrays, which increased by one object as long as the child was correct on half of the trials at a given array size. Memory span was again the largest array size for which at least half of the trials were correct. Scores on this missing object task were significantly related to semantic complexity ($r = .41$; $p < .05$) but only tended to be related to MLU ($r = .36$; $p > .05$). Regression analyses indicated that the relation between missing object scores and semantic complexity was not independent of age for the whole sample but was for the younger group of 12 children under 30 months ($F = 6.01$; $p < .04$). In fact, for this group, missing object scores accounted for 20% of the variance in semantic complexity beyond that accounted for by age (Blake, Quartaro, Austin, & Vingilis, 1989). Means and standard deviations for the younger and older groups on the memory and language measures are given in Table 7–2.

Because of the small size of the group for which the relationship between missing object scores and semantic complexity was found, a second experiment was conducted. The children in this sample of children also spoke only English at home but were more heterogeneous in their background. Thus, although the younger group of 14 children in this sample was close to the age of the older group in the previous sample, ranging in age from 32 to 41 months, their mean semantic complexity and MLU were in between the scores of the younger and older groups of the first experiment, as was their mean missing object memory span. Table 7–3 gives the means for all the language and memory measures administered in this experiment by age group. The older group in the second experiment contained 17 children, ranging in age from 44 to 59 months. For the whole sample of children, missing object scores were significantly correlated with MLU ($r = .47; p < .01$), but this correlation was not independent of age. Only for the younger

Table 7–2. Means and Standard Deviations in Memory and Language Measures for Younger and Older Children in Experiment 1

	Younger Group: 18–29 Mo. (N = 12)	Older Group: 30–44 Mo. (N = 15)
Missing object		
Means	2.08	3.13
SD	0.67	1.12
Position probe		
Means	3.30	3.64
SD	0.85	0.99
Semantic complexity		
Means	2.84	3.38
SD	0.46	0.24
MLU[a]		
Means	2.86	4.57
SD	0.96	0.78

[a] MLU = mean length of utterance.

Table 7-3. Means and Standard Deviations in Memory and Language Measures for Younger and Older Children in Experiment 2

	Younger Group: 32–41 Mo. (N = 14)	Older Group: 44–59 Mo. (N = 17)
Missing object		
Means	2.60	4.50
SD	0.63	1.92
Word span		
Means	3.14	3.47
SD	0.66	0.72
Semantic complexity		
Means	3.13	3.64
SD	0.39	0.51
MLU[a]		
Means	3.38	4.78
SD	0.84	0.73
Sentence imitation		
Means	36.87	52.09
SD	15.33	19.58

[a] MLU = mean length of utterance.

group of children did missing object scores predict MLU independently of age ($t = 2.76$; $p < .02$), accounting for 26% of the variance in MLU in addition to that accounted for by age. Missing object scores also tended to predict semantic complexity independently of age ($t = 2.06$; $p < .06$) in the younger group and accounted for 24% of the variance in semantic complexity beyond that attributable to age (Blake et al., 1989).

The third type of memory investigated was sequential auditory memory, namely, word span (Blake, Austin, Cannon, Lisus, & Vaughan, 1994, experiment 1). The children in the second experiment above heard a list of animal names that they were told to repeat. Trials began again with lists of two names, and the lists increased by one name as long as the child repeated one of three lists of a given length correctly in correct order. Memory span was the longest list for which two of three trials were correct.

In addition to MLU and semantic complexity based on spontaneous speech, these children's language ability was also measured with a sentence imitation task consisting of 22 sentences that varied in number of words, number of simple semantic propositions, number of phrases, and type of syntactic structure (see Blake, Austin, Cannon, & Vaughan, 1994, experiment 1). Repetition scores were based on the proportions of words, propositions, phrases, and syntactic structure retained; these proportions were then summed, the maximum score being 88.

For the whole sample, word span was highly correlated with sentence imitation ($r = .67$; $p < .0001$) but not with semantic complexity or MLU. Missing object scores were also correlated with sentence imitation scores ($r = .42$; $p < .05$) (Blake et al., 1989). However, regression analyses showed that only age and word span were significant independent predictors of sentence imitation scores for the whole sample ($t = 3.20$; $p < .003$ for word span). For the younger group of 14 children, word span and age together accounted for 54% of the variance in MLU, although neither was an independent predictor.

A third experiment was conducted to determine if the relationship between memory and language measures might be mediated by IQ. In this experiment, 23 children ranging in age from 23 to 38 months and all speaking only English at home were given the missing-object and word-span tasks, with the passing criterion on both tasks 50% of trials correct at a given array size or length. A speech sample was again recorded and scored for MLU and semantic complexity. In addition, the Merrill–Palmer Scale of Mental Tests (Stutsman, 1948) was administered. For this group, missing-object scores were correlated with both MLU ($r = .42$; $p < .05$) and semantic complexity ($r = .43$; $p < .05$) but not independently of age and mental age (Blake et al., 1989). Word span scores were more highly correlated with both MLU ($r = .66$; $p < .001$) and semantic complexity ($r = .56$; $p < .01$) than either age or mental age. Word span, in fact, was the only significant predictor of MLU ($t = 2.44$; $p < .02$) (Blake, Austin, Cannon, Lisus, & Vaughan, 1994, experiment 2). The mean word span for this group was 3.04 (SD = 0.77), and the mean MLU was 2.96 (SD = 0.80). Age, mental age, and word span together significantly accounted for 39% of the variance in semantic complexity ($F = 3.99$; $p < .02$), but none was a significant independent predictor. Similar results were obtained for semantic complexity in the equation with age, mental age, and missing-object scores.

Across these experiments, the findings demonstrate that for normally developing preschool children, spatial memory (as measured by the position probe task) is not related to productive language complexity except insofar as it is correlated with age. Memory for an array of objects involving the labeling of a missing object is moderately related to productive language, particularly to semantic complexity in the early stages of language acquisition. This relationship is not always independent of age or mental age, however. Memory for a list of words in sequence predicts sentence imitation independently of age across a wide preschool age range, whereas it predicts MLU better than age and mental age at the early stages of syntax. Although both word span and sentence imitation are repetition tasks, and in that sense similar, sentence imitation involves related words and knowledge of syntax, at least for correct repetition of the longer, more complex sentences. Furthermore, the strong relation between word span and the length of *spontaneous* sentences clearly indicates a quite general relationship between this measure of memory and early language. That children at later stages of language development no longer show a relation between word span and spontaneous language complexity is probably due to a greater automaticity of language programming.

If a relation between word span and spoken language complexity is entirely attributable to rate of articulation (Hulme, Thomson, Muir, & Lawrence, 1984), we should then expect a continuing relationship between word span and MLU in older children. In experiment 2, they were not related in the older group. Furthermore, the failure of articulation rate to explain differences between SLI children and matched normally developing children in the studies previously reviewed casts doubt on the usefulness of this factor.

In an attempt to compare primacy and recency effects in these children to the results for nonhuman primates presented in the first part of this chapter, serial position curves were plotted for the four-item series of the word span task separately for the 31 children in the second experiment (ranging in age from 32 to 59 months) and for the 14 children in the third experiment who completed the four-item trials (ranging in age from 28 to 38 months). These are plotted in Figure 7–4. The children in the two experiments overlap slightly in age but are labeled *old* (from experiment 2) and *young* (from experiment 3) on the graph. It should be kept in mind that these children had very few trials for each item length compared with the monkeys (three in experiment 2 and four in experiment 3). The figure appears to show a primacy effect for the older children and a recency effect for both older and younger children. This is what one would expect if the older preschool children are beginning to rehearse. In fact, for the older group, performance on position 1 only tended to be superior to position 3, $t(30) = 1.76$, $p <$

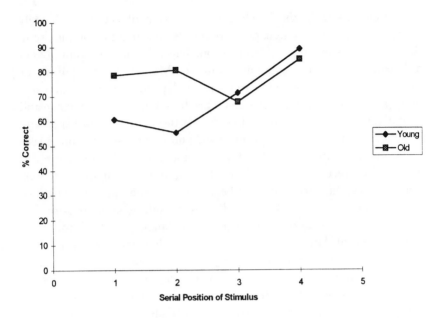

Figure 7–4: Mean percent correct recall of old versus young groups on four serial positions.

.09, but not to position 2. Performance on position 4 was significantly
superior to that on position 3, t (30) = 3.97, $p < .0001$. For the younger
group, performance on position 4 was superior to that on position 2, t
(13) = 3.98, $p < .002$. For the older children's curve, the quadratic component was significant, F (1, 30) = 7.45, $p < .01$, whereas for the
younger children's curve, the linear component was significant, F (1,13)
= 8.60, $p < .012$. Performance on the five-item trials is plotted only for
the 22 children in experiment 2 who completed this series. In Figure
7–5, the quadratic nature of the curve for this longer series is apparent,
with what seems to be a primacy effect for the first item presented and
a recency effect for the last. Although the quadratic component was
significant, F (1, 21) = 11.54, $p < .003$, and performance on position 5
was significantly superior to that on both position 3, t (21) = 3.47, $p <
.002$, and position 4, t (21) = 2.49, $p < .021$, performance on position
1 just tended to be superior to that on position 3, t (21) = 1.86, $p < .08$.
Thus, despite the significant quadratic component for both the four-
item and the five-item series, the older children did not yet show a clear
primacy effect, unlike the monkeys. Both groups of children did show
clear recency effects.

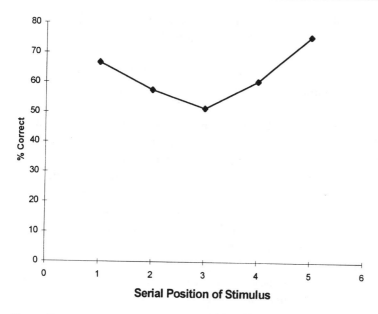

Figure 7–5: Mean percent correct recall of older group on five serial positions.

It is notable that these children overwhelmingly reported the items in order; their errors consisted of substitutions or omissions. Thus, there was no tendency to report the last item first, for example. A typical protocol for the word list *fox, sheep, bear, frog, fish* would be *fox, bear, fish*. Across the 66 five-item trials for these 22 children, only 5 contained a reversal of order. Across the 93 four-item trials in experiment 2, only 5 trials again contained reversals.

We have also administered these three memory tasks – position probe, missing object, and word span – to 14 preschool SLI children between 3 and 5 years and to 14 NL children matched individually to each SLI child on sex, on chronological age (CA; within 3 months), and on nonverbal mental age (MA; within 3 months) based on the Leiter International Performance Scale (Arthur, 1952; Kushnir & Blake, 1996). The SLI children had scores on both the Expressive and the Receptive Language Scales of the Reynell that were significantly lower than those of controls, but their language age on the receptive scale was not delayed. The memory tasks were administered using the same procedures as those described above except that the criterion for passing a position probe and missing object series at a given size was three of five trials. Also, on the missing-object task, a pail was used to cover the item that the child was to name. Again, no objects were used that a child could not label. The SLI children had significantly lower scores than their matched counterparts in missing-object and word-span scores but not in position-probe scores. The MLU was again determined from spontaneous speech samples. Across both groups of children, position-probe scores were unrelated to MLU, to Reynell Expressive scores, or to Reynell Receptive scores. Regression analyses determined that word span was the only significant predictor of MLU ($t = 4.75$; $p < .0001$), accounting for .58 of the variance, and of Reynell Expressive scores ($t = 3.17$; $p < .004$), accounting for .50 of the variance. Mental age and missing object scores did not account for a significant amount of variance in either productive language measure. Mental age was correlated with Reynell Receptive scores ($r = .61$; $p < .001$), and so were both missing-object scores ($r = .67$; $p < .001$) and word span ($r = .70$; $p < .001$). Again, memory as measured by the word-span task was the best predictor of spontaneous productive language complexity. In this study, word span was also the best predictor of standardized expressive language scores.

In contrast to the results of Raine et al. (1991) and Wyke & Asso (1979), SLI children in this study were not deficient in position memory. Our position-probe task differed from both of the tasks used in these earlier studies in that sequential responding was not required.

When 13 of the SLI children in this study were matched post hoc on MLU to younger children with normal language from the third experiment described above, the SLI children were still significantly lower on word span ($t = 2.52$; $p < .03$) but not on missing-object scores. These findings as a whole, then, clearly implicate auditory sequential memory in the language deficit of SLI children.

In a recent study (Mason, 1997), we examined whether it was the auditory or sequential aspect of the word-span task that was critical to SLI. Thirteen older SLI children between 5 and 9 years of age were matched to a CA/MA control group and to a younger LM group. MA was based on the Leiter and language matching on the Reynell or the Test of Language Development. We gave all three groups the same word-span task described above plus a visual analogue in which pictures of the same animals named in the word-span task were presented one at a time and placed facedown. The child was then shown an array of the animal pictures and asked to point to the pictures she/he had seen in order. This task was thus similar to the position-probe task in terms of picture presentation but different in response requirements. The child had to remember *what* she/he had seen (in order) and not simply *where* a picture was located. The visual-span task turned out to be more difficult than the auditory-span task for all groups, perhaps because of interference from the other response items. It is apparent from Figure 7–6 that all groups performed similarly on the visual task, whereas the SLI children were deficient on the auditory task compared with both control groups. The difference in auditory memory between the SLI children and the CA/MA controls was significant – t (12) = 2.52, p < .03; the difference between the SLI children and LM controls was not. If these results are not simply due to a floor effect on the visual task, they imply that it is *not* the sequential nature but the auditory nature of the word-span task that is critical.

The fact that these SLI children do not differ significantly from LM controls in auditory memory in this study is in agreement with the findings of van der Lely and Howard (1993). However, in both studies, SLI children do underperform their LM counterparts. Whereas one might argue from our findings, as van der Lely and Howard did, that language level is the crucial factor in auditory memory performance, it is notable that in our study, the LM controls were much younger (by a mean age difference of 20 months) than their matched SLI counterparts. Thus, more of them were in preschool and did not yet have avail-

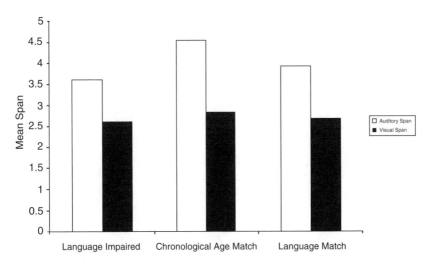

Figure 7–6: Mean auditory memory span and mean visual memory span for specifically language-impaired children, their chronological age–/mental age–matched group, and their language-matched group.

able to them the memory strategies that elementary school children typically use in these tasks.

Conclusions

At this point it seems unlikely that there is a general relationship between memory and language; there appears to be a more specific one between auditory memory and productive language. The fact that monkeys have such difficulty with auditory memory tasks underlines again its potential importance as a precursor for language, although we need more information about the great apes. At any rate, it is clear that spatial memory, although obviously critical for survival, has little bearing on language. Visual memory for an array may have some relationship to language, particularly its semantic aspects, and, one assumes, the visual aspects of communication (gestures), though the last relationship remains to be established.

There is a lack of research relating *delayed* imitation directly to language acquisition, although we know that immediate vocal imitation (accommodation) as stressed by Locke (1993) and Nottebohm (1975) is clearly important. Nonhuman primates are capable of the former but not of the latter, at least in any extensive way.

CHAPTER EIGHT

Origins of Language

There is an abundance of hypotheses about the origins of language. In this chapter, I examine some of them and attempt to relate them to the research findings that have been reviewed in the previous chapters. Although the field is often – necessarily – speculative, new findings about the brain have enabled some progress beyond speculation. The hypotheses I address here are focused on brain–body ratio and brain structure, gestures, cognitive culture, information donation, symbolic reference, and the "hopeful monster" theory (the label applied by Deacon, 1997, to the Chomskian theory of language origins).

Brain–Body Ratio and Brain Structure

The brain–body ratio in humans greatly exceeds that in nonhuman primates (although not apparently that in mice and other small mammals [Deacon, 1997]). Although prenatal brain growth in humans follows the typical primate pattern, it grows more than would be expected after birth, but body growth is truncated. If our bodies had continued along the ape ratio, we would be giants. Most of the "extra" brain is an expansion of the prefrontal cortex, with the human cerebellum also displaying a proportionate increase in size (Elman et al., 1996). Recently, the role of both of these areas in language has been emphasized. Most proponents of the brain–body ratio hypothesis of language origin view the increase in this ratio as causal in the evolution of language. Species with a greater ratio have more brain free for nonsomatic functions – that is, cognitive ones. Deacon (1997) has presented a different, novel outlook on the relationship. For him, it is not just a question of an increase in capacity as it is for Gibson (1990). According to Deacon, the shift in growth toward a larger cerebral cortex and cerebellum must occur early in neuroembryogenesis, because both structures originate from the dorsal side of the neural tube. In fetal development, the relative proportions of peripheral and central nervous system structures are altered in humans, what Deacon has called displacement. This results in altered connection patterns because in the competition for axons and synapses, larger neuronal populations will recruit more afferent and efferent connections. The expanded numbers of cortical axons should then mean more recruitment of targets in lower systems during development. For example, the prefrontal cortex, although having no apparent sensory or motor function, contains projections back to every modality, including the limbic cortex, basal ganglia, and midbrain. It also has expanded interconnectivity with cerebellar systems, making them part of vocal–auditory control processes. The cerebellum appears to be important in timing and may play a role in rapid, semiautomatic language processes; it is probably more involved with sound analysis in humans than in other species (Deacon, 1997). Most importantly, because of displacement, cortical axons should recruit more brain stem and spinal cord targets, particularly face and tongue muscle nuclei and visceral muscle nuclei. The latter include motor neurons that control the larynx and breathing. According to Deacon (1997, p. 250), "the human ability to speak is probably a consequence of all these systems being brought under common cortical control" – that is, facial and tongue muscles, laryngeal movements, and respiration.

Call production in nonhuman primates is subject to some cortical control from the anterior cingulate cortex, located between the limbic cortex and the neocortex, but this is limited to inhibition of calling or relaxation of such inhibition (see chapter 1). Although human laryngeal movements also are under the control of the visceral muscle systems (limbic), for humans (as for birds and cetaceans) the skeletal muscle control system is largely in charge, allowing flexibility, learning, and intentional control, according to Deacon. This shift in control of vocalizations away from emotional (limbic) systems, as well as cerebellar input into the rapidity of vocal–auditory processes, is reflected in the differences in vocal production between nonhuman primates and human infants discussed in chapter 1. The hypothesis of displacement as a cause of greater cortical control in human development needs further confirmation, however.

Deacon has suggested that if the shift in brain–body ratio itself can be seen as implicating greater cortical control over vocal–auditory processes, particularly greater involvement of the prefrontal cortex, then vocal skills emerged first in *Homo habiles* (called Early *Homo* in Figure 8–1) at least 2 million years ago, because they are the first hominids to exhibit the shift in brain–body ratio. According to Deacon (1997), however, other precursors of language, namely symbolic communication, emerged earlier and brought about the shift, setting the pace for language evolution. Thus, the brain–body ratio shift for Deacon is not causal but a result of an emerging symbolic function. Elman et al. (1996) have also argued that experience brings about specialization of regions of the brain for various aspects of language (see chapter 6).

Gestures

The gestural theory of language origin, that language is based on a gestural substrate, has been widely embraced. According to Hewes (1973,

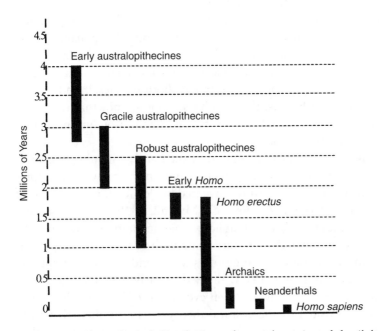

Figure 8–1: Chronological distribution of named species of fossil hominids. From Noble, W., and Davidson, I. (1996). *Human evolution, language and mind: A psychological and archaeological enquiry.* Figure 25. Cambridge, UK: Cambridge University Press. Reprinted with permission of Cambridge University Press.

p. 11), "manual communication . . . may come closer to representing the deep cognitive structure on which not only language but all of our intellectual and technological achievements rest." Although not denying that early hominids had a vocal call system, similar to the nonhuman primate call systems reviewed in chapters 1 and 2, Hewes did not view these calls as the "initial pathway to propositional communication" (p. 6). He cited as evidence for the primacy of gestures the fact that Broca's area seems to have been involved originally in precise sequential manual control (compare Greenfield, 1991). According to Hewes (1989, p. 303), modern humans, and to some extent other primates, have innate neural pathways "prefigured to receive and imitate visual information about . . . digital and manual movements." The link between the manual gesture system and vocal sounds is via the mouth gesture, and the impetus for the change to vocal communication is its increased capacity for vocabulary, increased speed of transmission, freeing of the hands for other labor, and capability of transmission in the dark and across greater distances.

Armstrong, Stokoe, and Wilcox (1995) stressed also the importance of visible and articulatory gestures as the roots of language. When bipedal locomotion freed the forelimbs for gesturing, this became a critical link between cognitive concepts and language in that gesture enabled "a set of signs for naming things, both to oneself and to others" (p. 228). Like Hewes, these authors proposed not that there was ever a mute, strictly manual gesture stage in hominid evolution but that visible gestures took the lead.

It seems reasonable to presume that such early "naming" gestures would have been similar to the symbolic gestures reviewed in chapter 4 and to the pantomimic gestures invented by deaf children deprived of sign language (Goldin-Meadow & Mylander, 1984). The studies reviewed in chapters 3 and 4 indicate that in human ontogeny, the majority of communicative gestures emerge before symbolic gestures and that most communicative gestures are found also in present-day nonhuman primates. It is likely, then, that early hominids first used communicative gestures, which then evolved into the symbolic "naming" gestures posited by the gestural theory. It is also likely that early communicative gestures were accompanied by vocalizations, as they are very soon after emergence in human infants and possibly in chimpanzees (Goodall, 1986). By *Homo erectus*, the vocal apparatus had changed sufficiently that humanlike speech was possible (Lieberman, 1984). Thus, only before this era is it likely that gestures were accompanied by simple calls, such as grunts. All australopithecines were bipedal (King, 1994), so it is possible that gestures plus calling originated with the australopithecines, prior to articulate speech. The equipotentiality that we now have for developing language in gesture and/or speech (Petitto, 1995) makes it likely that both modalities evolved in parallel, though it is certainly possible that in evolution the dominant modality shifted over time.

Interestingly, Darwin, as pointed out by Donald (1991), did not subscribe to the gestural theory despite his stress on continuity across species in facial expressions and postural signaling. Instead, as mentioned in chapter 1, he saw vocalization, particularly as expressed in rudimentary song, as the root of language. According to Donald (1991), Darwin believed that early hominids progressed from voluntary modulation of emotive sound (prosody) to vocal imitation of animals and other humans.

Opposition to the gestural theory is also found in more recent theories that make an abrupt distinction between verbal and nonverbal communication. For example, Burling (1993, p. 26) stated that "human language is almost as different from human nonverbal communication as it is from primate communication." Although admitting continuity between the nonhuman primate (and mammalian) gesture–call system and human nonverbal communication, he does not consider it plausible that language evolved from a gesture–call system. Locke (1993) posited two distinct modules in his dual specialization hypothesis, one for grammatical analysis and one for social cognition. Social cognition incorporates such important precursors as shared gaze, vocal turntaking, and vocal accommodation; it "preorients infants to the social and facial–vocal cues associated with speaking" (p. 357). Somewhat reminiscent of Darwin, Locke believes that the facial–vocal transmission of feeling and empathy is a biological imperative that has dictated our vocal (phonological) modality of language. Presumably, there is continuity with regard to this module to the extent that the precursors are present in other species. This social cognition module can holistically process and produce phonetic sounds, words, and stereotyped phrases. Abstract phonological rules and productive syntax belong in the module dedicated to grammatical analysis, for which precursors are not apparently relevant and therefore neither is continuity.

The gestural theory has the advantage of a close connection to a cognitive base. Such a connection can be seen also in the next three approaches, cognitive culture, information donation, and symbolic reference.

Mimetic to Mythic Culture

Similar to the gestural theory of language origin, Donald (1991) presented a view of the evolution of culture in which "elaborate systems of gestural symbolism might have preceded the speech adaptation" (p. 225). Like Noble and Davidson (1996; see below), he pointed to the fact that the originators of gestural signs had no models and had to create them de novo. Prior to this invention, the cognitive culture, both of apes and of the earliest hominids, was characterized as episodic – that is bound to concrete episodes. Donald suggested that with *H. erectus,* the cognitive culture became mimetic, allowing the invention of intentional, nonlinguistic representations to reenact an event. The primary form of mimetic expression is visuomotor; it involves postures, facial expressions, and gestures and not an arbitrary set of symbols. The facial musculature of *H. erectus* differed from that of australopithecines (Lieberman, 1984), such that the range of possible expressions was probably greater. Another form of mimesis is vocal, and "vocal mimesis would have allowed the self-cued regeneration of remembered utterances and their subsequent modification" (Donald, 1991, p. 183). Such vocal mimesis implicates also a vocal reproductive memory system and a process of rehearsal. Donald stressed that as part of speech adaptation, a new auditory adaptation was required. There had to be an increase in specialized auditory memory and a feedback mechanism for speech output. A necessary part of this adaptation was an articulatory (phonological) loop, as discussed in chapter 7, allowing for short-term storage and rehearsal. The most likely location of the mimetic controller is said to be in the prefrontal cortex, and this hypothesis is in line with the general emphasis of others (Deacon, 1997; Elman et al., 1996) on the importance of the prefrontal cortex in the evolution of language.

Donald situates the beginning of language somewhat earlier than 50,000 years ago when *Homo sapiens* appeared (at least in Europe, Asia, and Australia). In his view, it was a collective invention based on themes derived from concrete episodes. The primary focus was on thematic content, and this can still be seen in the myths that permeate everyday life in surviving Stone Age cultures. Like Wynn (1993), Donald postulated that most tool-use skills are transmitted to apprentices through mimetic modeling and that the use of language in this domain has always been limited. In evolution, language was most importantly a response to selective pressures to improve conceptual models about the universe. In modern culture, language and mimesis occur in parallel and are dissociable because "mimesis forms the core of an ancient root-culture" that is the logical basis of later culture (Donald, 1991, p. 189).

Although this is a compelling and intriguing view of the evolution of language, there is one problem, at least, in the depiction of mimetic culture. From the evidence presented in the last chapter on delayed imitation in rehabilitant orangutans from Russon (1996), it seems clear that mimetic culture is not restricted to humans. The repeated reenactments observed in these orangutans are clearly mimetic. Thus, although apes cannot be granted a mythic culture, apes who have some exposure to human culture can acquire a mimetic one. Whether they can do so without such exposure remains an open question, partly because the behaviors that unenculturated apes choose to reenact are often those which are prototypical for the species and thus possibly subject to genetic control. For example, Goodall (1986) described some infant chimpanzees reenacting slap-stamp elements of a charging display they had just observed in an adult chimpanzee. Because enactment of portions of a later species-typic behavior might be a reflection of a fixed-action pattern, this example apparently cannot be considered mimetic (Byrne, personal communication, 1996). Nevertheless, it seems likely that mimesis is not beyond the ability of unenculturated apes, although it may not always have a clear communicative function. This is also true of early mimesis in children.

Information Donation

The information donation theory of language origins (King, 1994) is focused on information transmission specifically directed from adults to immatures. According to King, information donation is implied by certain fossil findings. For example, the evidence of home-base activity during the period of late *H. erectus* suggests significant adult–immature hominid food sharing, which probably made information exchange important. Food sharing is found in nonhuman primates: Orangutan mothers put chewed food on their hands and then move their hands near the mouths of young infants; bonobo mothers strip skin from sugarcane and then hold it in their mouths until their young take it (King,

1994). King pointed out that after the development of home bases in hominid evolution, however, food sharing was probably no longer restricted to mothers and their offspring. An increase in information donation is also suggested by changes in the material culture, namely, hominid art and possibly tools with a standard form.

There were two turning points for information donation, according to King. First, like Parker and Gibson (1979), King stressed changes in foraging by both chimpanzees and early hominids, as compared to monkeys and other apes (but see Fox et al., 1999, discussed in chapter 5). The shift to dependence on embedded foods required "a significant investment by immatures in acquiring foraging skills and the information on which those skills depend" (p. 119). King emphasized similarities between chimpanzees and australopithecines in their tools and extractive foraging techniques and in their juvenile periods. The second shift applies only to hominid evolution and is seen in the material evidence from *H. erectus*. Despite her focus on these two important shifts, King held that "quantitative rather than qualitative differences exist in social information transfer across primate species" (p. 131). Evolutionary change in information donation is thus a matter of degree.

As discussed in chapter 3, gestures that share information – that is, comment gestures such as point and show – are precisely those gestures which are *not* found in wild apes. They *are* found in apes raised in a human environment (Miles, 1990). Why apes have the capacity to share information with manual gestures only when interacting with humans remains an interesting question (compare King, 1994, p. 134). Although one can argue that they share information nonverbally in the wild (e.g., by orienting themselves in the direction of incipient movement) and that the young learn to forage by observation, intentional and specifically directed information donation appears to be rare. Even in chimpanzees, clear observations of adult teaching – for example, in how to crack nuts – are very sparse, as discussed in chapter 5.

The case for information donation with regard to important signals in monkeys – for example, warning about predators reviewed in chapter 2 – depends on showing that they are directed by adults to immatures (King, 1994). One example from Boinski and Fragaszy (1989, cited in King, 1994) is an observation of an adult wild Peruvian squirrel monkey's placing himself between a caterpillar and some infants while giving bark vocalizations (caterpillars can be toxic). She also cited four cases from Caro and Hauser (1992) in which an incorrect alarm call from an infant vervet monkey was punished by its mother by biting or slapping. For the most part, however, King noted that immature vervet monkeys must learn these alarm calls themselves, despite their importance because of high predation.

Caro and Hauser (1992) defined teaching more functionally: An individual is teaching "if it modifies its behavior only in the presence of a naïve observer . . . without obtaining an immediate benefit for itself" (p. 153). Such teaching might provide an example or explicit encouragement/discouragement, so that the naïve observer learns a skill more rapidly. The only examples of discouragement in nonhuman primates are the four cases above and also some observations of adults removing suspect food from their young. According to Caro and Hauser, there is as yet evidence neither of faster skill acquisition from any such teaching nor of acquisition of the skill in the absence of any adult facilitation.

Symbolic Reference

In Deacon's (1997) view, "symbol acquisition abilities provide the pacemaker for language evolution" (p. 255) and for "prefrontalization of the brain in hominid evolution" (p. 336). Prefrontal areas appear to be essential for hierarchical associative learning; prefrontally damaged patients are characterized by concreteness in comprehension (p. 267). Australopithecines were not symbol users until toward the end of their era, Deacon postulated, when the beginning of stone tool use brought about very different learning biases. "Stone tools and symbols must both, then, be the architects of the *Australopithecus–Homo* transition, and not its consequences" (p. 348). The brain sizes of australopithecines suggest, however, that they were unable to exert cortical control over the muscles of the tongue and larynx. Thus, the major modality for the earliest symbolic communication was probably not vocal, but neither were the earliest hominids likely to have been silent. Deacon hypothesized that they carried out most of their communication using calls and display behaviors like those of modern apes. (See also the discussion of gestural theory earlier in this chapter.) As my colleagues and I have argued elsewhere (Blake et al., 1997), Deacon speculated that gesture was important in early communication but that it was always accompanied by vocal communication. Furthermore, like many developmental psycholinguists, as discussed in chapter 3, he stressed the importance of pointing in the transition to language.

H. erectus successfully adapted across the Old World, and the range of habitats suggested to Deacon that symbolic communication would have been essential for sharing of information necessary for survival. This view is supported also by a significant trend toward increasing brain size across the era of *H. erectus*. The first direct expression of symbol use is, of course, the cave paintings and carvings that emerged only about 30,000 to 40,000 years ago; but, according to Deacon, these do not correlate with any neurological changes in the brain and do not reflect the origin of symbolic communication.

Noble and Davidson (1996) represent the other extreme opinion with regard to the emergence of symbols in hominids. They claimed that symbols were not evident until the first colonization of Australia about 60,000 years ago, when both the planning of the emigration (building the boat) and the evidence of symbolic decoration among the early settlers of Australia make symbolic behavior undeniable. They hypothesized that prior to this colonization, plan-based behavior might have emerged between 70,000 and 100,000 years ago. The stone tools of hominids before this time, they argued, do not indicate planning the way the later evidence of ground bone tools and carvings of bone and ivory does. According to the authors, these later artifacts show a clear "concept of the final, intended form" (p. 205). Such planning, in their view, must be verbal, though certainly Piagetians would argue that nonverbal planning is quite possible not only in human infants, as we have seen in chapters 4 and 5, but also in many adult endeavors. These authors, however, have embraced a discontinuity view with regard to the relationship between nonverbal and verbal communication (see King & Shanker, 1997).

According to Noble and Davidson, increases in brain size over 1.5 million years were not accompanied by any changes in behavior, except perhaps for greater motor control of the forelimbs. A major difference from Deacon's view is that they believe that changes in skeletal morphology "will generally be earlier than the signs of the behavior which made it successful" (p. 142). Thus, unlike Deacon, who emphasized symbolic behavior effecting brain changes, these authors postulated that behavior is not what brought about morphological changes, although it did restrict the range of variation in these changes. They also argued that until about 50,000 years ago, there were no well-preserved skeletons, so that cranial capacity and body size in earlier fossils have rarely been measured from the same individual. This appears to be a difficult argument for proponents of the brain–body ratio hypothesis to answer.

Noble and Davidson's definition of a symbol is something that stands for something else *by convention or social custom* [my emphasis]. This definition would, it appears, include neither the early sound–meaning mappings in infants described in chapter 2 nor the idiosyncratic symbolic gestures discussed in chapter 4. It is true that neither of these behaviors is necessarily intended to communicate, and Noble and Davidson's focus was on symbolic communication. Furthermore, symbolic communication for them must be all or none; there is no partial meaning or protolanguage possible in evolution. Protolanguage in children is possible because they are surrounded by language users who transmit to them the idea of language. According to Noble and Davidson, language is a clear case in which ontogeny cannot recapitulate phylogeny because early humans had no language models. In evolution, symbol use had to be sudden, a view that seems concordant with the "hopeful monster" theory. (See the next section and also comments of King & Shanker, 1997). Chomskians also do not admit the possibility of gradual development. At the same time, however, Noble and Davidson also have claimed that their views are based in an evolutionary context, meaning that they see language as emerging from precursors, such as directed throwing and pointing. These actions then led to "iconic" gestures, but such gestures are apparently not considered to be symbolic, though most researchers treat *iconic gestures* (as the term is used with humans) and *symbolic gestures* as synonymous. It also seems quite unlikely that pointing emerged from throwing as they maintained; it certainly does not do this ontogenetically, as infants generally point before they throw. Body language, such as miming, is considered to be symbolic as in Donald's (1991) theory, but only when conventionalized.

The "Hopeful Monster" Theory

A "hopeful monster" theory is "the evolutionary theorist's counterpart to divine intervention, in which a freak mutation just happens to produce a radically different and serendipitously better-equipped organism" (Deacon, 1997, p. 35). The champion of this type of theory is Chomsky, who has argued that humans have a built-in language organ containing the universal rules of grammar. This organ arrived in one fell swoop, and the threshold to humanity was crossed (Deacon, 1997). Because we know little about mutations, according to Chomsky, we may never understand how the language organ actually came about.

Since its arrival, however, the human embryo has at its earliest stages the potential structure of language in the same way as it has the potential structure of the heart (Chomsky in Rieber, 1983).

Many years ago, Chomsky (1968) stated that "the native speaker has acquired a grammar on the basis of very restricted and degenerate evidence" (p. 23) This has come to be known as the poverty of the stimulus argument, which precludes the possibility of learning. Further, in attempting to understand how the human mind achieved its particular form of innate organization, Chomsky (1968, p. 83) stated that "it is perfectly safe to attribute this development to 'natural selection,' so long as we realize that there is no substance to this assertion." Later, he commented that "it is important not to fall prey to illusions about evolution and its adaptive miracles" (Chomsky, 1991a, p. 39). Thus, neither phylogenetic evolution nor ontogenetic learning is particularly informative.

For Chomsky (1991b, p. 7), "the language faculty is regarded as a particular component of the human mind/brain. It has an initial state, an element of the human biological endowment that appears to be subject to little variation apart from severe pathology, and is also apparently unique to the species in essentials." Further, for language *and conceptual development* [my emphasis], learning "seems to have little if any place" (p. 17). Even "the growth of the lexicon must be inner-directed to a substantial extent," because children acquire words "at an extraordinary rate" and "under quite ambiguous circumstances" (p. 29). Concepts, also, "must be available prior to experience, in something like their full intricacy" (Chomsky, 1991a, p. 29).

Chomsky argued that the issue of innateness versus learning is an empirical one, but he ignored developmental evidence showing the relation between early vocabulary acquisition and maternal input (e.g., Harris, Barrett, Jones, & Brookes, 1988). The type of evidence he seemed to want was not psychological but neuropsychological. The language organ should be treated as other physical systems and receive a similar scientific approach (i.e., rationalist), as in the physical sciences. Chomsky asked, "Why should we abandon the approach we take for granted in studying the body when we turn to the study of the mind?" (in Rieber, 1983, p. 56).

Pinker (1994) also supported a language organ, which he said, on the basis of evidence from aphasics and brain imaging studies, is located in the left perisylvian region of the cortex. (In Figure 1–2, the Sylvian fissure is located in the line through the center just below

Broca's area.) The front of the perisylvian region (including Broca's area) is said to be concerned with grammatical processing and the rear (including Wernicke's) with the sounds of words, particularly of nouns. Beyond that degree of localization he has as yet been unwilling to go. Pinker also has appeared to favor genes for grammatical abilities but has admitted that the current evidence is only suggestive.

Pinker has departed from Chomsky's views in believing that although human language ability is totally discontinuous from the abilities of nonhuman primates, "language could have had a gradual fade-in" (p. 346) among hominids – that is, *after* the branch leading to *H. sapiens* split off from the one leading to chimpanzees. "If language evolved gradually, there must have been a sequence of intermediate forms, each useful to its possessor" (p. 365), so that the newer forms were each favored by natural selection, in turn. There was not a sudden mutation enabling universal grammar, but the gradual changes in neural circuitry were genetically controlled. This view seems to differ from that of Noble and Davidson in allowing intermediate forms but not gestural precursors.

Language functions have long been identified with Broca's and Wernicke's areas in the brain (see Figure 1–2), but Lieberman (1984) and Deacon (1997), among others, have emphasized that these areas did not emerge in humans specifically to serve language. There are no new areas in the human brain without homologous areas in the nonhuman primate brain. It is a case of "old" brain being used for new functions. Furthermore, language cannot be specifically located in these areas. In normal development, the "left temporal area [Wernicke's] recruits left frontal cortex [Broca's] into an integrated system that permits the fluent and efficient comprehension and production of speech" (Elman et al., 1996, p. 311). At the same time, language functions are dependent on interactions among many different areas of the brain, allowing simultaneous processing of different aspects of language (Deacon, 1997). There are also individual differences in how language functions are distributed across brain regions, variations that appear in aphasias and in brain-imaging procedures with language stimuli (see Elman et al., 1996). The effects of damage to the so-called language areas are unpredictable across patients, and aphasia can be caused by injury to other areas (Donald, 1991). The evidence from aphasics thus appears to indicate less clear-cut relationships between brain areas and language disabilities than Pinker has implied.

Thus, there is no language organ that can be identified, nor is there any trace of a sudden mutation (Deacon, 1997). Furthermore, for genetic assimilation to occur, the behavior must be invariant across generations, like nest building in birds (Deacon, 1997). The only candidate for such invariance, according to Deacon, is phoneme processing, particularly of consonants. Many consonantal phonemes, especially stop consonants, like alarm calls in vervet monkeys, appear to be quite regularized across individuals and across languages (see chapter 1). Thus, this aspect of language, according to Deacon, may have undergone a degree of genetic assimilation in evolution.

Conclusions

The most reasonable conclusion given the state of our knowledge of brain organization and of fossils seems to be that language evolved gradually across hominid evolution with many intermediate forms. Because we know that environment and behavior have a major impact on brain development in many species, it does seem logical that communicative behavior affected the organization of neural circuits – that is, that the behavior came first. Gestures and calls/grunts were available to the earliest hominids, we presume, because they are part of the repertoire of current-day great apes. When the critical comment gestures evolved is unknown, but they must have been at least related to a cooperative, close-knit culture, perhaps toward the end of the australopithecine era, as Deacon has suggested. True symbolic gestures, of the kind that I have described in chapter 4, clearly precede *verbal* planning and drawing in ontogeny. It seems likely, then, that simple, depictive gestures would have been in the repertoire of early hominids before words (but not before vocalizations). Although to argue from infant development to evolutionary development may be risky, we at least know that symbolic gestures are somewhat easier than words.

The evolution of vocalizations was clearly restricted by the evolution of the upper vocal tract and by changes in the neural circuits controlling respiration and movements of the larynx, tongue, and mouth. The pace of articulatory development, then, had a more important biological basis than that of symbolic gestures, although the abstract component of these gestures may have depended on changes in the prefrontal cortex. Milo and Quiatt (1994) argued that rapidly spoken phonemic speech appeared late in evolution (in anatomically modern humans) but that the ability to manipulate symbols and to think abstractly evolved over at least 1.5 million years.

A continuity view across hominid evolution, I think, implicates necessarily a continuity view across primate species. It is only if language can be divorced from its precursors that phylogenetic discontinuity, in the Pinkerian sense, is possible. Whether one chooses a continuity or discontinuity view, then, ultimately depends on the degree to which one views language proper as grounded in early cognitive and communicative development. It is in these abilities that continuity across species is found.

CHAPTER NINE

Recapitulation

In this book, I have compared directly the evidence available on non-human primates and human infants/children with regard to several precursors of language: prelinguistic vocalizations, sound–meaning correspondences, communicative gestures, symbolic gestures and symbolic play, tool use and object permanence, representation, and memory. I think that this comparison has made it clear that the great apes differ very little from human infants in many communicative gestures, in tool use and object concept, in delayed imitation, and in the mental representation implied by their advanced abilities in these domains. Nonhuman primates can also be said to exhibit the necessary frequency modulation for prosody, as well as turn taking in dialogues. Where human infants depart from nonhuman primates is in their vocalization ability after age 4 months and particularly after the onset of CB containing true consonants at 7 months. Facility in combining such consonants in babbling is important not only for early word acquisition but also for later sentence production. Unlike nonhuman primates in the wild, human infants also show object sharing gestures that are related to early vocabulary acquisition and information-sharing gestures that are related to later word comprehension. A decrease in primitive gestures, such as protest and reach-request, also has long-term implications for later communicative competence and productive language complexity.

Human infants also exceed apes in their ability to map sounds onto many different situations, and they exhibit invented symbolic gestures and complex symbolic play not found in apes. These findings support those views which focus on the importance of symbol development for language, both in ontogeny and in evolution. Infants do not always use their symbols communicatively, however; their early sound–meaning mappings and their representations of an object or action by a gesture are often idiosyncratic and not conventional. Thus, as Piaget and Halliday both have stressed, these early symbols or protosymbols are not specifically learned. The abstraction (distancing) process involved in complex symbolic gestures and play may be an expression of the different hierarchical learning biases in humans that Deacon discussed. At any rate, it seems clear that apes do not play with sound–meaning correspondences or with symbols in this way. Any sound–meaning mapping that has been discovered in the wild is quite invariant across individuals and is probably genetically controlled. Symbolic gestures seen in apes who have had much exposure to human culture appear to be more conventional than invented (with the exception of Chantek's cooking), more similar to the largely imitated symbolic gestures of human infants at the beginning of the second year.

Thus, symbolization is a precursor that probably should not be attributed to apes. Although it is obvious that linking sounds to meaning and symbolizing objects/actions are important for language, the findings reviewed in chapters 2 and 4 nevertheless indicate that those human infants who display more sound–meaning correspondences, earlier symbolic gestures, or more advanced symbolic play are not necessarily accelerated in language acquisition. It may be that some of these infants are using these modes of expression as alternatives to recognizable words in part because of difficulty in matching their articulations to adult models. Some relationships between symbolic gestures and language and between stages of symbolic play and language have been found: the simultaneous emergence of symbolic gestures and words, sequencing in symbolic play and combining words in language, planning in play and productive word combinations. The relationships may be reciprocal, however, and symbolic play can be performed by children with a language deficit in a fashion that is not distinguishable from children with normal language.

Studies using Piagetian methodology have revealed few differences between captive apes and human infants in tool use. It is doubtful, however, that tool use in wild chimpanzees can be said to be equivalent to that of adult Tasmanian aborigines, as McGrew (1992) claimed. Their "tool kits" are viewed as similar in demonstrating neither complex forms nor compound implements. The aborigines showed considerable strategic planning in their animal traps, however – for example, setting spears on trails to catch kangaroos – and they created seemingly complex tools, such as ladders and baskets. Human infants would not be able to engage in this level of strategic planning or to create such complex tools, either. Thus, it is human infants and young children who provide McGrew's "bridgeable" comparison to apes and not adult aborigines. In human infants, specific tool use and object permanence abilities at stage 5 – that is, obtaining an object with a string and visible displacements – were linked to indicative communicative gestures and sophisticated request gestures involving cognizance of adult agency. The representation required in invisible displacements tasks was related to representational and relational words and to a vocabulary spurt.

Apes are more advanced than humans in spatial memory, and monkeys are quite proficient at visual sequential memory if highly trained. Neither of these abilities, however, appears to be important for language acquisition. In addition to symbolization and vocal articulation, the other area of species difference seems to be in auditory memory. Although the capacity of normally developing children in auditory memory span tasks increases with age, their performance in these tasks nevertheless seems quite effortless. Even very young children find these tasks easy as compared to other types of memory tasks, as long as they have the vocabulary needed. In contrast, monkeys seem to find auditory memory tasks very difficult. Unfortunately, we have little knowledge about the great apes in this domain. Thus, we might tentatively conclude that nonhuman primates are biased toward visual memory, and humans, toward auditory memory (and this bias is matched by differences in the size of the visual cortex). Auditory memory, then, may have been an exceedingly important precursor of language in evolution, as Donald (1991) suggested. Certainly, across several research studies, it emerges as an important deficit in SLI children, who are otherwise like their NL peers on tests of other cognitive abilities. In children acquiring language normally, auditory memory is related to many forms of productive language: sentence imitation, spontaneous sentence complexity as measured by MLU, and standardized measures of expressive language. Since monkeys have sensitive hearing, then an auditory memory bias in humans cannot have just a sensory basis. The central processing of auditory input must have evolved differently in humans, along with rapid vocal articulation, to enable automatic registration of sound sequences. Undoubtedly, the feedback loop played a role in this development, and the evidence from a tracheostomized infant (see chapter 1) attests to its importance. The larger cerebellum in humans and its incorporation into the neural circuits controlling language may have been critical in this regard, if, as Deacon suggested, this means that it is more involved in sound analysis and rapid processing than it is in other primates.

In conclusion, nonhuman primates possess many of the cognitive representational precursors for language. They lack rapid vocal articulation and consonants, largely because of their restricted vocal tract; they lack spontaneous, idiosyncratic symbols, perhaps because of different learning biases or cultural demands; and they lack automatic auditory memory capabilities. Both a continuity and a discontinuity view can then be supported, but to embrace total discontinuity would be to disregard the large overlap in precursors that is evident in the work reviewed in this book.

References

Acredolo, L. P., & Goodwyn, S. W. (1988). Symbolic gesturing in normal infants. *Child Development, 59,* 450–466.

Acredolo, L. P., & Goodwyn, S. W. (1990). Sign language in babies: The significance of symbolic gesturing for understanding language development. *Annals of Child Development, 7,* 1–42.

Acredolo, L., & Goodwyn, S. (1992, May). Symbolic gestures vs. words in early vocabulary acquisition. Paper presented at the Biennial Meeting of the International Conference on Infant Studies, Miami.

Adams, A-M., & Gathercole, S. E. (1995). Phonological working memory and speech production in preschool children. *Journal of Speech and Hearing Research, 38,* 403–414.

Adams, A-M., & Gathercole, S. E. (1996). Phonological working memory and spoken language development in young children. *The Quarterly Journal of Experimental Psychology, 49A,* 216–233.

Antinucci, F. (1989). *Cognitive structure and development in nonhuman primates.* Hillsdale, NJ: Lawrence Erlbaum.

Antinucci, F. (1990). The comparative study of cognitive ontogeny in four primate species. In S. T. Parker & K. R. Gibson (Eds.), *"Language" and intelligence in monkeys and apes: Comparative developmental perspectives* (pp. 157–171). New York: Cambridge University Press.

Armstrong, D. F., Stokoe, W. C., & Wilcox, S. E. (1995). *Gesture and the nature of language.* New York: Cambridge University Press.

Arthur, G. (1952). *The Arthur Adaptation of the Leiter International Performance Scale.* Washington, D.C.: Psychological Services Center Press.

Atkinson, R. C., Hansen, D. N., & Bernbach, H. A. (1964). Short-term memory with young children. *Psychonomic Science, 1,* 255–256.

Baddeley, A., Gathercole, S., & Papagno, C. (1998). The phonological loop as a language learning device. *Psychological Review, 105,* 158–173.

Baillargeon, R. (1987). Object permanence in $3^1/_2$- and $4^1/_2$-month-old infants. *Developmental Psychology, 23,* 655–664.

Baillargeon, R. (1995). A model of physical reasoning in infancy. In C. Rovee-Collier & L. P. Lipsitt (Eds.), *Advances in Infancy Research, 9,* 305–371.

Baillargeon, R., & DeVos, J. (1991). Object permanence in young infants: Further evidence. *Child Development, 62,* 1227–1246.

Baillargeon, R., Spelke, E. S., & Wasserman, S. (1985). Object permanence in five-month-old infants. *Cognition, 20,* 191–208.

Bard, K. A. (1990). "Social tool use" by free-ranging orangutans: A Piagetian and developmental perspective on the manipulation of an animate object. In S. T. Parker & K. R. Gibson (Eds.), *"Language" and intelligence in monkeys and apes: Comparative developmental perspectives* (pp. 356–378). New York: Cambridge University Press.

Bard, K. A. (1993). Cognitive competence underlying tool use in free-ranging orangutans. In A. Berthelet & J. Chavaillon (Eds.), *The use of tools by human and non-human primates: A Fyssen Foundation Symposium* (pp. 103–117). Oxford: Clarendon.

Barnhart, C. L. (Ed.) (1948). *The American college dictionary.* New York: Random House.

Bastian, J. R. (1965). Primate signaling systems and human languages. In I. DeVore (Ed.), *Primate behavior: Field studies of monkeys and apes* (pp. 585–606). New York: Holt, Rinehart & Winston.

Bates, E. (1976). *Language and context: The acquisition of pragmatics.* New York: Academic Press.

Bates, E. (1979). *The emergence of symbols: Cognition and communication in infancy.* New York: Academic Press.

Bates, E. (1996, April). Language and the infant brain. Invited address. International Conference on Infant Studies, Providence, RI.

Bates, E., Benigni, L., Bretherton, I., Camaioni, L., & Volterra, V. (1977). From gesture to the first word: On cognitive and social prerequisites. In M. Lewis & L. Rosenblum (Eds.), *Origins of behavior: Communication and language* (pp. 247–307). New York: Wiley.

Bates, E., Bretherton, I., & Snyder, L. (1988). *From first words to grammar: Individual differences and dissociable mechanisms.* New York: Cambridge University Press.

Bates, E., Bretherton, I., Snyder, L., Shore, C., & Volterra, V. (1980). Vocal and gestural symbols at 13 months. *Merrill-Palmer Quarterly, 26,* 407–423.

Bates, E., Shore, C., Bretherton, I., & McNew, S. (1983). Names, gestures, and objects: Symbolization in infancy and aphasia. In K. E. Nelson (Ed.), *Children's language* (Vol. 4, pp. 59–123). Hillsdale, NJ: Lawrence Erlbaum.

Bates, E., & Snyder, L. (1987). The cognitive hypothesis in language development. In I. C. Uzgiris & J. McV. Hunt (Eds.), *Infant performance and experience: New findings with the ordinal scales* (pp. 168–204). Urbana: University of Illinois Press.

Bates, E., Thal, D., Whitesell, K., Fenson, L., & Oakes, L. (1989). Integrating language and gesture in infancy. *Developmental Psychology, 25,* 1004–1019.

Bauer, P. J., & Dow, G. A. (1994). Episodic memory in 16- and 20-month-old children: Specifics are generalized but not forgotten. *Developmental Psychology, 30,* 403–417.

Bauer, P. J., & Mandler, J. M. (1992). Putting the horse before the cart: The use of temporal order in recall of events by one-year-old children. *Developmental Psychology, 28,* 441–452.

Belsky, J., & Most, R. K. (1981). From exploration to play: A cross-sectional study of infant free play behavior. *Developmental Psychology, 17,* 630–639.

Blake, J., Austin, W., Cannon, M., Lisus, A., & Vaughan, A. (1994). The relationship between memory span and measures of imitative and spontaneous language complexity in preschool children. *International Journal of Behavioral Development, 17,* 91–107.

Blake, J., Borzellino, G., Osborne, P., Mason, D., & Macdonald, S. (1997, April). Predicting language at 3 years from infant babbling and gestures. Paper presented at the Biennial Meeting of the Society for Research in Child Development, Washington, D.C.

Blake, J., & de Boysson-Bardies, B. (1992). Patterns in babbling: A cross-linguistic study. *Journal of Child Language, 19,* 51–74.

Blake, J., & Dolgoy, S. (1993). Gestural development and its relation to cognition during the transition to language. *Journal of Nonverbal Behavior, 17,* 87–102.

Blake, J., & Fink, R. (1987). Sound-meaning correspondences in babbling. *Journal of Child Language, 14,* 229–253.

Blake, J., McConnell, S., Horton, G., & Benson, N. (1992). The gestural repertoire and its evolution over the second year. *Early Development and Parenting, 1,* 127–136.

Blake, J., Olshansky, E., Vitale, G., & Macdonald, S. (1997). Are gestures the substrate of language? *Evolution of Communication, 1,* 261–282.

Blake, J., O'Rourke, P., & Borzellino, G. (1994). Form and function in the development of pointing and reaching gestures. *Infant Behavior and Development, 17,* 195–203.

Blake, J., Osborne, P., Borzellino, G., & Macdonald, S. (1995, April). Variation in babbling: Potential sources and consequences. Paper presented at the Biennial Meeting of the Society for Research in Child Development, Indianapolis.

Blake, J., & Quartaro, G. (1990). *Manual for analyzing the complexity of spontaneous speech samples.* Toronto: York University Department of Psychology Report No. 189.

Blake, J., Quartaro, G., Austin, W., & Vingilis, E. (1989, April). Does memory span constrain language complexity? Paper presented at the Biennial Meeting of the Society for Research in Child Development, Kansas City.

Blake, J., Quartaro, G., & Onorati, S. (1993). Evaluating quantitative measures of grammatical complexity in spontaneous speech samples. *Journal of Child Language, 20,* 139–152.

Bloom, K. (1988). Quality of adult vocalizations affects the quality of infant vocalizations. *Journal of Child Language, 15,* 469–480.

Bloom, K., Russell, A., & Wassenberg, K. (1987). Turn taking affects the quality of infant vocalizations. *Journal of Child Language, 14,* 211–227.

Bloom, L. (1973). *One word at a time: The use of single-word utterances before syntax.* The Hague: Mouton.

Bloom, L. (1993). *The transition from infancy to language: Acquiring the power of expression.* New York: Cambridge University Press.

Bloom, L., Lifter, K., & Broughton, J. (1985). The convergence of early cognition and language in the second year of life: Problems in conceptualization and measurement. In M. Barrett (Ed.), *Children's Single-Word Speech* (pp. 149–178). New York: Wiley.

Bloom, P. (1991). What does language acquisition tell us about language evolution? Commentary on P. M. Greenfield, Language, tools and brain: The ontogeny and phylogeny of hierarchically organized sequential behavior. *Behavioral and Brain Sciences, 14,* 553–554.

Blurton Jones, N. G. (1972). Non-verbal communication in children. In R. A. Hinde (Ed.), *Non-verbal communication* (pp. 271–296). Cambridge, UK: Cambridge University Press.

Boesch, C. (1993). Aspects of transmission of tool-use in wild chimpanzees. In K. R. Gibson & T. Ingold (Eds.), *Tools, language and cognition in human evolution* (pp. 171–183). New York: Cambridge University Press.

Boesch, C., & Boesch, H. (1984). Mental map in wild chimpanzees: An analysis of hammer transports for nut cracking. *Primates, 25,* 160–170.

Boesch, C., & Boesch, H. (1993). Diversity of tool use and tool-making in wild chimpanzees. In A. Berthelet & J. Chavaillon (Eds.), *The use of tools by human and non-human primates: A Fyssen Foundation Symposium* (pp. 158–168). Oxford: Clarendon Press.

Bogartz, R. S., Shinskey, J. L., & Speaker, C. J. (1997). Interpreting infant looking: The event set × event set design. *Developmental Psychology, 33,* 408–422.

Bornstein, M. H., Haynes, O. M., O'Reilly, A. W., & Painter, K. M. (1996). Solitary and collaborative pretense play in early childhood: Sources of individual variation in the development of representational competence. *Child Development, 67,* 2910–2929.

Bornstein, M. H., Vibbert, M., Tal, J., & O'Donnell, K. (1992). Toddler language and play in the second year: Stability, covariation and influences of parenting. *First Language, 12,* 323–338.

Bower, T. G. R. (1974). *Development in infancy.* San Francisco: W. H. Freeman.

Bowey, J. A. (1996). On the association between phonological memory and receptive vocabulary in five-year-olds. *Journal of Experimental Child Psychology, 63,* 44–78.

Bradley, R. H., & Caldwell, B. M. (1984). 174 Children: A study of the relationship between home environment and cognitive development during the first 5 years. In A. Gottfried (Ed.), *Home environment and early cognitive development: Longitudinal research* (pp. 5–56). New York: Academic Press.

Braine, M. (1976). Children's first word combinations. *Monographs of the Society for Research in Child Development, 41* (Serial No. 164).

Bremner, J. G. (1994). *Infancy* (2nd ed.). Oxford: Blackwell.

Bretherton, I., & Bates, E. (1984). The development of representation from 10 to 28 months: Differential stability of language and symbolic play. In R. N. Emde & R. J. Harmon (Eds.), *Continuities and discontinuities in development* (pp. 229–261). New York: Plenum Press.

Bretherton, I., O'Connell, B., Shore, C., & Bates, E. (1984). The effect of contextual variation on symbolic play development from 20 to 28 months. In I. Bretherton (Ed.), *Symbolic play: The development of social understanding* (pp. 271–298). New York: Academic Press.

Brown, C. H. (1982). Auditory localization and primate vocal behavior. In C. T. Snowdon, C. H. Brown, & M. R. Petersen (Eds.), *Primate communication* (pp. 144–164). London: Cambridge University Press.

Brown, R. (1973). *A first language: The early stages.* Cambridge, MA: Harvard University Press.

Brown, R., & Bellugi, U. (1964). Three processes in the child's acquisition of syntax. In E. H. Lenneberg (Ed.), *New directions in the study of language* (pp. 131–161). Cambridge, MA: MIT Press.

Bruner, J. S. (1964). The course of cognitive growth. *American Psychologist, 19,* 1–15.

Buchanan, J. P., Gill, T. V., & Braggio, J. T. (1981). Serial position and clustering effects in a chimpanzee's "free recall." *Memory & Cognition, 9,* 651–660.

Buhr, R. (1980). The emergence of vowels in an infant. *Journal of Speech and Hearing Research, 23,* 73–94.

Burling, R. (1993). Primate calls, human language, and nonverbal communication. *Current Anthropology, 34,* 25–53.

Byrne, R. W., & Russon, A. E. (1998). Learning by imitation: A hierarchical approach. *Behavioral and Brain Sciences, 21,* 667–721.

Caldwell, B. M., & Bradley, R. H. (1984). *Home observation for measurement of the environment* (rev. ed.). Little Rock: University of Arkansas.

Call, J., & Tomasello, M. (1994). Production and comprehension of referential pointing by orangutans. *Journal of Comparative Psychology, 108,* 307–317.

Camaioni, L., Caselli, M. C., Longobardi, E., & Volterra, V. (1991). A parent report instrument for early language assessment. *First Language, 11,* 345–359.

Caro, T. M., & Hauser, M. D. (1992). Is there teaching in nonhuman animals? *Quarterly Review of Biology, 67,* 151–174.

Carter, A. (1974). *The development of communication in the sensorimotor period: A case study.* Unpublished doctoral dissertation, University of California at Berkeley.

Carter, A. (1978). From sensori-motor vocalizations to words: A case study of the evolution of attention-directing communication in the second year. In A. Lock (Ed.) *Action, gesture, and symbol: The emergence of language* (pp. 309–349). New York: Academic Press.

Case, R., & Kurland, M. (1980). A new measure for determining children's subjective organization of speech. *Journal of Experimental Child Psychology, 30,* 206–222.

Caselli, M. C. (1990). Communicative gestures and first words. In V. Volterra & C. J. Erting (Eds.), *From gesture to language in hearing and deaf children* (pp. 56–67). New York: Springer-Verlag.

Castro, C. A., & Larsen, T. (1992). Primacy and recency effects in nonhuman primates. *Journal of Experimental Psychology: Animal Behavior Processes, 18,* 335–340.

Cheney, D. L. (1984). Category formation in vervet monkeys. In R. Harré & V. Reynolds (Eds.), *The meaning of primate signals* (pp. 58–72). New York: Cambridge University Press.

Cheney, D. L., & Seyfarth, R. M. (1990). *How monkeys see the world: Inside the mind of another species.* Chicago: University of Chicago Press.

Chevalier-Skolnikoff, S. (1983). Sensorimotor development in orang-utans and other primates. *Journal of Human Evolution, 12,* 545–561.

Chiasson, L. (1987). Relationships of language, symbolic play, memory, and play styles in very young children. Unpublished master's thesis, York University, Toronto.

Chomsky, N. (1968). *Language and mind.* New York: Harcourt, Brace & World.

Chomsky, N. (1991b). Linguistics and adjacent fields: A personal view. In A. Kasher (Ed.), *The Chomskyan turn* (pp. 3–25). Cambridge, MA: Blackwell.

Chomsky, N. (1991a). Linguistics and cognitive science: Problems and mysteries. In A. Kasher (Ed.), *The Chomskyan turn* (pp. 26–53). Cambridge, MA: Blackwell.

Clark, R. A. (1978). The transition from action to gesture. In A. Lock (Ed.), *Action, gesture and symbol: The emergence of language* (pp. 231–257). New York: Academic Press.

Clement, C. J., & Koopmans-van Beinum, F. J. (1995). Influence of lack of auditory feedback: Vocalizations of deaf and hearing infants compared. *Proceedings of the Institute of Phonetic Sciences Amsterdam, 19,* 25–37.

Clement, C. J., Koopmans-van Beinum, F. J., & Pols, L. C. W. (1996). Acoustical characteristics of sound production of deaf and normally hearing infants. *Proceedings of the International Congress on Spoken Language Processing,* Philadelphia.

Corrigan, R. (1978). Language development as related to stage 6 object permanence development. *Journal of Child Language, 5,* 173–189.

Corrigan, R. (1979). Cognitive correlates of language: Differential criteria yield different results. *Child Development, 50,* 617–631.

Corrigan, R. (1981). The effects of task and practice on search for invisibly displaced objects. *Developmental Review, 1,* 1–17.

Corrigan, R. (1982). The control of animate and inanimate components in pretend play and language. *Child Development, 53,* 1343–1353.

Curtiss, S., & Tallal, P. (1991). On the nature of the impairment in language-impaired children. In J. F. Miller (Ed.), *Research on child language disorders: A decade of progress* (pp. 189–210). Austin, TX: Pro-Ed.

Dale, P. (1980). Is early pragmatic development measurable? *Journal of Child Language, 7,* 1–12.

D'Amato, M. R., & Colombo, M. (1985). Auditory matching-to-sample in monkeys (*Cebus apella*). *Animal Learning & Behavior, 13,* 375–382.

D'Amato, M. R., & Colombo, M. (1988). Representation of serial order in monkeys (*Cebus apella*). *Journal of Experimental Psychology: Animal Behavior Processes, 14,* 131–139.

Daneman, M., & Case, R. (1981). Syntactic form, semantic complexity, and short-term memory: Influences on children's acquisition of new linguistic structures. *Developmental Psychology, 17,* 367–378.

Darwin, C. (1965). *The expression of the emotions in man and animals.* Chicago: University of Chicago Press. (Original work published 1872).

Darwin, C. (1877). *The descent of man, and selection in relation to sex.* London: John Murray.

Davis, B. L., & MacNeilage, P. F. (1995). The articulatory basis of babbling. *Journal of Speech and Hearing Research, 38,* 1199–1211.

Deacon, T. W. (1997). *The symbolic species: The co-evolution of language and the brain.* New York: W. W. Norton.

de Blois, S. T., Novak, M. A., & Bond, M. (1998). Object permanence in orangutans (*Pongo pygmaeus*) and squirrel monkeys (*Saimiri sciureus*), *Journal of Comparative Psychology, 112,* 137–152.

de Boysson-Bardies, B. (1993). Ontogeny of language-specific syllabic productions. In B. de Boysson-Bardies, S. de Schonen, P. Jusczyk, P. MacNeilage, & J. Morton (Eds.), *Developmental neurocognition: Speech and face processing in the first year of life* (pp. 353–363). Dordrecht: Kluwer Academic.

de Boysson-Bardies, B., Halle, P., Sagart, L., & Durand, C. (1989). A crosslinguistic investigation of vowel formants in babbling. *Journal of Child Language, 16,* 1–17.

de Boysson-Bardies, B., Vihman, M. M., Roug-Hellichius, L., Durand, C., Landberg, I., & Arao, F. (1992). Material evidence of infant selection from the target language: A cross-linguistic phonetic study. In C. A. Ferguson, L. Menn, & C. Stoel-Gammon (Eds.), *Phonological development: Models, research, implications* (pp. 369–391). Timonium, MD: York Press.

Delack, J. B., & Fowlow, P. J. (1978). The ontogenesis of differential vocalization: Development of prosodic contrastivity during the first year of life. In N. Waterson & C. Snow (Eds.), *The development of communication* (pp. 93–110). New York: Wiley.

Deputte, B. L. (1982). Duetting in male and female songs of the white-cheeked gibbon (*Hylobates concolor leucogenys*). In C. T. Snowdon, C. H. Brown, & M. R. Petersen (Eds.), *Primate communication* (pp. 67–93). London: Cambridge University Press.

Desrochers, S., Morissette, P., & Ricard, M. (1995). Two perspectives on pointing in infancy. In C. Moore & P. J. Dunham (Eds.), *Joint attention: Its origins and role in development* (pp. 85–101). Hillsdale, NJ: Lawrence Erlbaum.

De Waal, F. B. M. (1988). The communicative repertoire of captive bonobos (*Pan paniscus*) compared to that of chimpanzees. *Behaviour, 106,* 183–251.

Diamond, A. (1991). Neuropsychological insights into the meaning of object concept development. In S. Carey & R. Gelman (Eds.), *The epigenesis of mind: Essays on biology and cognition* (pp. 67–110). Hillsdale, NJ: Lawrence Erlbaum.

D'Odorico, L. (1984). Non-segmental features in prelinguistic communications: An analysis of some types of cry and non-cry vocalizations. *Journal of Child Language, 11,* 17–27.

D'Odorico, L., & Franco, F. (1991). Selective production of vocalization types in different communication contexts. *Journal of Child Language, 18,* 475–499.

Donald, M. (1991). *Origins of the modern mind: Three stages in the evolution of culture and cognition.* Cambridge, MA: Harvard University Press.

Doré, F. Y., & Dumas, C. (1987). Psychology of animal cognition: Piagetian studies. *Psychological Bulletin, 102,* 219–233.

Dore, J., Franklin, M. B., Miller, R. T., & Ramer, A. L. H. (1976). Transitional phenomena in early language acquisition. *Journal of Child Language, 3,* 13–28.

Dunn, L. M., & Dunn, L. M. (1981). *The Peabody Picture Vocabulary Test.* Circle Pines, MN: American Guidance Service.

Eilers, R. E., Oller, D. K., Levine, S., Basinger, D., Lynch, M. P., & Urbano, R. (1993). The role of prematurity and socioeconomic status in the onset of canonical babbling in infants. *Infant Behavior and Development, 16,* 297–315.

Ekman, P., & Friesen, W. (1969). The repertoire of nonverbal behavior: Categories, origins, usage, and coding. *Semiotica, 1,* 49–97.

Elbers, L. (1982). Operating principle in repetitive babbling: A cognitive continuity approach. *Cognition, 12,* 45–63.

Elbers, L., & Ton, J. (1985). Play pen monologues: The interplay of words and babbles in the first words period. *Journal of Child Language, 12,* 551–565.

Elman, J. L., Bates, E. A., Johnson, M. H., Karmiloff-Smith, A., Parisi, D., Plunkett, K. (1996). *Rethinking innateness: A connectionist perspective on development.* Cambridge, MA: MIT Press.

Elowson, A. M., Snowdon, C. T., & Lazaro-Perea, C. (1998). Infant 'babbling' in a nonhuman primate: Complex vocal sequences with repeated call types. *Behaviour, 135,* 643–664.

Erting, C. J., & Volterra, V. (1990). Conclusion. In V. Volterra & C. J. Erting (Eds.), *From gesture to language in hearing and deaf children* (pp. 299–303). New York: Springer-Verlag.

Fein, G. (1975). A transformational analysis of pretending. *Developmental Psychology, 11,* 291–296.

Fenson, L., Dale, P. S., Reznick, J. S., Bates, E., Thal, D. J., & Pethick, S. J. (1994). Variability in early communicative development. *Monographs of the Society for Research in Child Development, 59* (Serial No. 242).

Ferguson, C. A. (1976). Learning to pronounce: The earliest stages of phonological development in the child. Paper presented at the Conference on the Early Behavioral Assessment of the Communicative and Cognitive Abilities of the Developmentally Disabled, Orcas Island.

Ferguson, C. A., & Farwell, C. B. (1975). Words and sounds in early language acquisition. *Language, 51,* 419–439.

Ferguson, C. A., & Macken, M. A. (1983). The role of play in phonological development. In K. E. Nelson (Ed.), *Children's language* (Vol. 4, pp. 231–254). Hillsdale, NJ: Lawrence Erlbaum.

Fillmore, C. J. (1968). The case for case. In E. Bach & R. T. Harms (Eds.), *Universals in linguisitic theory* (1–88). New York: Holt, Rinehart & Winston.

Fogel, A. (1981). The ontogeny of gestural communication: The first six months. In R. Stark (Ed.), *Language behavior in infancy and early childhood* (pp. 17–40). New York: Elsevier.

Fogel, A., & Hannan, T. E. (1985). Manual actions of nine- to fifteen-week-old human infants during face-to-face interaction with their mothers. *Child Development, 56,* 1271–1279.

Fossey, D. (1972). Vocalizations of the mountain gorilla. *Animal Behaviour, 20,* 36–53.

Fox, E. A., Sitompul, A. F., & van Schaik, C. P. (1999). Intelligent tool use in wild Sumatran orangutans. In S. T. Parker, H. L. Miles, & R. W. Mitchell

(Eds.), *The mentality of gorillas and orangutans*. Cambridge, UK: Cambridge University Press.

Franco, F., & Butterworth, G. (1991, April). Infant pointing: Prelinguistic reference and co-reference. Paper presented at the Biennial Meeting of the Society for Research in Child Development, Seattle.

Franco, F., & Butterworth, G. (1996). Pointing and social awareness: Declaring and requesting in the second year. *Journal of Child Language, 23*, 307–336.

Fry, D. B. (1966). The development of the phonological system in the normal and the deaf child. In F. Smith & G. A. Miller (Eds.), *The genesis of language: A psycholinguistic approach* (pp. 187–206). Cambridge, MA: M.I.T. Press.

Furth, H. G. (1969). *Piaget and knowledge: Theoretical foundations*. Englewood Cliffs, NJ: Prentice-Hall.

Gaffan, E. A. (1994). Primacy in animals' working memory: Artifacts. *Animal Learning & Behavior, 22*, 231–232.

Galdikas, B. M. F. (1982). Orang-utan tool-use at Tanjung Puting Reserve, Central Indonesian Borneo (Kalimantan Tengah). *Journal of Human Evolution, 10*, 19–33.

Gardner, R. A., & Gardner, B. T. (1969). Teaching sign language to a chimpanzee. *Science, 165*, 664–672.

Gathercole, S. E. (1995). Is nonword repetition a test of phonological memory or long-term knowledge? It all depends on the nonwords. *Memory and Cognition, 23*, 83–94.

Gathercole, S. E., & Baddeley, A. D. (1990). Phonological memory deficits in language disordered children: Is there a causal connection? *Journal of Memory and Language, 29*, 336–360.

Gathercole, S. E., & Baddeley, A. D. (1993). *Working memory and language*. Hillsdale, NJ: Lawrence Erlbaum.

Gathercole, S. E., & Baddeley, A. D. (1995). Short-term memory may yet be deficient in children with language impairments: A comment on van der Lely & Howard (1993). *Journal of Speech and Hearing Research, 38*, 463–466.

Gathercole, S. E., & Baddeley, A. D. (1997). Sense and sensitivity in phonological memory and vocabulary development: A reply to Bowey (1996). *Journal of Experimental Child Psychology, 67*, 290–294.

Gathercole, S. E., Hitch, G. J., Service, E., & Martin, A. J. (1997). Phonological short-term memory and new word learning in children. *Developmental Psychology, 33*, 966–979.

Gibson, K. R. (1990). New perspectives on instincts and intelligence: Brain size and the emergence of hierarchical mental constructional skills. In S. T. Parker & K. R. Gibson (Eds.), *"Language" and intelligence in monkeys and apes: Comparative developmental perspectives* (pp. 97–128). New York: Cambridge University Press.

Gibson, K. R. (1993). Tool use, language and social behavior in relationship to information processing capacities. In K. R. Gibson & T. Ingold (Eds.), *Tools, language and cognition in human evolution* (pp. 251–269). New York: Cambridge University Press.

Gillis, S., & De Schutter, G. (1986). Transitional phenomena revisited: Insights into the nominal insight. In B. Lindblom & R. Zetterstrom (Eds.), *Precursors of early speech* (pp. 127–142). New York: Stockton.

Ginsburg, G. P., & Kilbourne, B. K. (1988). Emergence of vocal alternation in mother–infant interchanges. *Journal of Child Language, 15,* 221–235.

Goldin-Meadow, S., McNeill, D., & Singleton, J. (1996). Silence is liberating: Removing the handcuffs on grammatical expression in the manual modality. *Psychological Review, 103,* 34–55.

Goldin-Meadow, S., & Morford, M. (1985). Gesture in early child language: Studies of deaf and hearing children. *Merrill-Palmer Quarterly, 31,* 145–176.

Goldin-Meadow, S., & Mylander, C. (1984). Gestural communication in deaf children: The effects and noneffects of parental input on early language development. *Monographs of the Society for Research in Child Development, 49,* (Serial No. 207).

Gomez, J. C. (1990). The emergence of intentional communication as a problem-solving strategy in the gorilla. In S. T. Parker & K. R. Gibson (Eds.), *"Language" and intelligence in monkeys and apes: Comparative developmental perspectives* (pp. 333–355). New York: Cambridge University Press.

Goodall, J. (1965). Chimpanzees of the Gombe Stream Reserve. In I. DeVore (Ed.), *Primate behavior: Field studies of monkeys and apes* (pp. 425–473). New York: Holt, Rinehart & Winston.

Goodall, J. (1986). *The chimpanzees of Gombe: Patterns of behavior.* Cambridge, MA: The Belnap Press of Harvard University Press.

Goodwyn, S. W., & Acredolo, L. P. (1993). Symbolic gesture versus word: Is there a modality advantage for onset of symbol use? *Child Development, 64,* 688–701.

Gopnik, A. (1984). The acquisition of *gone* and the development of the object concept. *Journal of Child Language, 11,* 273–292.

Gopnik, A., Choi, S., & Baumberger, T. (1996). Cross-linguistic differences in early semantic and cognitive development. *Cognitive Development, 11,* 197–227.

Gopnik, A., & Meltzoff, A. N. (1984). Semantic and cognitive development in 15- to 21-month-old children. *Journal of Child Language, 11,* 495–513.

Gopnik, A., & Meltzoff, A. N. (1986). Relations between semantic and cognitive development in the one-word stage: The specificity hypothesis. *Child Development, 57,* 1040–1053.

Gopnik, A., & Meltzoff, A. N. (1997). *Words, thoughts, and theories.* Cambridge, MA: MIT Press.

Goubet, N., & Clifton, R. K. (1998). Object and event representation in $6^{1}/_{2}$-month-old infants. *Developmental Psychology, 34,* 63–76.

Gouzoules, H., Gouzoules, S., & Ashley, J. (1995). Representational signaling in non-human primate vocal communication. In E. Zimmerman, J. D. Newman, & U. Jurgens (Eds.), *Current topics in primate vocal communication* (pp. 235–252). New York: Plenum Press.

Gouzoules, H., Gouzoules, S., & Marler, P. (1985). External reference and affective signaling in mammalian vocal communication. In G. Zivin (Ed.), *The development of expressive behavior: Biology–environment interactions* (pp. 77–101). New York: Academic Press.

Gratch, G. (1975). Recent studies based on Piaget's view of object concept development. In L. B. Cohen & P. Salapatek (Eds.), *Infant perception: From sensation to cognition* (Vol. 2, pp. 51–99). New York: Academic Press.

Greenfield, P. M. (1991). Language, tools and brain: The ontogeny and phylogeny of hierarchically organized sequential behavior. *The Behavioral and Brain Sciences, 14,* 531–551.

Greenfield, P. M., Nelson, K., & Saltzman, E. (1972). The development of rule-bound strategies for manipulating seriated cups: A parallel between action and grammar. *Cognitive Psychology, 3,* 291–310.

Greenfield, P. M., & Smith, J. H. (1976). *The structure of communication in early language development.* New York: Academic Press.

Haith, M. M. (1998). Who put the cog in infant cognition? Is rich interpretation too costly? *Infant Behavior and Development, 21,* 167–179.

Hall, K. R. L., & DeVore, I. (1965). Baboon social behavior. In I. DeVore (Ed.), *Primate behavior: Field studies of monkeys and apes* (pp. 53–110). New York: Holt, Rinehart & Winston.

Halliday, M. A. K. (1973, April). A sociosemiotic perspective on language development. Paper presented at the Fifth Child Language Research Forum, Stanford University, Palo Alto, CA.

Halliday, M. A. K. (1975). *Learning how to mean – explorations in the development of language.* London: Edward Arnold.

Hallock, M. B., & Worobey, J. (1984). Cognitive development in chimpanzee infants (*Pan troglodytes*). *Journal of Human Evolution, 13,* 441–447.

Hannan, T. E. (1987). A cross-sequential assessment of the occurrences of pointing in 3- to 12-month-old human infants. *Infant Behavior and Development, 10,* 11–22.

Harcourt, A. H., Stewart, K. J., & Hauser, M. (1993). Functions of wild gorilla 'close' calls: I. Repertoire, context, and interspecific comparison. *Behaviour, 124,* 89–122.

Harris, M., Barrett, M., Jones, D., & Brookes, S. (1988). Linguistic input and early word meaning. *Journal of Child Language, 15,* 77–94.

Harris, P. L., & Kavanaugh, R. D. (1993). Young children's understanding of pretense. *Monographs of the Society for Research in Child Development, 58,* 1 (Serial No. 231).

Hauser, M. D. (1996). *The evolution of communication.* Cambridge, MA: MIT Press.

Hauser, M. D., & Marler, P. (1992). How do and should studies of animal communication affect interpretations of child phonological development? In C. A. Ferguson, L. Menn, & C. Stoel-Gammon (Eds.), *Phonological development: Models, research, implications* (663–680). Timonium, MD: York Press.

Hayes, K. J., & Nissen, C. H. (1971). Higher mental functions of a home-raised chimpanzee. In A. M. Schrier & F. Stollnitz (Eds.), *Behavior of nonhuman primates* (Vol. 4, pp. 60–115). New York: Academic Press.

Hewes, G. W. (1973). Primate communication and the gestural origin of language. *Current Anthropology, 14,* 5–24.

Hewes, G. W. (1989). The gestural origin of language and new neurological data. In J. Wind, A. Jonker, R. Allott, & L. Rolfe (Eds.), *Studies in language origins* (Vol. 3, pp. 293–307), Amsterdam: John Benjamins.

Hockett, C. F. (1958). *A course in modern linguistics*. New York: MacMillan.

Holloway, R. (1986). *Mental capacity, language, and play: A neo-Piagetian exploratory study of aspects of cognitive development from 6 to 20 months.* Unpublished doctoral dissertation, York University, Toronto.

Holloway, R., Blake, J., & Pascual-Leone, J. (1987, April). Relations between cognitive and communicative abilities in infancy. Paper presented at the Biennial Meeting of the Society for Research in Child Development, Baltimore.

Holmgren, K., Lindblom, B., Aurelius, B. J., & Zetterstrom, R. (1986). On the phonetics of infant vocalization. In B. Lindblom & R. Zetterstrom (Eds.), *Precursors of early speech* (pp. 51–63). New York: Stockton.

Hulme, C., Thomson, N., Muir, C., & Lawrence, A. (1984). Speech rate and the development of short-term memory span. *Journal of Experimental Child Psychology, 38*, 241–253.

Ingmanson, E. J. (1996). Tool-using behavior in wild *Pan paniscus*: Social and ecological considerations. In A. E. Russon, K. A. Bard, & S. T. Parker (Eds.) *Reaching into thought: The minds of the great apes* (pp. 190–210). New York: Cambridge University Press.

Inoue-Nakamura, N., & Matsuzawa, T. (1997). Development of stone tool use by wild chimpanzees. *Journal of Comparative Psychology, 111*, 159–173.

Irwin, O. C. (1947). Infant speech: Consonantal sounds according to place of articulation. *Journal of Speech Disorders, 12*, 397–401.

Irwin, O. C. (1948). Infant speech: Development of vowel sounds. *Journal of Speech and Hearing Disorders, 13*, 31–34.

Iverson, J. M., Capirci, O., & Caselli, M. C. (1994). From communication to language in two modalities. *Cognitive Development, 9*, 23–43.

Jakobson, R. (1968). *Child language, aphasia, and phonological universals.* Trans. by A. R. Keiler. The Hague: Mouton. (Original work published 1941).

James, D., van Steenbrugge, W., & Chiveralls, K. (1994). Underlying deficits in language-disordered children with central auditory processing difficulties. *Applied Psycholinguistics, 15*, 313–328.

Jay, P. (1965). The common langur of North India. In I. DeVore (Ed.), *Primate behavior: Field studies of monkeys and apes* (pp. 197–249). New York: Holt, Rinehart & Winston.

Jurgens, U. (1995). Neuronal control of vocal production in non-human and human primates. In E. Zimmermann, J. D. Newman, & U. Jurgens (Eds.), *Current topics in primate vocal communication* (pp. 199–206). New York: Plenum Press.

Jusczyk, P. W. (1997). *The discovery of spoken language.* Cambridge, MA: MIT Press.

Karmiloff-Smith, A. (1992). *Beyond modularity: A developmental perspective on cognitive science.* Cambridge, MA: MIT Press.

Kendon, A. (1993). Human gesture. In K. R. Gibson & T. Ingold (Eds.), *Tools, language and cognition in human evolution* (pp. 43–62). New York: Cambridge University Press.

Kent, R. D. (1981). Articulatory-acoustic perspectives on speech development. In R. E. Stark (Ed.), *Language behavior in infancy and early childhood* (pp. 105–126). New York: Elsevier/North Holland.

Kent, R. D., & Bauer, H. R. (1985). Vocalizations of one-year-olds. *Journal of Child Language, 12,* 491–526.

Kent, R. D., and Murray, A. D. (1982). Acoustic features of infant vocalic utterances at 3, 6, and 9 months. *Journal of the Acoustical Society of America, 72,* 353–363.

Kessen, W., Levine, J., & Wendrich, K. A. (1979). The imitation of pitch in infants. *Infant Behavior and Development, 2,* 93–99.

Kimura, D. (1993). *Neuromotor mechanisms in human communication.* New York: Oxford University Press.

King, B. J. (1994). *The information continuum: Evolution of social information transfer in monkeys, apes, and hominids.* Santa Fe: Sar Press.

King, B. J., & Shanker, S. G. (1997). The expulsion of primates from the garden of language. A review of *Human evolution, language, and mind,* by W. Nobel & I. Davidson. *Evolution of communication, 1,* 59–99.

Köhler, W. (1927). *The mentality of apes* (2nd rev. ed.). Trans. by E. Winter. New York: Vintage Books.

Kramer, J. A., Hill, K. T., & Cohen, L. B. (1975). Infants' development of object permanence: A refined methodology and new evidence for Piaget's hypothesized ordinality. *Child Development, 46,* 149–155.

Krause, M. A., & Fouts, R. S. (1997). Chimpanzee (*Pan troglodytes*) pointing: Hand shapes, accuracy, and the role of eye gaze. *Journal of Comparative Psychology, 111,* 330–336.

Kushnir, C. C., & Blake, J. (1996). The nature of the cognitive deficit in specific language impairment. *First Language, 16,* 21–40.

Lancaster, J. B. (1968). Primate communication systems and the emergence of human language. In P. C. Jay (Ed.), *Primates: Studies in adaptation and variability* (pp. 439–457). New York: Holt, Rinehart, & Winston.

Langer, J. (1986). *The origins of logic: One to two years.* New York: Academic Press.

Langer, J. (1993). Comparative cognitive development. In K. R. Gibson & T. Ingold (Eds.), *Tools, language and cognition in human evolution* (pp. 300–313). New York: Cambridge University Press.

Langer, J. (1996). Heterochrony and the evolution of primate cognitive development. In A. E. Russon, K. A. Bard, & S. T. Parker (Eds.), *Reaching into thought: The minds of the great apes* (pp. 257–277). New York: Cambridge University Press.

Leavens, D. A., & Hopkins, W. D. (1998). Intentional communication by chimpanzees: A cross-sectional study of the use of referential gestures. *Developmental Psychology, 34,* 813–822.

Leavens, D. A., Hopkins, W. D., & Bard, K. A. (1996). Indexical and referential pointing in chimpanzees (*Pan troglodytes*). *Journal of Comparative Psychology, 110,* 346–353.

Legerstee, M. (1991). Changes in the quality of infant sounds as a function of social and nonsocial stimulation. *First Language, 11,* 327–343.

Legerstee, M., Corter, C., & Kienapple, K. (1990). Hand, arm, and facial actions of young infants to a social and nonsocial stimulus. *Child Development, 61,* 774–784.

Lempers, J. (1979). Young children's production and comprehension of nonverbal deictic behaviors. *The Journal of Genetic Psychology, 135,* 93–102.

Leslie, A. M. (1987). Pretense and representation: The origins of "Theory of Mind." *Psychological Review, 94,* 412–426.

Lethmate, J. (1982). Tool-using skills of orang-utans. *Journal of Human Evolution, 11,* 49–64.

Leung, E. H. L., & Rheingold, H. L. (1981). Development of pointing as a social gesture. *Developmental Psychology, 17,* 215–220.

Levitt, A. (1993). The acquisition of prosody: Evidence from French- and English-learning infants. In B. de Boysson-Bardies, S. de Schonen, P. Jusczyk, P. MacNeilage, & J. Morton (Eds.), *Developmental neurocognition: Speech and face processing in the first year of life* (pp. 385–398). Dordrecht: Kluwer Academic.

Lieberman, P. (1975). *On the origins of language: An introduction to the evolution of human speech.* New York: MacMillan.

Lieberman, P. (1980). On the development of vowel production in young children. In G. H. Yeni-Komshian, J. F. Kavanagh, & C. A. Ferguson (Eds.), *Child Phonology.* Vol. 1. *Production* (pp. 113–142). New York: Academic Press.

Lieberman, P. (1984). *The biology and evolution of language.* Cambridge, MA: Harvard University Press.

Lieberman, P. (1991). *Uniquely human: The evolution of speech, thought, and selfless behavior.* Cambridge, MA: Harvard University Press.

Lieberman, P. (1995). What primate calls can tell us about human evolution. In E. Zimmermann, J. D. Newman, & U. Jurgens (Eds.), *Current topics in primate vocal communication* (pp. 273–282). New York: Plenum Press.

Lieberman, P. H., Klatt, D. H., & Wilson, W. H. (1969). Vocal tract limitations on the vowel repertoires of rhesus monkey and other nonhuman primates. *Science, 164,* 1185–1187.

Lifter, K., & Bloom, L. (1989). Object knowledge and the emergence of language. *Infant Behavior and Development, 12,* 395–423.

Lillard, A. S. (1993). Pretend play skills and the child's theory of mind. *Child Development, 64,* 348–371.

Liska, J. (1994). The foundation of symbolic communication. In D. Quiatt & J. Itani (Eds.), *Hominid culture in primate perspective* (pp. 233–251) Niwot, CO: University Press of Colorado.

Lock, A. (1978). The emergence of language. In A. Lock (Ed.), *Action, gesture and symbol: The emergence of language* (pp. 3–18). New York: Academic Press.

Lock, A. (1980). *The guided reinvention of language.* New York: Academic Press.

Lock, A., Young, A., Service, V., & Chandler, P. (1990). Some observations on the origins of the pointing gesture. In V. Volterra & C. J. Erting (Eds.), *From gesture to language in hearing and deaf children* (pp. 42–55). New York: Springer-Verlag.

Locke, J. L. (1983). *Phonological acquisition and change.* New York: Academic Press.

Locke, J. L. (1993). *The child's path to spoken language.* Cambridge, MA: Harvard University Press.

Locke, J. L., & Pearson, D. M. (1990). Linguistic significance of babbling: Evidence from a tracheostomized infant. *Journal of Child Language, 17,* 1–16.

Lucksinger, K. L., Cohen, L. B., & Madole, K. L. (1992, May). What infants infer about hidden objects and events. Paper presented at the International Conference on Infant Studies, Miami.

MacDonald, S. E. (1994). Gorillas' (*Gorilla gorilla gorilla*) spatial memory in a foraging task. *Journal of Comparative Psychology, 108,* 107–113.

MacDonald, S. E., & Agnes, M. M. (1999). Orangutan (*Pongo pygmaeus abelii*) spatial memory and behavior in a foraging task. *Journal of Comparative Psychology, 113,* 1–5.

MacDonald, S. E., Pang, J. C., & Gibeault, S. (1994). Marmoset (*Callithrix jacchus jacchus*) spatial memory in a foraging task: Win-stay versus win-shift strategies. *Journal of Comparative Psychology, 108,* 328–334.

MacDonald, S. E., & Wilkie, D. M. (1990). Yellow-nosed monkeys' (*Cercopithecus ascanius whitesidei*) spatial memory in a simulated foraging environment. *Journal of Comparative Psychology, 104,* 382–387.

MacKinnon, J. (1974). The behaviour and ecology of wild orang-utans. *Animal Behaviour, 22,* 3–74.

Mandler, J. M. (1988). How to build a baby: On the development of an accessible representational system. *Cognitive Development, 3,* 113–136.

Mandler, J. M. (1990). Recall of events by preverbal children. In A. Diamond (Ed.), *The development and neural bases of higher cognitive functions* (pp. 485–516). New York: New York Academy of Sciences.

Mandler, J. M. (1998). Representation. In D. Kuhn & R. Siegler (Eds.), *Cognition, perception, and language* (pp. 255–308). Vol. 2 of W. Damon (Ed.), *Handbook of Child Psychology* (5th ed.). New York: Wiley.

Mandler, J. M., & McDonough, L. (1995). Long-term recall of event sequences in infancy. *Journal of Experimental Child Psychology, 59,* 457–474.

Marcos, H. (1987). Communicative functions of pitch range and pitch direction in infants. *Journal of Child Language, 14,* 255–268.

Marcos, H. (1991). Reformulating requests at 18 months: Gestures, vocalizations and words. *First Language, 11,* 361–375.

Marler, P. (1965). Communication in monkeys and apes. In I. DeVore (Ed.), *Primate behavior: Field studies of monkeys and apes* (pp. 544–584). New York: Holt, Rinehart, & Winston.

Marler, P. (1975). On the origin of speech from animal sounds. In J. F. Kavanagh & J. E. Cutting (Eds.), *The role of speech in language* (pp. 11–37). Cambridge, MA: MIT Press.

Marler, P. (1976). Social organization, communication, and graded signals: The chimpanzee and the gorilla. In P. P. G. Bateson & R. A. Hinde (Eds.), *Growing points in ethology* (pp. 239–280). London: Cambridge University Press.

Marler, P., & Mitani, J. (1988). Vocal communication in primates and birds: Parallels and contrasts. In D. Todt, P. Goedeking, & D. Symmes (Eds.), *Primate vocal communication* (pp. 3–14). Berlin: Springer-Verlag.

Marler, P., & Tenaza, R. (1977). Signaling behavior of apes with special reference to vocalization. In T. A. Sebeok (Ed.), *How animals communicate* (pp. 965–1033). Bloomington: Indiana University Press.

Marshack, A. (1979). Data for a theory of language origins. Commentary on S. T. Parker & K. R. Gibson, A developmental model for the evolution of language and intelligence in early hominids. *The Behavioral and Brain Sciences, 2,* 394–396.

Martinsen, H., & Smith, L. (1989). Studies of vocalization and gestures in the transition to speech. In S. von Tetzchner, L. S. Siegel, & L. Smith (Eds.), *The social and cognitive aspects of normal and atypical language development* (pp. 95–112). New York: Springer-Verlag.

Masataka, N. (1992a). Early ontogeny of vocal behavior of Japanese infants in response to maternal speech. *Child Development, 63,* 1177–1185.

Masataka, N. (1992b). Pitch characteristics of Japanese maternal speech to infants. *Journal of Child Language, 19,* 213–223.

Masataka, N. (1993). Effects of contingent and noncontingent maternal stimulation on the vocal behaviour of three- and four-month-old Japanese infants. *Journal of Child Language, 20,* 303–312.

Masataka, N. (1995). The relation between index-finger extension and the acoustic quality of cooing in three-month-old infants. *Journal of Child Language, 22,* 245–257.

Mason, D. (1997). Nonverbal communication and memory in language-impaired children. Unpublished master's thesis, York University, Toronto.

Masur, E. F. (1983). Gestural development, dual-directional signaling, and the transition to words. *Journal of Psycholinguistic Research, 12,* 93–109.

Mathieu, M., Bouchard, M.-A., Granger, L., & Herscovitch, J. (1976). Piagetian object-permanence in *Cebus capucinus, Lagothrix flavicauda,* and *Pan troglodytes. Animal Behaviour, 24,* 585–588.

Mathieu, M., Daudelin, N., Dagenais, Y., & Décarie, T. G. (1980). Piagetian causality in two house-reared chimpanzees (*Pan troglodytes*). *Canadian Journal of Psychology, 34,* 179–186.

Matsuzawa, T., & Yamakoshi, G. (1996) Comparison of chimpanzee material culture between Bossou and Nimba, West Africa. In A. E. Russon, K. A. Bard, & S. T. Parker (Eds.), *Reaching into thought: The minds of the great apes* (pp. 211–232). New York: Cambridge University Press.

McCune, L. (1995). A normative study of representational play at the transition to language. *Developmental Psychology, 31,* 198–206.

McCune, L., & Vihman, M. M. (1996, April). First words: Lexical and phonetic aspects. Paper presented at the International Conference on Infant Studies, Providence, RI.

McCune, L., Vihman, M. M., Roug-Hellichius, L., Delery, D. B., & Gogate, L. (1996). Grunt communication in human infants (*Homo sapiens*). *Journal of Comparative Psychology, 110,* 27–37.

McCune Nicolich, L. (1977). Beyond sensorimotor intelligence: Assessment of symbolic maturity through analysis of pretend play. *Merrill-Palmer Quarterly, 23,* 89–99.

McCune-Nicolich, L. (1981a). The cognitive bases of relational words in the single word period. *Journal of Child Language, 8,* 15–34.

McCune-Nicolich, L. (1981b). Toward symbolic functioning: Structure of early pretend games and potential parallels with language. *Child Development, 52,* 785–797.

McCune-Nicolich, L., & Bruskin, C. (1982). Combinatorial competency in symbolic play and language. In D. J. Pepler & K. H. Rubin (Eds.), *The play of children: Current theory and research* (pp. 30–45). Basel, Switzerland: Karger.

McGrew, W. C. (1992). *Chimpanzee material culture.* Cambridge, MA: Harvard University Press.

McGrew, W. C. (1993). The intelligent use of tools: Twenty propositions. In K. R. Gibson & T. Ingold (Eds.), *Tools, language and cognition in human evolution* (pp. 151–170). New York: Cambridge University Press.

McGuire, I., & Turkewitz, G. (1978). Visually elicited finger movements in infants. *Child Development, 49,* 362–370.

McNeill, D. (1992). *Hand and mind: What gestures reveal about thought.* Chicago: University of Chicago Press.

McShane, J. (1980). *Learning to talk.* Cambridge, UK: Cambridge University Press.

Meltzoff, A. N. (1985). Immediate and deferred imitation in fourteen- and twenty-four-month-old infants. *Child Development, 56,* 62–72.

Meltzoff, A. N. (1988a). Infant imitation after a 1-week delay: Long-term memory for novel acts and multiple stimuli. *Developmental Psychology, 24,* 470–476.

Meltzoff, A. N. (1988b). Infant imitation and memory: Nine-month-olds in immediate and deferred tests. *Child Development, 59,* 219–225.

Meltzoff, A. N., & Moore, M. K. (1998). Object representation, identity, and the paradox of early performance: Steps toward a new framework. *Infant Behavior and Development, 21,* 201–235.

Menn, L. (1976). The semantics of intonation contour. Paper presented at the Meeting of the Linguistic Society of America, Oswego, NY.

Menyuk, P., Liebergott, J. W., & Schultz, M. C. (1995). *Early language development in full-term and premature infants.* Hillsdale, NJ: Lawrence Erlbaum.

Menyuk, P., & Looney, P. (1976). A problem of language disorder: Length versus structure. In D. M. Morehead & A. E. Morehead (Eds.), *Normal and deficient child language* (pp. 259–279). Baltimore: University Park Press.

Menzel, E. W. (1973). Chimpanzee spatial memory organization. *Science, 182,* 943–945.

Menzel, E. W., & Johnson, M. K. (1975, September). Communication and cognitive organization in humans and other animals. Paper presented at the New York Academy of Sciences' Conference on Origins and Evolution of Language and Speech, New York.

Menzel, Jr., E. W., Premack, D., & Woodruff, G. (1978). Map reading by chimpanzees. *Folia primatol., 29,* 241–249.

Miles, H. L. W. (1990). The cognitive foundations for reference in a signing orangutan. In S. T. Parker & K. R. Gibson (Eds.), *"Language" and intelligence in monkeys and apes: Comparative developmental perspectives* (pp. 511–539). New York: Cambridge University Press.

Miles, H. L., Mitchell, R. W., & Harper, S. E. (1996). Simon says: The development of imitation in an enculturated orangutan. In A. E. Russon, K. A. Bard, & S. T. Parker (Eds.), *Reaching into thought: The minds of the great apes* (pp. 278–299). New York: Cambridge University Press.

Miller, J. A., & Siegel, L. S. (1989). Cognitive and social factors as predictors of normal and atypical language development. In S. von Tetzchner, L. S. Siegel, & L. Smith (Eds.), *The social and cognitive aspects of normal and atypical language development* (pp. 145–171). New York: Springer-Verlag.

Milo, R. G., & Quiatt, D. (1994). Language in the middle and late stone ages: Glottogenesis in anatomically modern *Homo sapiens*. In D. Quiatt & J. Itani (Eds.), *Hominid culture in primate perspective* (pp. 321–339). Niwot, CO: University Press of Colorado.

Mirak, J., & Rescorla, L. (1998). Phonetic skills and vocabulary size in late talkers: Concurrent and predictive relationships. *Applied Psycholinguistics, 19,* 1–17.

Mitani, J. C., & Gros-Louis, J. (1998). Chorusing and call convergence in chimpanzees: Tests of three hypotheses. *Behaviour, 135,* 1041–1064.

Mitani, J. C., & Nishida, R. (1993). Contexts and social correlates of long-distance calling by male chimpanzees. *Animal Behaviour, 45,* 735–746.

Mitchell, R. W. (1994). The evolution of primate cognition: Simulation, self-knowledge, and knowledge of other minds. In D. Quiatt & J. Itani (Eds.), *Hominid culture in primate perspective* (pp. 177–232). Niwot, CO: University Press of Colorado.

Mitchell, P. R., & Kent, R. D. (1990). Phonetic variation in multisyllabic babbling. *Journal of Child Language, 17,* 247–265.

Montgomery, J. W. (1995). Examination of phonological working memory in specifically language-impaired children. *Applied Psycholinguistics, 16,* 355–378.

Mori, A. (1983). Comparison of the communicative vocalizations and behaviors of group ranging in eastern gorillas, chimpanzees, and pygmy chimpanzees. *Primates, 24,* 486–500.

Morris, D., Collett, P. Marsh, P., O'Shaughnessy, M. (1979). *Gestures: Their origins and distribution.* New York: Stein and Day.

Müller, U., & Overton, W. F. (1998). How to grow a baby: A reevaluation of image-schema and Piagetian action approaches to representation. *Human Development, 41,* 71–111.

Munakata, Y., McClelland, J. L., Johnson, M. H., & Siegler, R. S. (1997). Rethinking infant knowledge: Toward an adaptive process account of successes and failures in object permanence tasks. *Psychological Review, 104,* 686–713.

Murphy, C. M. (1978). Pointing in the context of a shared activity. *Child Development, 49,* 371–380.

Murphy, C. M., & Messer, D. J. (1977). Mothers, infants and pointing: A study of gesture. In H. R. Shaffer (Ed.), *Studies in mother–infant interaction* (pp. 325–354). London: Academic Press.

Myers Thompson, J. A. (1994). Cultural diversity in the behavior of pan. In D. Quiatt & J. Itani (Eds.), *Hominid culture in primate perspective* (pp. 95–115). Niwot, CO: University Press of Colorado.

Nagell, K., Olguin, R. S., & Tomasello, M. (1993). Processes of social learning in the tool use of chimpanzees (*Pan troglodytes*) and human children (*Homo sapiens*). *Journal of Comparative Psychology, 107,* 174–186.

Natale, F. (1989). Causality II: The stick problem. In F. Antinucci (Ed.), *Cognitive structure and development in nonhuman primates* (pp. 121–133). Hillsdale, NJ: Lawrence Erlbaum.

Natale, F., Antinucci, F., Spinozzi, G., & Poti, P. (1986). Stage 6 object concept in nonhuman primate cognition: A comparison between gorilla (*Gorilla gorilla gorilla*) and Japanese macaque (*Macaca fuscata*). *Journal of Comparative Psychology, 100,* 335–339.

Nelson, C. A. (1995). The ontogeny of human memory: A cognitive neuroscience perspective. *Developmental Psychology, 31,* 723–738.

Netsell, R. (1981). The acquisition of speech motor control: A perspective with directions for research. In R. E. Stark (Ed.), *Language behavior in infancy and early childhood* (pp. 127–156). New York: Elsevier/North-Holland.

Newman, J. D., & Symmes, D. (1982). Inheritance and experience in the acquisition of primate acoustic behavior. In C. T. Snowdon, C. H. Brown, & M. R. Petersen (Eds.), *Primate communication* (pp. 259–278). London: Cambridge University Press.

Noble, W., & Davidson, I. (1996). *Human evolution, language and mind: A psychological and archaeological inquiry.* Cambridge, UK: Cambridge University Press.

Nottebohm, F. (1975). A zoologist's view of some language phenomena with particular emphasis on vocal learning. In E. Lenneberg & E. Lenneberg (Eds.), *Foundations of language development* (pp. 61–103). New York: Academic Press.

Ogura, T. (1991). A longitudinal study of the relationship between early language development and play development. *Journal of Child Language, 18,* 273–294.

Oller, D. K. (1980). The emergence of the sounds of speech in infancy. In G. H. Yeni-Komshian, J. F. Kavanagh, & C. A. Ferguson (Eds.), *Child phonology.* Vol. 1. *Production.* (pp. 93–112). New York: Academic Press.

Oller, D. K. (1981). Infant vocalizations: Exploration and reflexivity. In R. E. Stark (Ed.), *Language behavior in infancy and early childhood* (pp. 85–103). New York: Elsevier/North Holland.

Oller, D. K. (1986). Metaphonology and infant vocalization. In B. Lindblom & R. Zetterstrom (Eds.), *Precursors of early speech* (pp. 26–31). New York: Stockton.

Oller, D. K., Basinger, D., & Eilers, R. E. (1996, April). Intuitive identification of infant vocalizations by parents. Paper presented at the International Conference on Infant Studies, Providence, RI.

Oller, D. K., & Eilers, R. E. (1988). The role of audition in infant babbling. *Child Development, 59,* 441–449.

Oller, D. K., Eilers, R. E., Basinger, D., Steffens, M. L., & Urbano, R. (1995). Extreme poverty and the development of precursors to the speech capacity. *First Language, 15,* 167–187.

Oller, D. K., Eilers, R. E., Steffens, M. L., Lynch, M. P., & Urbano, R. (1994). Speech-like vocalizations in infancy: An evaluation of potential risk factors. *Journal of Child Language, 21*, 33–58.

Oller, D. K., Eilers, R. E., Urbano, R., & Cobo-Lewis, A. B. (1997). Development of precursors to speech in infants exposed to two languages. *Journal of Child Language, 24*, 407–425.

Oller, D. K., & Lynch, M. P. (1992). Infant vocalizations and innovations in infraphonology: Toward a broader theory of development and disorders. In C. A. Ferguson, L. Menn, & C. Stoel-Gammon (Eds.), *Phonological development: Models, research, implications* (pp. 509–536). Timonium, MD: York Press.

Oller, D. K., Wieman, L. A., Doyle, W. J., & Ross, C. (1976). Infant babbling and speech. *Journal of Child Language, 3*, 1–11.

Owren, M. J. (1990a). Acoustic classification of alarm calls by vervet monkeys (*Cercopithecus aethiops*) and humans (*Homo sapiens*): I. Natural calls. *Journal of Comparative Psychology, 104*, 20–28.

Owren, M. J. (1990b). Acoustic classification of alarm calls by vervet monkeys (*Cercopithecus aethiops*) and humans (*Homo sapiens*): II. Synthetic calls. *Journal of Comparative Psychology, 104*, 29–40.

Oxman, J., & Blake, J. (1980). Sign language use by autistic children: A pragmatic analysis. Paper presented at the Meeting of the American Psychological Association, Montreal.

Papousek, M., & Papousek, H. (1989). Forms and functions of vocal matching in interactions between mothers and their precanonical infants. *First Language, 9*, 137–158.

Parker, S. T. (1990). Origins of comparative developmental evolutionary studies of primate mental abilities. In S. T. Parker & K. R. Gibson (Eds.), *"Language" and intelligence in monkeys and apes: Comparative developmental perspectives* (pp. 3–64). New York: Cambridge University Press.

Parker, S. T., & Gibson, K. R. (1977). Object manipulation, tool use and sensorimotor intelligence as feeding adaptations in cebus monkeys and great apes. *Journal of Human Evolution, 6*, 623–641.

Parker, S. T., & Gibson, K. R. (1979). A developmental model for the evolution of language and intelligence in early hominids. *The Behavioral and Brain Sciences, 2*, 367–408.

Pascual-Leone, J., & Johnson, J. (1999). A dialectical constructivist view of representation: Role of mental attention, executives, and symbols. In I. E. Sigel (Ed.), *Development of mental representation: Theories and applications* (pp. 169–200). Hillsdale, NJ: Lawrence Erlbaum.

Petitto, L. A. (1987). On the autonomy of language and gesture: Evidence from the acquisition of personal pronouns in American Sign Language. *Cognition, 27*, 1–52.

Petitto, L. A. (1995, April). Language modality is set after birth: Implications for neurogenesis in the developing brain. Paper presented at the Biennial Meeting of the Society for Research in Child Development, Indianapolis.

Piaget, J. (1952). *The origins of intelligence in children.* Trans. by M. Cook. New York: International Universities Press.

Piaget, J. (1954). *The construction of reality in the child.* Trans. by M. Cook. New York: Basic Books. (Original work published 1937).

Piaget, J. (1962). *Play, dreams, and imitation in childhood.* Trans. by C. Gattegno & F. M. Hodgson. New York: Norton. (Original work published 1945).

Pierce, Jr., J. D. (1985). A review of attempts to condition operantly alloprimate vocalizations. *Primates, 26,* 202–213.

Pinker, S. (1994). *The language instinct.* New York: HarperPerennial.

Ploog, D. (1988). Neurobiology and pathology of subhuman vocal communication and human speech. In D. Todt, P. Goedeking, & D. Symmes (Eds.), *Primate vocal communication* (pp. 195–212). Berlin: Springer-Verlag.

Ploog, D., & Jurgens, U. (1980). Vocal behavior of nonhuman primates and man. In S. A. Corson, E. O. Corson, & J. A. Alexander (Eds.), *Ethology and nonverbal communication in mental health* (pp. 179–189). New York: Pergamon Press.

Plooij, F. X. (1978). Some basic traits of language in wild chimpanzees? In A. Lock (Ed.), *Action, gesture and symbol: The emergence of language* (pp. 111–131). New York: Academic Press.

Plooij, F. X. (1984). *The behavioral development of free-living chimpanzee babies and infants.* Norwood, NJ: Ablex.

Premack, D. (1978). Comparison of language-related factors in ape and man. In D. J. Chivers & J. Herbert (Eds.), *Recent advances in primatology, Behaviour* (Vol. 1, pp. 867–881). New York: Academic Press.

Quiatt, D., & Itani, J. (1994). Preface: Culture, nature, and the nature of culture. In D. Quiatt & J. Itani (Eds.), *Hominid culture in primate perspective* (pp. xiii–xvii). Niwot, CO: University Press of Colorado.

Raine, A., Hulme, C., Chadderton, H., & Bailey, P. (1991). Verbal short-term memory span in speech-disordered children: Implications for articulatory coding in short-term memory. *Child Development, 62,* 415–423.

Ramer, A. L. H. (1977). The development of syntactic complexity. *Journal of Psycholinguistic Research, 6,* 145–161.

Reynell, J. (1981). *Reynell Developmental Language Scales* (rev.). Windsor: N.F.E.R. Publishing.

Reynolds, V., & Reynolds, F. (1965). Chimpanzees of the Budongo Forest. In I. DeVore (Ed.), *Primate behavior: Field studies of monkeys and apes* (pp. 368–424). New York: Holt, Rinehart, & Winston.

Rieber, R. W. (Ed.) (1983). *Dialogues on the psychology of language and thought: Conversations with Noam Chomsky, Charles Osgood, Jean Piaget, Ulric Neisser, and Marcel Kinsbourne.* New York: Plenum Press.

Roberts, W. A. (1998). *Principles of animal cognition.* New York: McGraw-Hill.

Rome-Flanders, R., & Ricard, M. (1992). Infant timing of vocalizations in two mother–infant games: A longitudinal study. *First Language, 12,* 285–297.

Rönnqvist, L., & von Hofsten, C. (1994). Neonatal finger and arm movements as determined by a social and an object context. *Early Development and Parenting, 3,* 81–94.

Roth, F. P., & Clark, D. M. (1987). Symbolic play and social participation abilities of language-impaired and normally developing children. *Journal of Speech and Hearing Disorders, 52,* 17–27.

Roug, L., Landberg, I., & Lundberg, L.-J. (1989). Phonetic development in early infancy: A study of four Swedish children during the first eighteen months of life. *Journal of Child Language, 16,* 19–40.

Ruff, H. A., & Halton, A. (1978). Is there directed reaching in the human neonate? *Developmental Psychology, 14,* 425–426.

Russell, C. L., & Russnaik, R. N. (1981). Language and symbolic play in infancy: Independent or related abilities? *Canadian Journal of Behavioural Sciences, 13,* 95–104.

Russon, A. E. (1990). The development of peer social interaction in infant chimpanzees: Comparative social, Piagetian, and brain perspectives. In S. T. Parker & K. R. Gibson (Eds.), *"Language" and intelligence in monkeys and apes: Comparative developmental perspectives* (pp. 379–419). New York: Cambridge University Press.

Russon, A. E. (1995, November). Reaching into thought: The minds of the great apes. Invited Address, York University, Toronto.

Russon, A. E. (1996). Imitation in everyday use: Matching and rehearsal in the spontaneous imitation of rehabilitant orangutans (*Pongo pygmaeus*). In A. E. Russon, K. A. Bard, & S. T. Parker (Eds.), *Reaching into thought: The minds of the great apes* (pp. 152–176) New York: Cambridge University Press.

Russon, A. E. (1999). Orangutans' imitation of tool use: A cognitive interpretation. In S. T. Parker, H. L. Miles, & R. M. Mitchell (Eds.), *The mentalities of gorillas and orangutans.* Cambridge, UK: Cambridge University Press.

Sands, S. F., & Wright, A. A. (1980). Serial probe recognition performance by a rhesus monkey and a human with 10- and 20-item lists. *Journal of Experimental Psychology: Animal Behavior Processes, 6,* 386–396.

Sands, S. F., & Wright, A. A. (1982). Monkey and human pictorial memory scanning. *Science, 216,* 1333–1334.

Savage-Rumbaugh, E. S. (1979). Symbolic communication – its origins and early development in the chimpanzee. *New Directions for Child Development, 3,* 1–15.

Savage-Rumbaugh, S. (1990). Symbols: Their communicative use, comprehension and combination by bonobos (*Pan paniscus*). *Advances in Infancy Research, 6,* 221–278.

Savage-Rumbaugh, S., Shanker, S. G., & Taylor, T. J. (1998). *Apes, language, and the human mind.* New York: Oxford University Press.

Schaller, G. B. (1965). The behavior of the mountain gorilla. In I. DeVore (Ed.), *Primate behavior: Field studies of monkeys and apes* (pp. 324–367). New York: Holt, Rinehart & Winston.

Scollon, R. (1976). *Conversations with a one-year-old: A case study of the developmental foundation of syntax.* Hawaii: The University Press.

Seyfarth, R. M. (1984). What the vocalizations of monkeys mean to humans and what they mean to the monkeys themselves. In R. Harré & V. Reynolds (Eds.), *The meaning of primate signals* (pp. 43–56). New York: Cambridge University Press.

Seyfarth, R. M., & Cheney, D. L. (1993). Meaning, reference, and intentionality in the natural vocalizations of monkeys. In H. L. Roitblat, L. M. Herman, &

P. E. Nachtigall (Eds.), *Language and communication: Comparative perspectives* (pp. 195–219). Hillsdale, NJ: Lawrence Erlbaum.

Shore, C. (1986). Combinatorial play, conceptual development, and early multiword speech. *Developmental Psychology, 22,* 184–190.

Shore, C., O'Connell, B., & Bates, E. (1984). First sentences in language and symbolic play. *Developmental Psychology, 20,* 872–880.

Siegel, L. S. (1981). Infant tests as predictors of cognitive and language development at two years. *Child Development, 52,* 545–557.

Sigman, M., & Ungerer, J. A. (1984). Cognitive and language skills in autistic, mentally retarded, and normal children. *Developmental Psychology, 20,* 293–302.

Sininger, Y. S., Klatzky, R. L., & Kirchner, D. (1989). Memory scanning speed in language-disordered children. *Journal of Speech and Hearing Research, 32,* 289–297.

Skarakis-Doyle, E., & Prutting, C. (1982, August). A description of symbolic play in the language-disordered child. Paper presented at the Meeting of the American Speech-Language-Hearing Association, Toronto.

Smith, B. L., Brown-Sweeney, S., & Stoel-Gammon, C. (1989). A quantitative analysis of reduplicated and variegated babbling. *First Language, 9,* 175–190.

Smolak, L. (1982). Cognitive precursors of receptive vs. expressive language. *Journal of Child Language, 9,* 13–22.

Smolak, L., & Levine, M. P. (1984). The effects of differential criteria on the assessment of cognitive-linguistic relationships. *Child Development, 55,* 973–980.

Snowdon, C. (1982). Linguistic and psycholinguistic approaches to primate communication. In C. T. Snowdon, C. H. Brown, & M. R. Petersen (Eds.), *Primate communication* (pp. 212–238). London: Cambridge University Press.

Snowdon, C. T. (1993). Linguistic phenomena in the natural communication of animals. In H. L. Roitblat, L. M. Herman, & P. E. Nachtigall (Eds.), *Language and communication: Comparative perspectives.* Hillsdale, NJ: Lawrence Erlbaum.

Snyder, L. (1978). Communicative and cognitive abilities and disabilities in the sensorimotor period. *Merrill-Palmer Quarterly, 24,* 161–180.

Speidel, G. E. (1993). Phonological short-term memory and individual differences in learning to speak: A bilingual case study. *First Language, 13,* 69–91.

Spelke, E. S. (1982). Perceptual knowledge of objects in infancy. In J. Mehler, M. Garrett, & E. Walker (Eds.), *Perspectives on mental representation* (pp. 409–430). Hillsdale, NJ: Lawrence Erlbaum.

Spelke, E. S. (1991). Physical knowledge in infancy: Reflections on Piaget's theory. In S. Carey & R. Gelman (Eds.), *The epigenesis of mind: Essays on biology and cognition* (pp. 133–169). Hillsdale, NJ: Lawrence Erlbaum.

Spelke, E. S. (1994). Initial knowledge: Six suggestions. *Cognition, 50,* 431–445.

Spelke, E. S. (1998). Nativism, empiricism, and the origins of knowledge. *Infant Behavior and Development, 21,* 181–200.

Spelke, E. S., Breinlinger, K., Macomber, J., & Jacobson, K. (1992). Origins of knowledge. *Psychological Review, 99,* 605–632.

Spencer, P. E. (1996). The association between language and symbolic play at two years: Evidence from deaf toddlers. *Child Development, 67,* 867–876.

Spinozzi, G., & Natale, F. (1989). Early sensorimotor development in Gorilla. In F. Antinucci (Ed.), *Cognitive structure and development in nonhuman primates* (pp. 21–38). Hillsdale, NJ: Lawrence Erlbaum.

Spinozzi, G., & Poti, P. (1989). Causality I: The support problem. In F. Antinucci (Ed.), *Cognitive structure and development in nonhuman primates* (pp. 113–119). Hillsdale, NJ: Lawrence Erlbaum.

Stark, R. E. (1978). Features of infant sounds: The emergence of cooing. *Journal of Child Language, 5,* 379–390.

Stark, R. (1980). Stages of speech development in the first year of life. In G. H. Yeni-Komshian, J. F. Kavanagh, & C. A. Ferguson (Eds.), *Child phonology* (pp. 73–92). Vol. 1. *Production.* New York: Academic Press.

Stark, R. (1981). Infant vocalization: A comprehensive view. *Infant Mental Health Journal, 2,* 118–128.

Stark, R. E., Rose, S. N., & McLagen, M. (1975). Features of infant sounds: The first eight weeks of life. *Journal of Child Language, 2,* 205–221.

Stark, R. E., & Tallal, P. (1988). *Language, speech, and reading disorders in children: Neuropsychological studies.* Boston: Little, Brown.

Steckol, K. F., & Leonard, L. B. (1981). Sensorimotor development and the use of prelinguistic performatives. *Journal of Speech and Hearing Research, 24,* 262–268.

Steklis, H. D. (1985). Primate communication, comparative neurology, and the origin of language re-examined. *Journal of Human Evolution, 14,* 157–173.

Stewart, K. J., & Harcourt, A. H. (1994). Gorillas' vocalizations during rest periods: Signals of impending departure? *Behaviour, 130,* 29–40.

Stoel-Gammon, C. (1988). Prelinguistic vocalizations of hearing-impaired and normally hearing subjects: A comparison of consonantal inventories. *Journal of Speech and Hearing Disorders, 53,* 302–315.

Stoel-Gammon, C. (1989). Prespeech and early speech development of two late talkers. *First Language, 9,* 207–224.

Stoel-Gammon, C. (1992). Prelinguistic vocal development: Measurement and predictions. In C. A. Ferguson, L. Menn, & C. Stoel-Gammon (Eds.), *Phonological development: Models, research, implications* (pp. 439–456). Timonium, MD: York Press.

Stoel-Gammon, C., & Cooper, J. A. (1984). Patterns of early lexical and phonological development. *Journal of Child Language, 11,* 247–271.

Struhsaker, T. T. (1967). Auditory communication among vervet monkeys (*Cercopithecus aethiops*). In S. A. Altmann (Ed.), *Social communication among primates* (pp. 281–324). Chicago: University of Chicago Press.

Studdert-Kennedy, M. (1991). Language development from an evolutionary perspective. In N. A. Krasnegor, D. M. Rumbaugh, R. L. Schiefelbusch, & M. Studdert-Kennedy (Eds.), *Biological and behavioral determinants of language development* (pp. 5–28). Hillsdale, NJ: Lawrence Erlbaum.

Stutsman, R. (1948). *The Merrill–Palmer Scale of Mental Tests.* Chicago: Stoelting.

Sugiyama, Y. (1993). Local variation of tools and tool use among wild chimpanzee populations. In A. Berthelet & J. Chavaillon (Eds.), *The use of tools by human and non-human primates: A Fyssen Foundation symposium* (pp. 175–187). Oxford: Clarendon Press.

Tamis-LeMonda, C. S., & Bornstein, M. H. (1990). Language, play, and attention at one year. *Infant Behavior and Development, 13,* 85–98.

Tamis-LeMonda, C. S., & Bornstein, M. H. (1994). Specificity in mother–toddler language–play relations across the second year. *Developmental Psychology, 30,* 283–292.

Tamis-LeMonda, C. S., Bornstein, M. H., Cyphers, L., Toda, S., & Ogino, M. (1992). Language and play at one year: A comparison of toddlers and mothers in the United States and Japan. *International Journal of Behavioral Development, 15,* 19–42.

Tamis-LeMonda, C., Kahana-Kalman, R., Damast, A. M., Baumwell, L., & Bornstein, M. H. (1992, April). Associations between patterns of language acquisition and symbolic play across the first two years. Paper presented at the Conference of Human Development, Atlanta.

Tanner, J. E., & Byrne, R. W. (1996). Representation of action through iconic gesture in a captive lowland gorilla. *Current Anthropology, 37,* 162–173.

Terrace, H. S. (1979). How Nim Chimpsky changed my mind. *Psychology Today,* 65–76.

Terrace, H. S. (1993). The phylogeny and ontogeny of serial memory: List learning by pigeons and monkeys. In Symposium on animal cognition. *Psychological Science, 4,* 162–169.

Terrace, H. S., & McGonigle, B. (1994). Memory and representation of serial order by children, monkeys, and pigeons. *Current Directions in Psychological Science, 3,* 180–185.

Terrell, B. Y., & Schwartz, R. G. (1988). Object transformations in the play of language-impaired children. *Journal of Speech and Hearing Disorders, 53,* 459–466.

Thal, D., & Bates, E. (1988). Language and gesture in late talkers. *Journal of Speech and Hearing Research, 31,* 115–123.

Thelen, E., & Fogel, A. (1986). Toward an action-based theory of infant development. In J. J. Lockman & N. L. Hazen (Eds.), *Action in social context: Perspectives on early development* (pp. 23–63). New York: Plenum.

Thorpe, W. H. (1978). *Purpose in a world of chance.* London: Oxford University Press.

Tinklepaugh, O. L. (1932). Multiple delayed reaction with chimpanzees and monkeys. *Journal of Comparative Psychology, 13,* 207–243.

Tomasello, M. (1990). Cultural transmission in the tool use and communicatory signaling of chimpanzees. In S. T. Parker & K. R. Gibson (Eds.), *"Language" and intelligence in monkeys and apes: Comparative developmental perspectives* (274–311). New York: Cambridge University Press.

Tomasello, M. (1996). Do apes ape? In C. M. Heyes & B. G. Galef, Jr. (Eds.), *Social learning in animals: The roots of culture* (pp. 319–346). New York: Academic Press.

Tomasello, M., & Call, J. (1997). *Primate cognition.* New York: Oxford.

Tomasello, M., Call, J., Nagell, K., Olguin, R., & Carpenter, M. (1994). The learning and use of gestural signals by young chimpanzees: A trans-generational study. *Primates, 35,* 137–154.

Tomasello, M., Call, J., Warren, J., Frost, G. T., Carpenter, M., & Nagell, K. (1997). The ontogeny of chimpanzee gestural signals: A comparison across groups and generations. *Evolution of Communication, 1,* 223–259.

Tomasello, M., & Camaioni, L. (1997). A comparison of the gestural communication of apes and human infants. *Human Development, 40,* 7–24.

Tomasello, M., & Farrar, M. J. (1984). Cognitive bases of lexical development: Object permanence and relational words. *Journal of Child Language, 11,* 477–493.

Tomasello, M., & Farrar, M. J. (1986). Object permanence and relational words: A lexical training study. *Journal of Child Language, 13,* 494–505.

Tomasello, M., George, B. L., Kruger, A. C., Farrar, M. J., & Evans, A. (1985). The development of gestural communication in young chimpanzees. *Journal of Human Evolution, 14,* 175–186.

Tomasello, M., Gust, D., & Frost, G. T. (1989). A longitudinal investigation of gestural communication in young chimpanzees. *Primates, 30,* 35–50.

Trevarthen, C. (1977). Descriptive analyses of infant communicative behavior. In H. R. Schaffer (Ed.), *Studies in mother–infant interaction* (pp. 227–270). London: Academic Press.

Trevarthen, C., & Hubley, P. (1978). Secondary intersubjectivity: Confidence, confiding and acts of meaning in the first year. In A. Lock (Ed.), *Action, gesture and symbol: The emergence of language* (pp. 183–229). New York: Academic Press.

Tulkin, S. R. (1977). Social class differences in maternal and infant behavior. In P. H. Leiderman, S. R. Tulkin, & A. Rosenfeld (Eds.), *Culture and infancy: Variations in the human experience* (pp. 494–537). New York: Academic Press.

Tutin, C., & Fernandez, M. (1983). Gorillas feeding on termites in Gabon, West Africa. *Journal of Mammology, 6,* 530–531.

Ungerer, J. A., & Sigman, M. (1984). The relation of play and sensorimotor behavior to language in the second year. *Child Development, 55,* 1448–1455.

Uzgiris, I. C. (1987). The study of sequential order in cognitive development. In I. C. Uzgiris & J. McV. Hunt (Eds.), *Infant performance and experience: New findings with the ordinal scales* (pp. 131–167). Urbana: University of Illinois Press.

Uzgiris, I. C. & Hunt, J.McV. (1975). *Assessment in infancy: Ordinal scales of psychological development.* Chicago: University of Illinois Press.

van der Lely, H. K. J., & Howard, D. (1993). Children with specific language impairment: Linguistic impairment or short-term memory deficit? *Journal of Speech and Hearing Research, 36,* 1193–1207.

van Hooff, J. A. R. A. M. (1973). A structural analysis of the social behaviour of a semi-captive group of chimpanzees. In M. von Cranach & I. Vine (Eds.), *Social communication and movement: Studies of interaction and expression in man and chimpanzee* (pp. 75–162). London: Academic Press.

Van Lawick-Goodall, J. (1968). A preliminary report on expressive movements and communication in the Gombe Stream Chimpanzees. In P. C. Jay (Ed.), *Primates: Studies in adaptation and variability* (pp. 313–374). New York: Holt, Rinehart, & Winston.

Vauclair, J. (1996). *Animal cognition: An introduction to modern comparative psychology.* Cambridge, MA: Harvard University Press.

Vibbert, M., & Bornstein, M. H. (1989). Specific associations between domains of mother–child interaction and toddler referential language and pretense play. *Infant Behavior and Development, 12,* 163–184.

Vihman, M. M. (1991). Ontogeny of phonetic gestures: Speech production. In I. G. Mattingly & M. Studdert-Kennedy (Eds.), *Modularity and the motor theory of speech perception* (pp. 69–84). Hillsdale, NJ: Lawrence Erlbaum.

Vihman, M. M. (1992). Early syllables and the construction of phonology. In C. A. Ferguson, L. Menn, C. Stoel-Gammon (Eds.), *Phonological development: Models, research, implications* (pp. 393–422). Timonium, MD: York Press.

Vihman, M. M. (1996). *Phonological development: The origins of language in the child.* Oxford: Blackwell.

Vihman, M. M., Ferguson, C. A., & Elbert, M. (1986). Phonological development from babbling to speech: Common tendencies and individual differences. *Applied Psycholinguistics, 7,* 3–40.

Vihman, M. M., & Greenlee, M. (1987). Individual differences in phonological development: Ages one and three years. *Journal of Speech and Hearing Research, 30,* 503–521.

Vihman, M. M., Macken, M. A., Miller, R., Simmons, H., & Miller, J. (1985). From babbling to speech: A reassessment of the continuity issue. *Language, 61,* 397–445.

Vihman, M. M., & Miller, R. (1988). Words and babble at the threshold of language acquisition. In M. D. Smith & J. L. Locke, (Eds.), *The emergent lexicon: The child's development of a linguistic vocabulary* (pp. 151–183). New York: Academic Press.

Visalberghi, E., Fragaszy, D. M., & Savage-Rumbaugh, S. (1995). Performance in a tool-using task by common chimpanzees (*Pan troglodytes*), bonobos (*Pan paniscus*), an orangutan (*Pongo pygmaeus*), and capuchin monkeys (*Cebus apella*). *Journal of Comparative Psychology, 109,* 52–60.

Visalberghi, E., & Limongelli, L. (1996). Acting and understanding: Tool use revisited through the minds of capuchin monkeys. In A. E. Russon, K. A. Bard, S. T. Parker (Eds.), *Reaching into thought: The minds of the great apes* (pp. 57–59). New York: Cambridge University Press.

Vitale, G. R. (1998). *Maternal responsivity at 9 and 15 months and subsequent language outcomes in a sample of Italian-Canadian mother–child dyads.* Unpublished doctoral dissertation, York University, Toronto.

Volterra, V., & Caselli, M. C. (1985). From gestures and vocalizations to signs and words. In W. Stokoe & V. Volterra (Eds.), *Proceedings of the III international symposium on sign language research* (pp. 1–9). Silver Springs, MD: Linstok Press.

von Hofsten, C. (1984). Developmental changes in the organization of prereaching movements. *Developmental Psychology, 20,* 378–388.

Werner, H., & Kaplan, B. (1963). *Symbol formation.* New York: Wiley.

Whalen, D. H., Levitt, A. G., & Wang, Q. (1991). Intonational differences between the reduplicative babbling of French- and English-learning infants. *Journal of Child Language, 18,* 501–516.

Whiten, A. (1998). Imitation of the sequential structure of actions by chimpanzees. (*Pan troglodytes*). *Journal of Comparative Psychology, 112,* 270–281.

Winitz, H., & Irwin, O. C. (1958). Syllabic and phonetic structure of infants' early words. *Journal of Speech and Hearing Research, 1,* 250–256.

Wright, A. A., & Rivera, J. J. (1997). Memory of auditory lists by rhesus monkeys (*Macaca mulatta*). *Journal of Experimental Psychology: Animal Behavior Processes, 23,* 441–449.

Wright, A. A., Santiago, H. C., Sands, S. F., Kendrick, D. F., & Cook, R. G. (1985). Memory processing of serial lists by pigeons, monkeys, and people. *Science, 229,* 287–289.

Wyke, M. A., & Asso, D. (1979). Perception and memory for spatial relations in children with developmental dysphasia. *Neuropsychologica, 17,* 231–238.

Wynn, T. (1993). Layers of thinking in tool behavior. In K. R. Gibson & T. Ingold (Eds.), *Tools, language and cognition in human evolution* (pp. 389–406). New York: Cambridge University Press.

Zinober, B., & Martlew, M. (1985). Developmental change in four types of gesture in relation to acts and vocalizations from 10 to 21 months. *British Journal of Developmental Psychology, 3,* 293–306.

Author Index

Subject Index

Alarm calls, 45, 49, 51, 220–221
Ape language studies, 114–115
Auditory memory, sequential,
　205–207, 230
Australopithecines, 215, 217, 221,
　226
Autistic children, 115

Babbling. *See also* Vocalizations,
　prelinguistic
　canonical, 16–19, 31, 35, 228
　environmental influences on,
　　35–39
　features of, 30–32
　and first words, 32–34
　and later language, 34–35
　identification of phonetically
　　consistent forms in, 52
　phonetic preferences in, 20–30
Babbling drift, 37–39
Baboons
　spatial memory in, 188–189
　vocalization in, 2
Bayley Mental Development Indices
　(MDI), 108
Belching, 3, 45, 47
Belsky—Most play scale, 131
Birdsong, 5
Bistratal system, 42
Bonobos

communicative gestures in, 83,
　85, 86, 89, 91
food sharing by, 219
tool use among, 146–147, 152
volcalization in, 2–4, 6, 11, 12,
　16, 47, 48
Bossou, 144–146
Brain, 140, 167, 225, 230–231
　evolution of human, 221–222
　of human infants, 171
　and representation, 183
　and vocalization, 9–10
Brain—body ratio, 213–215
Broca's area, 9–10, 140, 167, 225
Budongo Forest, 2, 44

Calls, nonhuman primate, 2–6,
　43–51
　great apes, spontaneous calls of,
　　2–6, 43–48
　playback experiments, 48–51
Campo, 145–146
Canonical babbling (CB), 16–19,
　31, 35, 228
Capuchin monkeys
　object concept in, 156–157
　tool use among, 152–153
CB. *See* Canonical babbling
Cebus monkeys
　object concept in, 157

269